War Orphan
in San Francisco

Letters Link a Family Scattered by World War II

*To Judy
A long-time dear friend
Love Phyllis*

by

Phyllis Helene Mattson

ii

Published by Stevens Creek Press
P.O. Box 305
Cupertino, California 95015
www.stevenscreekpress@pacbell.net

Published 2005
Printed in the United States of America

ISBN 0-9761656-0-0

Library of Congress Cataloguing-in-publication data

    Mattson, Phyllis Helene.
    War Orphan in San Francisco: Letters Link a Family Scattered by World War II /
    Phyllis Helene Mattson. — 1st ed. — Cupertino, Calif. : Stevens Creek Press,
    2005.
        p. ; cm.
        Includes bibliographical references.
        1. Mattson, Phyllis Helene. 2. World War, 1939-1945 — Refugees —
    Austria. 3. World War, 1939-1945 — Personal narratives. 4. Jewish children in
    the Holocaust. 5. Foster children — California — San Francisco. 6. Jewish
    orphanages — California — San Francisco. I. Title.

D811.5.M38 2005
940.54/81436/13—dc22   0501

In Memory of My Parents
Laura and Samuel Finkel
Victims of the Holocaust

Dedicated to My Children
Laurel Davis and Jeffrey Mattson
So they may know their history

With Heartfelt Gratitude to My Rescuers
Aunt Laura and the Jewish Charities
Who cared about saving children during the World War II

v

ACKNOWLEDGEMENTS

No book is the product of one person's effort—it takes many to see the project to completion. Indeed, countless people have contributed to my undertaking in so many different ways, and I want to thank each and every one for helping me.

I am grateful to my writing teachers, Nina Holzer, Mary Jane Moffat, and Kate Breslau in whose classes I began to develop this memoir, and who patiently taught me to write more details. Thanks to my writing group, Lorraine Macchello, Ginny McKim, Jane Paull, Verna Spinrad and Mary Whitman for listening and contributing suggestions chapter by chapter.

Several people kindly read my manuscript and gave comments. Among these, Jeanne Ricket was most generous with her detailed comments and suggestions and for helping me with the photo reproductions. Maggie Blackford, Dave Donald, Prof. Hill Gates, Judy Pugh and Alice Story read and commented on the memoir, and gave much of their time encouraging me. Other loyal friends, Pepper Bonneau, Jane Eckman, Juliana Richmond, and Jean Sutherland patiently listened to me report on my progress. Al and Bev Nowack helped me remember Homewood Terrace. Thanks also to Eva Maiden for connecting me to Holocaust affairs.

Another source of help for which I am grateful came from Iris Posner, founder and director of One Thousand Children, Inc., an organization devoted to telling the history of the roughly 1000 children, of which I am one, who came to America without their parents during the Hitler era. Through this organization I was able to find some sources to fill in the voids of my memory of those times. This organization also published an anthology of these children's experiences in *Don't Wave Goodbye: The Children's Flight from Nazi Persecution to American Freedom* (Praeger, 2004) and which contains two of my chapters.

Special thanks to the people in Australia: "Dunera Boys"—Henry Lippman, Mike Sondheim, and Eric Eckstein—for informing me about their experiences and hosting me while I searched for my father's footsteps, Sister Dacy of the Jewish Museum of Sydney and Mrs. Lurline Knee of the Wartime Camps Research Office in the Tatura Historical Museum for helping me search for Dunera memorabilia. Similarly, I want to thank to Bettina Brockman for her translations of my mother's letters, and to Dorothy Foglia, my book designer, who worked so patiently with me to produce such a nice book.

I appreciate, more than I know how to express, the support Laurie and Jeff, my children, gave me in this long-term project.

TABLE OF CONTENTS

Going to America

Chapter 1   Journey to America 1

The World I Left Behind

Chapter 2   Growing Up Through Letters 8
Chapter 3   My Home 17
Chapter 4   My Family 25
Chapter 5   Daily Life 35
Chapter 6   Summers in Poland 45
Chapter 7   Hitler Comes to Austria 52

My Father's Plight

Chapter 8   Journey to Australia 64

Life in San Francisco

Chapter 9   The First Six Months 75
Chapter 10   My First Foster Home 103
Chapter 11   Life in an Orphanage 137
Chapter 12   Cottage #42 153
Chapter 13   Making It 175
Chapter 14   Choosing a Career 187
Chapter 15   Good News, Bad News 194
Chapter 16   My Nemesis 221
Chapter 17   Another Foster Home 229
Chapter 18   High School 254
Chapter 19   More Troubles 277

The Post-War Period

Chapter 20   Life With Father 290
Chapter 21   Search for My Family 308
Chapter 22   I Never Cried for My Mother 320
Chapter 23   Visit From My Dad 333
Chapter 24   Epilogue 338
Time Line   343

Poem by Laura Finkel to her daughter, Lizzi, about to leave for America,
Vienna, 18 March 1940

Farewell, the hour of taking leave draws near.

Remember often your old, once beloved country!

God bless you and guide you safely to the free land

May He soon unite our torn-apart band.

Now, as you travel far away from home

May luck be at your side and

Shine on you like the stars in the sky.

With great sorrow I see you leaving here,

So I wish to give you some good lessons for your path

Keep things in order; use your time well,

That brings contentment and sunshine to your heart.

Be honest, joyful, and a valuable human being,

Preserve your innocent soul from every fault.

Love truth, may this virtue grace you

Just as your youth graces you.

Check your thought before you give it voice

And you'll avoid a troublesome burden

Since an inconsiderate mouth

Brings many a painful hour.

When you follow my advice

You'll have a successful life.

Be good, be helpful

The loved God will be with you!

Remember your strict,
but loving you beyond all words, devoted Mutti

1

S.S. Washington

JOURNEY TO
SAN FRANCISCO

*I*t is March 20, 1940. It is freezing tonight as I stand on the
train station platform waiting to leave Vienna. I rub my
hands and shuffle my feet. There are many bright lights, many
people and many soldiers carrying guns.

I am starting on a long journey from war to safety, from Vienna
to America, in a group of ten children, but I am the only one
going to San Francisco, to stay with a distant relative. Our
escort is a lady who is going on the same ship, but she is a

stranger to us. We huddle around her waiting to board the train. Parents couldn't come to see us off because Jews can't be out at night.

I am ten and a half, the youngest of our group, but I am already a seasoned traveler. When I was younger I often went to Poland to visit my relatives. This time is different—I won't be cushioned by my mother's comforting arms, but I am not afraid because she has prepared me for my upcoming adventure. She told me to not to cry, to be brave.

"I'll be coming as soon as I get the papers for immigration," my mother had assured me and then commanded, "You must write to me and Papa weekly, giving all the details. Remember to be good and grateful and helpful. The poem I have written for you will be a guide for your new life."

I am cold and impatient to get started on this journey, so I am glad when we can finally get on the train and leave this scary place.

The train was packed with people fleeing Nazi persecution, some crying, all somber, clutching their few possessions. We carried food for the two-day trip to Genoa, Italy, where we would embark for New York. The seats on the train were wooden and very uncomfortable. The slow train lurched, throwing us from side to side as it went to its destination stopping at many stations. I ran frequently to the toilet to throw up, suffering from severe motion sickness. We slept sitting up for two nights, likely leaning on each other. In Genoa we stayed in a hotel, my first ever. My only remembrance of it is that the toilet was just a hole in a tile floor creating anxiety for me with each use.

Contrary to the train, the ship, the SS Washington, an American luxury ship, was astounding in its elegance to my unsophisticated eyes. Crystal chandeliers and beautiful furniture in the dining room were new to me, but it was the food that was especially great. There was even kosher food, and the cook wanted to spoil us by piling on the rich food—and some got tummy aches from it. We had had so little food except potatoes and noodles since Hitler had occupied Austria two years before, so I enjoyed meat and fruit as well as the variety and quality at mealtimes. It was wonderful. The ship was fun as it rocked gently in the Mediterranean the first two days, but when we entered the Atlantic, the rocking was no longer fun. I became very seasick and for the next three days spent most of my time in the cabin I shared with other girls. Motion sickness on trains and even streetcars had plagued me since I was a very young child. One scary time I couldn't open the door of the toilet stall to get out, so I had to crawl under it. Still, I liked the ship.

Finally, early one morning I heard "New York...New York" and many other unintelligible words over the loudspeaker. I only understood New York, enough to know that I should hurry to the deck. It was Monday, April 1, a gray, overcast and very cold day as our ship eased into the New York harbor. I ran up to the deck, squeezing in between other equally excited passengers to get a closer look at the Statue of Liberty. There she was before me, green, huge, dramatic and beautiful, and I gasped with wonder. Towering buildings of the New York skyline came into sight, equally incredible. I was eager and excited to see the famous sights that my mother had told me about as she prepared me for my solo journey to America—my new life without her. Hopefully, very soon, we would be reunited with my father, already in England, who had been forced to leave Austria the year before. Thus, full of wonder and excitement I took in the sights of the New York skyline, realizing how lucky I was.

Admiring the view from the ship, I was glad the ten-day voyage was over, and that, at last, I had arrived in New York! I was wearing my best dress, made by my mother. It was maroon velvet with a white lace collar and buttons to the waist. Today, I wonder if I wore it the whole time I was on the ship, or even slept in it. I wonder if I changed my underwear, washed my clothes or took a bath or shower.

I wouldn't have known how to do any of those things unless somebody on the trip showed me; in Vienna, our apartment did not have a bathroom, and weekly baths were in a metal tub, water brought from the hall spigot and heated on the stove. How did I learn about showers or bathtubs or even sinks with running water?

Miss Liberty loomed large as the ship slipped by, and sailing past I was amazed with her size and stunned by the skyline, never having seen such high buildings. Passengers pointed to this and that, surprised by the view before us.

✦ ✦ ✦

I had no idea what would happen next, except that I was going to San Francisco to stay with Aunt Laura whom I had never met. Soon the ship docked and everybody rushed to get off. It was very cold. Some nicely dressed ladies greeted us and took care of the disembarkation; I did not know who they were, but later I learned they were from a Jewish Welfare Committee that sponsored our immigration. They were friendly, but I could not speak with them because I only knew a few words of English, such as "thank you, please, how do you do, and good morning." One lady asked me something with the word "cold," a word I knew, but I was not cold, so I said "No." She pointed to my nose, and then I guessed that she was talking about my runny nose and cough, a perennial cold I had brought with me from Vienna.

A taxi took us to the George Washington Hotel on 23rd St. in Manhattan. I understood taxi, for it is a

Hotel George Washington

German word, but I had never been in one, or any car, for that matter. In Vienna, I had seen some cars and wondered how it would be to ride in one. This one was fast, but very nice. America must really be a rich country, I concluded, because the streets were full of cars and so many big buildings.

Even the hotel was a skyscraper! This hotel was much nicer than the one in Genoa. Red carpets, fancy chairs and tables and gold on the pillars in the lobby, all impressed me. Then we went up the elevators, high, high, while my stomach stayed behind, almost like getting seasick. I shared a large, lovely room with another girl, surprised by the big bed just for me. At home, I had a very little bed, the size of a crib. When I looked out the window, I saw many more big buildings and the taxis looked very small. It was all much more astounding than my mother had told me. I wished that my parents could be with me, but we were so busy with fun things to see and do, that I didn't think about them very long.

The dining room at the top of the hotel was another beautiful room, like the palace rooms in Cinderella. The tables had pink tablecloths, flowers, and beautiful glasses on thin legs. Black waiters in white uniforms served us great food elegantly. I had seen a black person only once before in Vienna. People on the street had called out "schwarze" (black) and pointed at him because he was so strange. I had stared too, then, but now I did not think the waiters were strange; they seemed very friendly. A waiter served us, like on the ship, and that was also a new experience. The waiter put the napkin on my lap; I didn't know how to be proper in such a fine place. Though I couldn't understand him, I thought he was nice.

After lunch the welfare ladies took us to the Rockefeller Center, one of those super high skyscrapers I had noticed from the ship. This time it took two different elevators to get to the top, going so fast, leaving my stomach behind and causing my ears to pop, but I was getting used to the elevators and the jerks on my stomach. It was thrilling to be on the observation deck near the top looking down on the street and seeing the cars looking as small as fleas. Yet, one building was even higher than ours: I learned it was the Empire State Building.

Our next stop was a giant theater, Radio City Music Hall, where we saw a movie, Pinocchio; it was about a boy whose nose grew long, but since I didn't understand English, I was just amused by the cartoon figures and enjoyed the pretty music. Later, many beautiful ladies, the Rockettes, danced in a long line, all doing the same thing. I had been to a few movies in Vienna, but there had not been live dancers, and this theater was so-o much bigger. There were even two organs playing wonderful music. Everything in New York was big!

After that, we were taken to a restaurant for some sweets. An ice cream soda was ordered for me, and I can still remember the funny sensation when the soda came up my nose. I loved ice cream. When my father rewarded me for good marks in school, ice cream was the special treat. It had been a long time since I'd had ice cream. This was a great day, one adventure and thrill after another!

The next day I was put on a train to begin my journey to San Francisco. I was the only child to go to the West Coast since all others had relatives in the New York area. Now I was really alone, couldn't speak English, didn't know what would happen next, but unworried and excited about the new wonders yet to come. Somebody was my guardian, perhaps the porter, because I was taken off the train in Chicago where I spent the night at the Palmer House Hotel. I wrote each of my parents a postcard, but I don't remember who bought it and the stamp for me, as I had no money.

I resumed my train journey the next day. I had a soft seat by myself next to the window where I could see America go by. We traveled a long time over a snow-covered plain, and then we started to climb huge mountains. Periodically, the kind, black conductor brought me to the dining room. Since I was functionally deaf and dumb, not understanding English, I ate what was given to me, all delicious. I spent three more days on the train, climbing on a ladder to an upper berth to sleep—how amazing American trains were! I did not get motion sickness even once! And what beautiful scenery! I was impressed with America's size since it took so many days to go to San Francisco. I especially remember the beautiful mountains still in snow, so many tunnels and the steep mountainsides.

It was a beautiful, clear, sunny day when the train stopped in Oakland early on the morning of April 6 and I was put on a ferry to San Francisco. I wondered what Aunt Laura and her family would be like. My mother had told me that as a young girl she had known Auntie and that she was very nice. As the ferry approached the city, instead of skyscrapers I saw many hills. I loved everything I saw: the famous bridges, the water, the hills, the white and pastel buildings in the shimmering morning sun, reflecting it and sparkling like glass. San Francisco was so beautiful! Everything was more enchanting than I had imagined. I felt very lucky to have come to San Francisco.

If I felt anxious, worried, or lonesome during my journey to my new home so many years ago, I have forgotten it, remembering only the wonder of America on my first trip. I am thankful that my mother prepared me for this journey, making it something marvelous instead of a dreaded separation. I am grateful to my parents for having taught me independence and especially trust, so that instead of the panic of being alone, I was comfortable and could savor the miracle of America. This journey set the tone for my life—looking forward with excitement of good things to come, feeling lucky for my experiences and forgetting the bad. Thus, anticipating a new and better life with optimism, I did not look back. This memorable journey to America inspired my lifelong wanderlust.

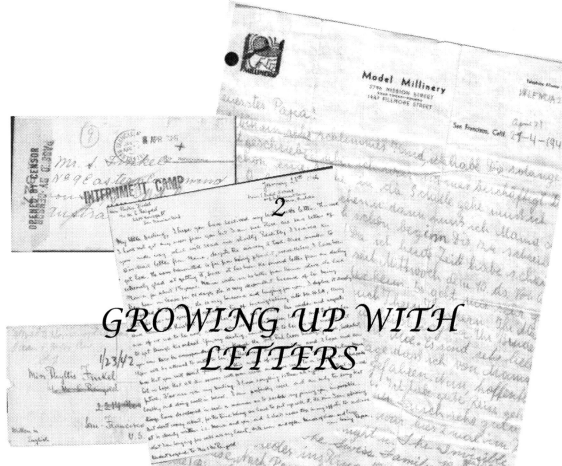

GROWING UP WITH LETTERS

2

In 1940 Europe was in chaos. Hitler was taking over countries boldly—Austria in 1938, then Czechoslovakia, then Poland in 1939. Besides annexing countries for more *Lebensraum*—more living room—he was bent on ridding his domain of Jews. As early as 1933, when he came to power, Jews began to lose some of their civil rights; later they would be denied their livelihood if not their lives. Those who could, left. Those left behind tried desperately to find a way to escape. Some, like my father, were forced to leave or face concentration camps. Thus, he left Vienna in 1939, finding refuge in England, only to be sent to Australia in 1940 as a British Prisoner of War.

✦ ✦ ✦

In order to save the children from the horrors of war and from death, Jewish, Quaker, Unitarian and other benevolent organizations sought ways to get them out of Germany and Austria. My best friend was among some children sent to France on a *Kindertransport* (child transport). As the danger mounted, 10,000 children were accepted by England without any sponsoring papers.[1] However, few other countries, including the United States, were willing to accept refugee children unless the children actually had a visa and a sponsoring family to live with. Altogether, from 1933 to 1945—Hitler's time—roughly 1,000 children in small Kindertransports were brought to America, without fanfare or publicity because there was opposition to Jewish immigrants.[2][3] Despite the severity of the times, however, children were told the separation from parents would be short, and to hope and pray that this chaos would soon end.

I was one of these children. I did not know about foreign policies, immigration limits, quotas, visas, rules and regulations; I was just a child sent to the new Promised Land—America—to escape the imminent danger to Jews. I was told of America's wonders and opportunities, the beautiful cities, the good schools, the good life, and that our family would soon be reunited.

✦ ✦ ✦

In the hundreds of times that I have told my story of coming to America alone, without my parents, I have always been asked, "Weren't you scared?" I have no recollection of fear. I expected our separation to be short. As I told my story, I told it as though it happened to another child, factually without emotion, a way to distance myself from the tragedy that I had experienced, and the way I still talk about my experiences. I did not want people to feel sorry for me, nor did I want to brag about my bravery. After all, many children had been sent to safety during the war, but perhaps only a few would go so far alone. Besides, it somehow felt bad to admit to

---

[1] Harris, Mark J, and Deborah Oppenheimer, (Ed): *Into the Arms of Strangers: Stories of the Kindertransport*, New York; London: Bloomsbury Pub.: St. Martin's Press, 2000

[2] Baumel, Judith T: *Unfulfilled Promise: Rescue and Resettlement of Jewish Refugee Children in the United States*, 1934-1945, Denali Press, Juneau, 1990

[3] Jason, Philip K, and Iris Posner, (Ed.): *Don't Wave Goodbye: The Children's Flight from Nazi Persecution to American Freedom*, Greenwood Publishing Group, 2004

being alone and without parents, of being an orphan, a feeling I tried to keep even from myself. At the same time I was telling my story, I was also memorizing it, perhaps inventing it, or at least not remembering things that were painful to recall.

✦ ✦ ✦

Minding my mother's command that I write often and in detail, I began a lifetime of letter writing. Letters became a big part of my life: my way of having family, as well as a way of expressing myself to those who cared about me. Usually I wrote to my mother and father every week, or more truthfully, every two weeks. I had a duty to write, but I also wanted to tell my parents about my extraordinary new life. In my first letter to my father, in a postscript, I asked him to save my letters and bring them to me when he came to America. I don't know what prompted me to make this request. Perhaps my mother had suggested it. I saved all incoming letters. Together with mine, they are a record of my life from 1940 to 1946, and a source of many recollections of my first years in America. I have 251 letters altogether, 124 that I wrote, 86 from my father and 41 from my mother. Some have been lost. Not all of them are included in the book.

Letters from my mother in Austria were full of hopes and promises of coming to me soon. They were written in German on such thin paper that the ink bled through. She filled every inch of the paper, not making paragraphs or margins. German censors opened and read them, sometimes blacked out parts, sometimes cut out bits. Her letters were loving and scolding, hopeful and then tragically desperate as her hopes of coming to America disappeared with the entrance of the United States into war with Germany in December 1941; the letters stopped at that time. I cannot read her letters now without tears forming and great sorrow overwhelming me.

My father and I wrote to each other for six years, our letters also opened by censors. I tried to make him see my world, the world of an adolescent, a virtual orphan, in an unfamiliar country, among strangers. He was concerned about my progress in school, which at first was very good, but increasingly became less so. His greatest worry, however, was my troublesome behavior which had me expelled from four fosters homes and three cottages at an orphanage. Perhaps he feared I'd be thrown out on the streets, but it had never occurred to me that I could be made homeless. I took for granted that I would be taken care of.

Most of my father's letters were written in excellent English, the language required by the Australian censors, not his first langugage, but a language he had learned in school. His letters first show a loving, caring, teasing, indulgent parent. Later they became nagging, authoritative with harsh tones, sometimes all in the same letter. In my lifetime I had remembered mainly the nagging, but re-reading the letters now verify how much he really loved me, how patient he was, and how he tried to encourage me. He tried to parent me long-distance, and only rarely disclosed his way of life in exile. He was not a complainer, but accepted life as it happened—sometimes mournfully. Perhaps he wasn't permitted to vent his anger due to the censorship. Most likely it was his nature to accept his fate, and not to reveal himself. He did not tell me much about his work, his friends or recreation although I repeatedly asked him to tell me of his life. In all the letters, however, his and mine, were the hopes of his coming to America and delivering me from my predicament of being an orphan.

✦ ✦ ✦

I grew strong. My letters show me as a pragmatic, fiercely independent, confident, truthful child growing through adolescence. As I worked with these letters, I was often surprised by the young girl who wrote them. Was I that girl? I had the strange experience of somehow being detached from her, as though she was a stranger that I was just meeting, not someone I really knew.

Most frustrating for us was the delay in the mail—sometimes taking up to ten weeks—worrisome, and always making our communication askew. In the text, I have tried to put the letters in some order of relationship to each other, usually as answers to <u>my</u> letters, but it wasn't always possible due to the time lag in responding. Thus, sometimes I will be writing, say in May; however, a response might not be written until June or July and received by me in August or September. I couldn't always tell when I received them.

My parents designated me to be the central communication link between them and others, a job I did not perform as well as they wished. Yet when I see the quantity of letters I did write, I have to give my young self credit for diligence. Besides letters to my parents, I had some correspondence with my Uncle Max, my father's brother who was also on the move, as well as Viennese friends of my parents, Anny and Arno Bick, already living in Baltimore, who worked tirelessly to get affidavits for my parents.

Later, I started writing letters to myself on special occasions such as my sixteenth birthday, or a momentous event such as the end of World War II, or at New Year to review of my experiences of the past year. These were like a journal that I sealed in an envelope with a command "not to be opened until ten years later" or "when I am married." When I'm troubled, I write a letter, not always mailed. Sometimes I write letters to my deceased parents.

I consider letters a gift from one person to another. I hold the paper the other person held, searching for understanding when different interpretations are possible; I look forward to them with anxiety or hope, considering how to write a response. I will keep the letters, to cherish, to re-read later, and sometimes, to destroy in rage. Letters allow time to consider the answer, thereby crafting it rather than blurting it out. Sometimes writing is a chore taking time from other duties or pleasures, sometimes a chance to vent frustrations, to share experiences or to brag about accomplishments. Because letters are such a gift, people keep letters as treasured objects, like jewels, in special places. I find our letters precious, like fragments of us, broken off and saved. Now that I am a parent, I understand their letters more. Even as I re-read them, I discover new information about us during those years when we were separated. Letters formed a safety net around me connecting me to the people I loved. As I think about it now, being a temporary orphan, it must have been very important for me to keep the letters as the only physical connections to my family. I might have been afraid of disappearing in such a big world, but by writing letters I kept connected, and did not feel as a true orphan, although others thought of me as such.

Although my letters sometimes disclosed my loneliness or my indignation, they often rejoiced in my new experiences such as going to the World Fair or participating in sports. Many times I reported on my new culture, such as the ritual of holidays, throwing in a bit of history. My letters are very long, giving details that might bore, but which described my life as a teenage immigrant becoming American. I often explained my life like an anthropologist describes a remote tribe, objectively, but other times, my impartial reporting gives way to explosions of anger or exuberant patriotism. I liked the reporting style—I still like the emotional distance it gives me, preventing an emotional display.

It is no wonder that I actually became an anthropologist whose work is on the edge between two cultures—observer and participant at the same time. I lived my life that way during my adolescence. Now, in my writing I am an archeologist digging in the potsherds—the letters—to reconstruct my early life, to analyze my motives and examine my disappointments, trying to figure out who I was or what I tried to be. Thus, with the continuous stream of writing and receiving letters, I grew to maturity. If I sometimes complained about having to write them, I was always glad to receive them, connecting me to my family. If I didn't always like what they said, I had a chance to express myself without interruption. I had a chance to show my love in words, if not with hugs and kisses, and to receive my parents' love repeatedly.

◆ ◆ ◆

I was most struck by the damage that the war did to my family, as it did to millions of others as I studied the letters. I was too young to comprehend the scope of the tragedy at the time, but now I can tally the misfortune. My immediate family was continents apart—my father in Australia, my mother in Europe and I in America, while my extended family—aunts and uncles, grandparents and cousins—was also dispersed, and many died. I become sad, and even remorseful that later my father and I didn't discuss our family history or our lives during the separation. Like many others who experienced the war, my father wanted the past left behind, and I, because of my youth and by disposition, looked only to the future. In fact, at that time I did not think of our letters as precious, although I knew they were important, so I stored all of them in a small, old, slightly mildewed cardboard briefcase, put it in a metal footlocker kept in the garage, covered with heavy objects so that the insides were kept out of my sight and out of mind, but safe. Fortunately, they were in excellent condition when I resurrected them a few years ago as I started writing my memoirs.

◆ ◆ ◆

When I came as a war orphan, I needed to adapt to America immediately. I had to learn everything anew, even my name, as if I were just born. I only knew a few words of English. The various people who took care of me in the first weeks didn't speak to me in a language I knew, but I learned quickly, as many children do. I had left my culture, my history, my language, my world, my relatives and friends behind. As I forgot the old culture, even memories disappeared, for they are kept alive when people move in groups, reminding each other by talking of the past: "...remember when you were a little girl, you were always..." or "when I was young we used to..." When I lost my language I also lost the meanings conveyed with tones as well as words, including conversations with my parents. I am not able to reconstruct a conversation with my parents from my years in Vienna. Many scenes of my childhood have just vanished. Perhaps retelling my story has helped me to keep some memories alive, even though they may not be correct.

Although I wasn't aware of it, besides the language, I lost what is fundamental to life's fullness: sharing lives through gatherings and memories and by belonging to families. I grew up in San Francisco without a single close relative in the United States. My real family was separated by oceans. Therefore, also missing from my childhood were the celebrations, aunts and uncles, cousins, tales of childhood, weddings, funerals and even grieving. I never missed these gatherings and connections when I was young, at least consciously, but in my old age I see how the lack of these associations impacted my life.

I came to minimize the importance of families, and I wondered why other people were so dependent on theirs. I also noticed that many families weren't good to each other, so what was this thing called "family loyalty?" Later, I disliked going to weddings and funerals, even my college graduation because I sensed my aloneness. At my father's death in 1970 I could not assemble the required *minyon*, ten Jewish men, to conduct a proper burial; it didn't matter to me at that time, since I had long ago ceased to care about traditions. My marriage was private, and I begged my children to elope, but they wanted to enjoy their traditional weddings, rich in relatives and friends. I felt alone for lack of my larger family's presence.

I want to mourn for my losses, but grieving alone now doesn't help; rather it intensifies my feelings of deficiency, of lacking family. As I think about these terrible losses today, I realize that I learned to forget unpleasant things, to block them out, and not dwell on the past. Instead, desperately, I tried to make my own connections with friends and lived for the future. I survived my losses by the thin strands of letters to and from my parents, and by the lucky aptitude for making deep friendships.

❖ ❖ ❖

My story is just one more move in the *Diaspora,* the dispersal of Jews throughout history. Moving is part of my ethnic history though I wasn't aware of it at the time I came to America. Jews were the wandering people from the start of history, forced to move rather than choosing to because other populations decreed them undesirable, *personae non grata.* Moving became a way of life for me in my youth, even as I was adapting and acculturating to a new way of life. Between 1940 and 1947, I moved ten times. My parents were also on the move during that time. After that, I was still on the move, but by inclination instead of force. Even during my young years, sometimes, moving was an escape. Later, as an adult, a move more often was a thrill of new opportunities, new adventures, new friends to be made, new cultures to be encountered. If moving is the magic carpet of my life, then letters and friends are the bright threads that run through it.

3

MY HOME

Riesenrad

My father has taken me to the Prater, Vienna's amusement park as a reward for good marks at school. I am seven years old. I love going places with my Papa. We are now going for a ride on the Riesenrad, the giant Ferris wheel. We sit in a big box with windows all around and we can see the city as the wheel turns higher and higher into the air.

"Look, Lizzchen," my father says as he points at landmarks. Below me I see buildings as far as the sky. "Where is our house?" I ask. "Look there, do you see the building with the funny roof? That is the Volksoper, where we sometimes go to see the fairy tales, and if you look a little to the right, you will see Nüssdorferstrasse where we live." I recognize the Volksoper and our street, but I can't find our apartment house.

He continues pointing and telling, and I begin to recognize some streets where we have walked. "See, he says, "that is the 1st district, the most beautiful. "Look, there is the Opera House, and that building is the Hofburg Palace" and he mentions other important buildings, still pointing. As the wheel turns slowly in its giant circle, new vistas appear. "Below is the Danube, and those are the Vienna Woods in the distance."

"Look at this beautiful view" he exclaims with a sweep of his hand and an animated voice. He really loves Vienna. The ride is slow and it takes long to go around, so we have many chances to find landmarks. It is most amazing to look down on big buildings. I can see that Vienna is mostly flat, and goes on forever until it touches the sky.

*M*y father tells me that Vienna is the most beautiful city in Europe, and we are lucky to live here. He promises that we will visit many of the places he has pointed out to me so that I can learn all about our lovely Vienna.

◆ ◆ ◆

As a child I often walked among the beautiful buildings that we saw from the Riesenrad, but I was unaware of the importance of Vienna in world history because I was so young. I liked Vienna because I lived there. Then I did not know Vienna's rich history, but its history is important to my own.

Vienna, capital of Austria, is not a big city as world cities go, although it is very famous for its rich culture and history. Its million and a half residents are 20 percent of the country's population, now about eight million, but once when Austria was an empire it had 50 million people. Like many European cities most of the important buildings are in one district, the 1st, and in Vienna are surrounded by a broad boulevard called the Ring; each section of it has its own label, such as Statsring, where all the government buildings are located, or Opernring, which holds the Opera house. The world famous art and science museums, beautiful buildings in their own right, are also located on the Ring. The architecture is grand and imposing, from the gothic, spired Rathaus (City Hall) and Stephansdom whose landmark spire can be seen far away, to the neo-classic Parliament with its many columns, resembling the Parthenon of Greece. Baroque, with its ornate decorations, is the most widespread architectural style, as seen in the Burg Theater, the Opera, and the graceful Hofburg Palace.

Streetcars run on the Ring connecting all the parts. One side of the Ring is a small muddy channel of the Danube. The Prater, Vienna's amusement park with the famous giant Ferris wheel is on the other side of the channel, the 2nd district. The main river, one of the longest in the world, is above the city, some distance away, continuing its journey through Budapest, Hungary, and many other famous cities in southeastern Europe before emptying into the Black Sea. Beautiful gardens with statues of famous Viennese—soldiers, emperors, as well as musicians—surround the historic buildings, while fenced-off lawns declare that stepping on the grass is forbidden. The main cathedral, Stephansdom and its plaza, is a gathering place for many demonstrations, and there are many other notable churches are in this district.

It is a great walking city. Cafes are everywhere, in good weather serving at small tables outside, always crowded with espresso drinkers, and somewhere nearby musicians fill the air with old and new favorites. "Eine kleine schwarze" is how one asks for the espresso, while a regular coffee, still strong in flavor is "Eine grosse braune" meaning large with milk. Delicious pastries filled with whipped cream and iced in dark chocolate are temptations to the dieter, but pleasantly enjoyed by everybody. Social life is conducted in cafes. The café house is an old tradition in Vienna. My father, using a dreamy, reminiscing tone, used to tell me about going to them; there for the price of a coffee, he could stay for hours reading the many free newspapers that were part of the ambiance. People had their favorite café houses each with its own club atmosphere and patrons could spend the evening playing cards, only buying coffee and perhaps a sandwich or a sweet; the waiters dressed formally in crisp black and white uniforms, addressed the patrons with "gnadiger Herr", (gracious sir) showing respect.

There are many popular images of Vienna derived from movies and music. These include visions of beautiful people in elaborate palaces waltzing in luxurious gowns. Its blue Danube river—not really blue—is celebrated by a waltz. Its art and artists, as well as its outstanding classical music and musicians such as Mozart, Schubert, Beethoven, Strauss, and Mahler are world famous. The city was also a world center of science and medicine spawning many Nobel Prizes, as well as the beginning of psychotherapy by the world-famous Dr. Freud.

✦ ✦ ✦

Located in the valley of the Danube but close to hills and woods, Vienna is a northern city—it has very cold winters and hot sticky summers with overcast skies. Its history began as a Roman outpost because of its strategic river location. Later it became the headquarters of the Catholic Church for its northern and eastern frontiers. For many centuries the city protected Europe from the eastern invaders—the Ottoman Empire and its Moslem religion. Austrians take great pride in having saved Europe for Christianity.

Following the Napoleonic Wars in 1804, Austria became an empire. Later, in 1867, the great Hapsburg Empire ruled large areas of central and eastern Europe, including the countries we now know as Poland, Hungary, Romania, Serbia, Croatia, Slovakia, the Czech Republic, part of The Ukraine and part of Italy, including Trieste on the Adriatic Sea. As a result, Vienna became a cosmopolitan city enticing geniuses, craftsmen and energetic migrants from all the provinces. For awhile Austria even had its hands on Mexico, as Archduke Maximillian appointed by Napoleon, became its ruler in 1864, only to be assassinated. The beautiful feathered headpiece worn by Montezuma, a Mexican treasure, found its home in a dark corner of the Kunstmuseum in Vienna. The assassination of Archduke Ferdinand, heir to the Austrian throne, started World War I in 1914, involving all of Europe as well as the United States and Russia.

As a result of the Versailles Peace Treaty following the defeat of Austria and Germany and the end of World War I, the Austrian-Hungarian Empire was dissolved leaving just the current Austria, a small, landlocked and powerless country in the center of Europe, basically broke.

The post-war period saw super-inflation, then depression, and great discontent in the land. Hitler, born in Linz, Austria, who had fought in the war, got his political start at this time. He had spent some years prior to the war in Vienna developing his artistic talents, but was not recognized by the critics; he, in turn, never liked the city because it was so cosmopolitan. It was here that he first wrote about his hatred of Jews:

> I was repelled by the conglomeration of races which the capital showed me, repelled by this whole mixture of Czechs, Poles, Hungarians,

Ruthenians, Serbs, and Croats, and everywhere the eternal mushroom of humanity—Jews, and more Jews. To me the giant city seemed the embodiment of racial desecration… The longer I lived in this city the more my hatred grew for the foreign mixture of peoples which had begun to corrode this old site of German culture. [1]

In 1938, some years after Hitler became Chancellor of Germany, he annexed Austria to Germany in a coup, without much opposition or firing a shot and was accepted joyously by most inhabitants. World War II started in September 1939 after which he initiated the most horrific genocide against Jews and some other groups he felt should not live, such as Gypsies, homosexuals, and deformed or mentally deficient people. Six million Jews were killed in monstrous schemes of annihilation.

The Allies bombed Vienna, but spared many of its famous landmarks. After the war, Austria was governed jointly by Russia, England, France and the United States. It regained its independent status in 1955.

✦ ✦ ✦

MY HOME, 1929 to 1939

Our apartment—this is the only place that I can recall living in—was on the second floor of a big, dark gray corner building that had four stories altogether. Residences were above shops on the ground floor, such as the leather shop below us. The upstairs was reached by going through a dark, musty-smelling foyer that led to a courtyard, or by turning left, to a wide stone circular staircase. Our apartment was close to the landing, but the

---

[1] Shirer, William L.: *The Rise and Fall of the Third Reich,* Fawcett, 1959:p.49, quoting *Mein Kampf,* Hitler's manifesto, here pertaining to his pre-political era, around 1912.

corridor continued on and around forming two sides of a square around the court-yard. Other buildings formed the remaining sides of the square.

Our apartment faced the street, and one of my favorite pastimes was to stand at the window, watching the world go by as I rested my elbows on window pillows kept between the double windows to block out the bitter winter. Streetcars passed frequently, as well as bicycles, shoppers and an occasional car.

The front door to our apartment opened to a smallish room separated length-wise by a curtain that hid the kitchen. There was no window in this room, no built-in cabinets or closets, no stove, no running water. A cupboard against the wall held utensils and food; a two-burner cooking surface and a table with three chairs filled up the kitchen. On the other side of the curtain was my crib, the only bed I remem-ber. This side of the room was also the hallway to the next room, which was twice as big, but also divided by a curtain. Behind it were my parents' bed, my mother's cutting table, dress form, ironing board and sewing machine, the latter being near one window to catch the light for her work. Two chairs were close together near the sewing machine used by my mother and her helper, Anny, in their sewing work.

In the main part of this room a big wardrobe held our clothes, while close to the dividing curtain near the second window was a chaise lounge with a small table with fashion magazines neatly displayed. An armchair was nearby and full-length mirror was mounted on the wall. There weren't any rugs on the wooden floor. The walls were white, the ceilings, high. I don't remember any pictures on the wall. Everything was simple, perhaps inadequate, but that is from my current viewpoint. I don't remember comparing our place to those better-furnished ones of my friends.

The other tenants—unwanted intruders—were bedbugs that made nightly forage for my blood. My skin was very sensitive to their bites and they itched un-comfortably. It's creepy to have bugs biting you when you sleep, but awkward when they venture forth in daytime. I recall my mother's great embarrassment once when a bedbug came out from behind the mirror as a customer was being fitted for a dress. I am sure my father sprayed the mattresses, but apparently it didn't help, at least not permanently.

There was no bathroom. The toilet was across the hall and used by several other families, and water was obtained from a spigot in the hall. We took our infrequent baths in a metal tub in our kitchen, also used for washing clothes. A washbasin served us for our daily ablutions. Washing my hair was quite an ordeal since I had lice that refused to go away despite tar soap and turpentine rinses. My head was held over the washbasin while water, chamomile rinses, or the unpleasant turpentine were poured over my hair. Then, my hair had to be carefully searched for the dreadful little bugs with a fine-tooth comb, the cliché coming from this ancient activity. Finally it was dried and combed. I was around four years old when my fine black hair was shaved off to deal with the lice. I remember having a picture of myself with no hair. Otherwise, I usually wore my straight hair short and don't remember any time in my life when it was longer than shoulder length. Miraculously, my hair became wavy in my teens.

We did not have a radio, but my father was always reading newspapers. I don't remember any toys, not even books, and although I had a doll I do not recall what she looked like. It was not a cozy place, by my standards of today, but in my childhood I was comfortable and happy living there with my parents.

4

MY FAMILY

My parents and me at different ages.

I was the first person in my family to be born in Vienna. My father, Samuel Finkel, and my mother, Laura Hermann, met in Vienna, but they were not born there. They came from Eastern Europe, the area known as Galicia, then part of the large Austrian-Hungarian Empire. Emperor Franz Joseph and his beautiful wife Elizabeth presided over a rich and powerful country whose stamp is still felt today in the architecture and urban designs, interest in music and the arts.

I once heard a joke on the radio that encapsulates eastern European history, especially Galicia, the wellspring of my family.

> A man was being interviewed for having lived in so many places. The interviewer asked: "Where were you born?" to which the man replied, "Austria."
> Interviewer: "Where did you go to school?
> The Man: "Poland."
> "And where did you get married?"
> "Germany," was the answer.

"And where did you work then?"

"Russia"

"And now where do you live?"

"The Ukraine"

Interviewer, amazed: "My, you have moved around a lot in your life!"

The Man: "Not me! I've never moved! I've lived in the same village all my life."

In fact, these changes were experienced in my parent's hometowns in the 20th century.

◆ ◆ ◆

My father, Samuel, was born on August 20, 1901, in Leipzig, Germany, at the home of his mother, Dresel (born Dora Goldstaub) at Georgenstrasse 6. She came from a prosperous family that was in the fur business. His father, Abraham, a green-grocer, however, came from a city then called Lemberg, part of the Austrian Empire. He had lived in Leipzig where he was introduced to my grandmother. It was probably an arranged marriage.

When my father was five years old the family moved to Lemberg, still part of Austria. Lemberg was a big city, fashioned after Vienna with beautiful baroque buildings and wide boulevards. In 1918, the region where my parents had grown up became part of Poland. Their citizenship was Polish, and the language of the land, Polish. Lemberg's name was changed to L'vov which is what I remember calling it when I was young. Ukranians were the dominant nationality in Galicia, which today is part of The Ukraine. In the places where my parents lived, Ukrainians were mostly very poor tenant farmers and were discriminated against by the Poles. There were many Jews in that area too, living in small towns or villages, despised by Poles and Ukranians alike. In 1940, Germany and Russia divided eastern Europe, Russia getting parts of Poland, including Galicia. In September 1941, Hitler changed his mind and invaded this area, but it was re-occupied by the Russians after World War II. Since the breakup of the Soviet Union in 1991, Galicia became part of a new country, The Ukraine, and the city is now called L'viv.

Uncle Max & Aunt Tillie

My father was the middle child of three, having an older brother, Max, and a younger sister, Hannah. Max did not stay in Lemberg at maturity, but returned to Leipzig to join his mother's family in the fur business. He married a first cousin, Tillie, and because of that, chose not to have children. Max was so successful that he was able to support my father's higher education in Vienna at the Business College in International Trade (Hochschule fur Welthandel). My father received his diploma in March 1924. After graduating, and because of his language skills, he worked as a correspondent for a bank dealing with foreign banks. He had chosen to study and work in Vienna because he was drawn to the urban, sophisticated life abounding there. He often spoke of his love of Vienna, its culture and worldliness, and its wonderful café houses. He especially loved opera, which he knew in detail, and often reminisced about how he, as a student, had bought standing-room tickets, not caring if he could see the actors because, to him, the music itself was the most important part. He often hummed arias while working around the house.

✦ ✦ ✦

My mother, Laura Hermann, was born on April 7, 1903 in Lawoczne, a little village in the same general area as L'viv, but very close to the Hungarian border. A rail line passed through the town, carrying timber from the Carpathean Mountains south to Hungary and north to L'viv. Her father, because of his early blindness, committed suicide before I was born, but his sister, Mrs. Laufer, lived in Vienna, where she rented a room to my father. When my mother immigrated to Vienna to find work as a seamstress, she lived with her aunt, and through her met my father.

My mother had an older brother, Heshu (Henry) and a younger brother, Dzuniu (David). (More about that family in "Summers in Poland," a later chapter.)

♦ ♦ ♦

Thus, my parents were immigrants to Vienna, as Polish citizens, although I was never conscious of it while growing up; perhaps they didn't act or feel like immigrants because they had been born in the Empire, and identified with the assimilated, educated Jews who came mainly from the German-speaking parts. Perhaps my parents were less religious and did not segregate themselves as much. I surmise that we were an acculturating Viennese family, living in a mixed neighborhood, and not surrounded only by other Jewish immigrants.

Austria had had a large subculture of Jews before World War I—many were well assimilated into Austrian culture. In the 19th century many Jews had been able to assimilate and to participate in the richness of the culture in all fields, owning property, and holding important jobs, such as scientists, doctors, university professors, and some even were Nobel Prize winners. Some were army officers who had fought in WWI, or served in government positions. After the war, they continued to succeed. By 1934, Vienna had over 175,000 Jews, only 2% of the population, but "Jewish businesses and financial institutions managed much of the country's economic life...over 50% of Austria's attorneys, physicians, and dentists were Jewish."[1] For those assimilated, successful Jews, life was very rewarding and pleasant—they were part of the country's elite. My father came to Vienna hoping to share in these opportunities for a good life. The Jews' successes, enabled by a previously benign government, however, became a source of prejudice in the hard times of worldwide depressions. In Hitler's time these feelings erupted into mass discrimination.

My father was twenty-eight and my mother, twenty-five when they married. My father was very tall to my young eyes, but he was only 5'10". He had a big frame and

---

[1] Bukey, Evan Burr: *Hitler's Austria: Popular Sentiment in the Nazi Era, 1938-1945,*
  Univ. of No. Carolina Press, 2002, p. 131

carried his weight well. Already when I was a small child, he was bald except for a ring of thin brown hair from ear to ear in the back of his head. He shaved his facial hair, but was hairy on his chest and arms. He had small brown eyes, a big nose in a big head—not handsome—but his smile and open, friendly demeanor invited connection. His hygiene and dress were meticulous and he took good care of his clothes and possessions. He smoked cigarettes, and I remember him rolling his own. He was slow and deliberate in his movements, never in a rush for anything and always had time for me.

My mother was petite, perhaps five feet tall with very beautiful wavy black hair, light eyes, a pale complexion with some freckles which were a constant source of irritation to her and which she treated with cucumber packs to no avail. I resemble her. She had a nice disposition, making for harmony in the house.

I don't know how long my parents had known each other before they married on November 4, 1928, in Lawoczne, Poland, my mother's home village. It had been considered a "good marriage match", my father told me, because of his education and prospects for success, and her good looks and skills as a seamstress. Aunt Laufer may have acted as a marriage broker. My father told me of the marriage negotiations that had taken place regarding a dowry that according to customs of those times should have established him in some business. Once or twice he later recalled, with some sorrow and even bitterness, that her family had never come through with their promises.

◆ ◆ ◆

I was born in a hospital in Vienna, the first and only offspring of this union, on August 9, 1929. It was not an auspicious year, for in October, stock markets crashed catapulting the Western world into depression after many brutal years of super inflation. My given name was Felicitas, which implies happiness, but I was called Lizzi and many endearing derivatives like Lizzili and Lizzchen. It is an Eastern Jewish custom to name a child after a deceased relative; it might have been my father's grandmother, Frumme, because her name started with F. I don't really know where Felicitas came from for it was not a common name. I was a chubby baby with little hair. When I did get more hair, it was black. I had hazel eyes, like my mother. Later, in adolescence, my hair got thicker, shiny and wavy, eliciting compliments.

I have always assumed my first language was German, but when I reflect on my parents' origins, especially my mother's more rural background, I wonder if Polish, or Ukranian or Yiddish weren't spoken at home. When my parents went to school in the early years of the 20th century, living in Galicia, German was the official language but the local languages were Ukrainian, Polish and the lingua franca of Europe, Yiddish, a derivative of German. Thus, my parents were schooled in German, but were fluent in the other languages as well. I have no recollection of these other languages. Although I know some German now—learned in high school and college—I speak with a bad accent and no fluency. My father and I never spoke German after we came to the States.

✦ ✦ ✦

Except for Tante Laufer, my mother's aunt, and her husband, we had no other relatives in Vienna. We visited the Laufer's fairly often, and though I don't remember the aunt, I do remember her husband since one incident is engraved in my memory with guilt. He was blind and I was often asked to take him on a walk. My job was to tell him when to step up and down at curbs. On one occasion when I was seven or eight years old as we were walking, my attention wandered, and I failed to alert him to the step; he fell forward, breaking his dark glasses, and hurting his knees in the fall. I was reprimanded for my negligence. I felt remorse for my inattention, and the memory of it still pains me.

Though the family was small, my parents did have some friends; however, they did not come for dinner since only relatives shared meals. Anny, my mother's helper, and later her husband-to-be, Arnold Bick, were at our apartment often. These were the dear people who worked tirelessly to secure visas for my parents. Dr. Murmelstein, Rabbi of a Jewish congregation visited us. He had been a beau of my mother's and she had considered marrying him, and even though she married my

*Arnold &
Anny Bick*

father, they still remained friends. Dr. Murmelstein liked playing with me. He was a big man with red hair and beard, and he often became my "horse" as we romped around the room. He may have been instrumental in my joining the children's transport going to America. Another of my mother's close friends was Rosie, also a seamstress, who may have come from Galicia. She and her husband, Max Engel lived around the corner from us and I visited them, or perhaps I stayed there when my parents had other things to do. I was in touch with them later when they immigrated to New York. These people constitute a very small world of connection—perhaps there were more, but I don't remember them, even though many other names were mentioned by my mother in her letters to me later. None of the ones I remembered had children, so I was "it", their token child.

✦ ✦ ✦

The Jewish religion has been an important factor in my life, not for my practice of it, but because being Jewish makes it a central issue of every Jew's life. Had it not been for history's dislike and persecution of Jews, I would not have been separated from my parents at a young age, nor would they have been persecuted and banished from their home. Later, my father disowned me when I didn't marry a Jew.

Is it possible to define who or what is a Jew? Is it a race or religion? Many people consider being Jewish as mainly a tribal or ethnic association—by blood—not always a religious one. On the other hand, in history, even conversion to another religion did not free Jews from persecution and relegation to inferior if not hated status because of blood ties. Even in Israel, a Jewish state, the religious Jews are at odds with the secular, non-religious Jews, both claiming they are Jews. Differences in geographic origins also make for rivals, yet they are all Jews. In Israel, there are Jews of all colors with many variations to the practice of their religion.

So it was in Vienna too. Jews had been in Austria for centuries, sometimes well accepted, sometimes not. Many Jews with a long history in Austria considered themselves first as Austrian, of Jewish faith rather than the national Catholic faith. For these Jews it was a shock when anti-Semitism became so flagrant. Many Jews had converted generations ago, but for Hitler, that didn't matter, and they were subject to persecution. On the other hand, many Jews who had come to Vienna, especially after the first World War, did not wish to assimilate. They came with their orthodox religion, provincial outlooks and costumes, and planned to keep to their old culture and ethnicity and never thought of themselves as Austrians.

✦ ✦ ✦

My parents were trained in the Jewish traditions, but I don't remember much involvement in religious practices when I was young—that just might be my poor memory of my childhood. Since my parents were immigrants from Galicia, where the concentration of Jews in small towns created strong communities and strong Jewish traditions, I believe that they considered their religion very important. I was exposed to Hebrew classes for a while and at one point remember being imbued with an idealistic desire to go to Palestine. My fantasy included working on a kibbutz, stooped over, tilling and planting in the field under the hot sun. Attending to my garden is the closest I have come to fulfilling such a fantasy. From their letters to me later, I know that religion was significant to them as my mother showed her religiosity in her letters, and my father reminded me to study Hebrew.

Nevertheless, I just don't remember much of the Jewish traditions in my early life, although I remember saying prayers every night. My friends in school were Jewish since we were a distinct minority in our class. When the other children had Catholic lessons, we were excused to do some other work, but I do not recall any harassment about religion until after Hitler came.

We observed Chanuka and I vaguely recall some observance of Passover. I do not remember if my mother lit candles on Friday night, but I have the feeling that she did because once, when I was visiting in Israel, I had occasion to learn that prayer. I was startled when Hebrew words came pouring out of my mouth, words I must have known when I was a child. I was astonished by the tears that engulfed me and which I took as a sign of deeper remembrance. Actually, Jewish or Hebrew melodies have a profound effect on me, almost always bringing hard-to-hold-back tears, yet I do not recall where or when I may have heard those melodies. I don't remember attending Temple in Vienna; my parents may have gone for the High Holidays, but considering how little money they had (and one must buy tickets to attend the Temple for observance of those holidays) they might not have been able to afford it. However, Rabbi Murmelstein may have helped them with access to the Temple for the holidays.

I don't believe that we kept a kosher kitchen, though we didn't eat pork, nor meat and milk dishes at the same meal. I knew nothing of the beliefs of Christians, only that we were different. However, once, when Christian neighbor girls, much older than I, came to our door around Christmas with some small gifts for me, I was allowed to accept them.

Religion was not central for me as a child until Hitler declared that to be a Jew was to be inferior, undesirable and to be gotten rid of, which made me conscious of my Jewishness. Whatever religious connection I felt as a youngster eroded after I came to America.

5

DAILY LIFE

My School

The overriding feeling I have of my childhood in Vienna is that life was pleasant and essentially happy. I was very much loved, and I took it for granted. It is a feeling of great comfort to me, even now. Although my parents may have experienced financial hardships, they sheltered me from want. Now, when I consider our life style then, I know that we were poor, but my parents did not impart a "poor" mentality to me, one that would make me feel inferior in facing the world, probably because they had not grown up poor, and expected their fortunes to improve. I did not feel poor vis-à-vis my fellow students at school, nor when I came to the United States. My friends had nicer furniture in their homes, perhaps nicer clothes, but I was never conscious of envying them when I was a child. I am so grateful to my parents for the good outlook on life that they shared with me.

◆ ◆ ◆

Despite my father's promise of a bright future because of his education, in my earliest memories my father did not work. However, according to an affidavit he wrote for some legal purposes later, and mentioned to me later, he had worked for two fur companies as a bookkeeper and correspondent with Slavic-language countries since he was proficient in many languages. In 1928 he started his own business selling motorcycles and bicycles. That would have been a good business, since automobiles were still very scarce in Vienna. I had heard him speak of this business, but I don't remember his having such a business; my guess is that he lost it in the early 1930s. Austria in the 1920's had experienced super-inflation, followed by a severe depression in the 30's. I recall his great enthusiasm once for getting a job of selling stoves with ovens, a new item for households, but it came to nothing, as people had no money for such luxury. He did not seem to be distressed with his inability to work and since there was income from my mother's work, he seemed to settle into his unemployment status. His outlook on life took one day at a time and always with optimism.

He had a gentleness about him, a pleasant, even personality with no signs of a temper, and infinite patience. I can recall some slight arguments between my parents, but never any shouting. If anything, he would have retreated into silence and sulked if he was angry, but I don't remember that from my childhood, only in our later relationship. Nevertheless, he was opinionated, and wouldn't consider another point of view. He enjoyed conversation, even arguing, and was outgoing. He was never in a hurry and I cannot remember even one occasion where he rushed. He wasn't always at home either, so I guess that like other Viennese men he went to the cafe houses to read papers, play cards and visit with friends.

My father was my hero, and I his princess, his "Puppele" (little doll, a name which he continued to call me until he died). He spoiled me, I think, and his attention and approval were very important to me. I re-experienced his attentions when I observed him interact with my children. He adored my first-born, Laurie. He was delighted by her and showered her with presents and love.

He was patient. For example, when he taught my son, Jeff, to play chess, he always explained his moves, and managed his pieces in such a way that Jeff would be able to see the correct move by himself. I noticed that my father always lost; when I asked him why, he said, "I want to build Jeff's confidence." I knew how to play chess when I was little, and I feel he must have taught me in the same patient way. Although he was patient with my children when they were learning something and presumably with me when I was young, he had little patience for self-determination in children, especially when it came to food. In fact, he would brag about how he had disciplined me as a child when I refused to eat something (spinach and tomato sauce are the things I recall not liking). This often came up at dinners when my son refused to eat many things.

"I would not give her anything else to eat until she had finished that first", he would brag to our friends when we discussed the raising of children. "If she didn't want it," he would continue, talking about me, "all right, but at the next meal, that's what she was given. That's how she learned her lesson." Unfortunately, that behavior—eating everything that is put before me—has been a lifelong burden in terms of controlling my weight. Of course, in my childhood eating what was available was prudent—without refrigeration food would not keep; with our very limited income, wasting food would be unthinkable. My father felt I should impose the same standards on my finicky son, but I didn't.

He was proud of the discipline he had exercised in my upbringing, but I can only recall the issues of food and time. He was adamant about punctuality. He was equally proud of how he "broke" my mother of her habit of being late for their appointments. "I told her that I would not wait for her anymore, and one day I simply did not wait," he told us with glee. He relished telling me the story when I was young, and to my children a generation later. I heard his demand for punctuality very clearly, and for fear of being punished, I was hardly ever late.

Other than those two examples of possible misbehavior, I was a good little girl; quiet, as little girls should be, but not shy; polite, anxious to please, but self-assured and not much trouble. If there were punishments for my misdeeds, I do not recall them, and although I probably was spanked for transgressions, I cannot recall being hit. I did show my stubborn streak a couple of times that I remember. Once, I was loafing on the lounge, and my mother asked me to go across the street to get some bread. I refused. My mother blamed my father for spoiling me, and an argument ensued, but I did not go and wasn't punished for it. Another time, my father wanted me to fetch some milk, and I refused, but after a long argument between my parents about my being spoiled, I finally did as I was told.

My father was liberal with approval, enjoyed my accomplishments in school for which I was usually rewarded with some treat, such as ice cream. I liked pleasing him. Nevertheless, I was quite independent. I was allowed to go to my friends' houses in the afternoons by myself, and was not forced to study or to help with things around the house. However, I wasn't allowed to be angry, nor did I ever share some of my fears. I learned that only pleasantness was a suitable emotion, another attribute of training I recalled painfully when my father demanded that my daughter smile. "Nobody likes a girl who doesn't smile," he told her one day as she was pouting and expressing some angry feelings at the dinner table. Still today, I have trouble even recognizing that I am angry, and I keep my fears to myself. Others think of me as having a pleasant disposition and being brave and fearless—so I smile, and bury anger and fear deeply.

It was my mother who supported us with her dressmaking. She was sweet and quiet, but serious, and because she was working she didn't spend much time with me. Eventually, she had enough business to hire an apprentice, Anny, who became a family friend. Anny and my mother chatted endlessly while sewing, mostly about getting Anny a husband.

My mother sewed me some special outfits that I remember clearly. One was a velvety dress of a leopard print, and when I was very small I had a piece of that material which I rubbed on my face when I needed comfort. Another time she made me a red and blue checked cape and had a milliner make a cap, with a point in front and back, like a private's hat, to match. The cape was finished, but she was short on money to pay for the cap. One day she asked me to run an errand to pick up payment from one of her customers. I took it upon myself to take some of the money to pay the milliner. My mother was devastated that I had done that, for the money was meant to pay the rent, but I wasn't punished for my independent decision!

She traded some sewing for other goods or services. Our next-door neighbor, who was an artist, painted a border of flowers on a black, silky, dirndl for me; in exchange, my mother sewed something for his wife. I was photographed in that dress, and still own it, a sweet reminder of my mother. She traded sewing for dance lessons and for piano lessons. Unfortunately, I was a klutz and the dance lessons ended soon; I couldn't carry a tune, so the piano lessons stopped too. Despite these loving acts on my behalf, I cared for my father more probably because he spent more time with me. He was always patient and interested in my thoughts and activities. Relatives and friends of my parents would often ask: "Who do love more, your mother or your father?" It was an awkward question which I always answered "the same", but in my heart, I knew better. Perhaps that is a European, or perhaps a Jewish kind of question, for I was startled when my cousins later asked me which of my children was my favorite.

While my mother sewed, my father spent his days cooking our meals, taking care of me, cleaning the apartment or reading the paper. I am not sure how my mother felt about working and supporting us, but I don't remember any arguments. In fact, it was not until Hitler disturbed our lives that I was aware of some disagreements, and perhaps resentments.

Our daily routine started with a simple breakfast of fresh rolls from the little bakery across the street and hot cocoa. My mother often asked me to tell her my dreams, and she was especially interested if there were any numbers in them so she could buy a good lottery ticket. Then I went to school from 8:00 to 12:00, including Saturdays. School was a public school, a big gray stone building sandwiched in among other big stone buildings on a small street around the corner from us. I don't remember much of the school, except that I was told not to sing when the class was singing because I could not carry a tune. I recall learning to sing *Santa Lucia*; when I hear it occasionally on the radio, I am immediately transported to my classroom in Vienna where a man is conducting our singing. I was taught to knit and crochet, and we would spend hours in class doing such handiwork. I think most classes were segregated by sex. Although I knew some of the boys, I never played with them after school. There was no recess or a playground.

When I came home it was time for the big dinner of the day. Viennese cooking is delicious, and my father was a good cook. Our meal would have had noodles or potatoes, some meat such as a Wiener Schnitzel, which is a fried veal cutlet, or Hungarian Goulash, a spicy veal stew, or perhaps chicken. In most of Europe, veal is the preferred meat. Vegetables might have been cauliflower or string beans or my hated spinach. Mealtimes were usually pleasant, unless I refused to eat something that was put on my plate, thereby creating a big scene.

Then everybody would take a nap. We had the afternoon free for homework and play and I most often would go out to visit with my school friends, returning at an appointed time, 5:00 or 6:00 o'clock when we had another meal, perhaps leftovers, or a light soup purchased from the restaurant next door, or some bread and cheese and salad.

I was a healthy child, except I had a cough every winter when the weather was cold and damp. I was not taken to the doctor often, but finally, when I was seven, it was decided that my tonsils should be removed. The hospital was close by in our district, a big imposing building, and the operation was done as an outpatient procedure. I remember my father carrying me home, and then often feeding me the prescribed ice cream to speed the convalescence. I continued to have the cough as long as I lived in Vienna, but never again once I lived in California.

The same hospital was also the dental clinic. I had bad teeth and had to have many fillings. Usually, I did not cry with the pain of drilling, and one time the dentist used me as a model in order to quiet a boy who was screaming. Of course, that day, I cried too, to her big disappointment. My feet were not so good either, so I had to wear arch supports. In my pictures I can see my fallen arches and turned-in knees explaining my clumsiness.

✦ ✦ ✦

In the afternoons I usually went to a friend's apartment. My friends hardly ever came to my house because my mother's work required customers to come for fittings, and there would have been no place to play. I was free to go where I liked, I think, and considering the busy street that I lived on, and the others nearby, I often wonder if it wasn't careless of my parents to let me roam at will. Of course, that question comes from the perspective of my present world in which I, and most other suburban mothers, did not give our kids that much freedom; we always needed to know where the kids were and with whom, and that they were supervised by an adult.

I had two favorite friends, Elfie and Lizzi, who lived about 15 minutes away. At Elfie's house, her mother was usually present and we would read, and play games and perhaps knit or crochet together while chatting. At Lizzi's apartment there were no adults present, and we found similar ways to amuse ourselves, and some additional ones as well. Lizzi, whose full name was Alice, was my best friend, and we never tired of each other's company. Friends were a very important part of my life, even then.

Sex education came early in my life, but not from my parents who were extremely modest and I never saw either of them in any state of undress. (It was ironic that the first time I should see my father's genitals was in his very last week of life in the nursing home. His room faced the entrance patio, his bed next to the window; and one day as I approached the front door of the home, there was my father totally exposed for the whole world to see. I felt humiliated for him.)

Although my parents were modest, I was exposed to men's genitalia on the streets where it was common for men to urinate in the gutter and against walls of buildings. Not only that, but there were several men who just stood around exposing themselves. One such man often stood in the narrowest part of the circular staircase in our apartment house, hidden from view until I just came upon him at the turn. It frightened me; I did not know what that red thing was sticking out of his body. I would run back down the stairs waiting for him to leave, which could take a long time, and it caused me to be late. One day another friend, Anne Rozencranz, was with me when that happened, and she ran up the stairs to tell my parents. I was scolded for not telling them, but they never patrolled the steps when I was due to come home, nor did they ever ask me about such an occurrence again, although it happened several times. I was not alone in this experience. In a story written for children by a Viennese girl, there is an episode of an exposed man offering gum to a girl to touch his penis.[1]

I was curious as well as frightened by these encounters. My curiosity about men's strange anatomy was satisfied somewhat by pictures my friend Lizzi found among her parents' things. These were pictures of naked men and women in strange positions so as to clearly expose the anatomy. She and I spent countless hours looking at these pictures. These pictures were erotic and stimulated some feelings that we didn't understand, but by rocking back and forth on our hands and knees we found the secret pleasure of our bodies. We were pretty sure that our parents would not favorably receive our activities since the pictures had been hidden and obviously not meant for our curious eyes, but we didn't really feel naughty.

---

[1] Orgel, Doris, *The Devil in Vienna*, Dial, 1978

Although I had learned the pleasures of my body, I also knew that my private parts should be private. Yet another man lurked in our stairway, fully clothed, who would wait for me to come up the stairs, then reach under my dress and into my pants and fondle me. I knew this was not right, but I didn't know how to tell my parents. I lived in dread of daily homecoming, lest this awful man be there, and compounded by my fear of therefore being late, and sure to be punished for my tardiness by my father. Once I knocked his hat off and he ran away, but that didn't deter him from coming back another time. I kept this secret to myself—somehow guilt-ridden by it—for the next forty years when I read about such an experience in one of Saul Bellow's novels. Reading that others had had such experiences finally permitted me to release this immense burden. Later, when I worked as a sex educator, I learned that most children don't tell because they feel they are somewhat responsible for this occurrence, thus allowing the assaults to continue.

✦ ✦ ✦

Despite our poverty, which I really never felt or identified with, there were times of recreation. I was taken to the Prater, Vienna's famous playground. The Riesenrad (Ferris wheel) described earlier was an enormous treat, and maybe just a one-time experience. My father enjoyed our outings as much as I. Later, I noticed his pleasure when he took his grandchildren to amusement parks eagerly and lovingly. Not far from my house was the Volksoper, an opera house for less classical works where on some weekend afternoons they would perform children's tales. My favorite story was the Princess and the Pea. I would go inside alone because we couldn't afford tickets for my father, but he would take me and pick me up and we would enjoy talking about these performances. Occasionally we went to the movies. Children were limited to certain movies such as Shirley Temple's or Nelson Eddy and Jeanette McDonald musicals such as *Maytime.*

The few pictures I have of myself from that time, show an attractive girl, far from beautiful, but also not homely, of average build, short black hair, with legs slightly turned in and fallen arches. My mouth is never open to show my smile; had it been, it would have shown crooked teeth and many that were filled. The pictures are posed so the look is somewhat serious, and I think I was and am a rather serious person. My body position in these pictures does not show assertiveness or shyness. I have only one photo that wasn't posed: It shows my father holding me, then about 2 years-old, in front of our apartment house. His smile as he looks at me is adoring, and on the back of the picture it says "the precious Lizzi". I felt precious in his presence. In some ways I must have been spoiled because I have always thought of myself as someone special, an image no doubt created by my parents who did love me.

In Jewish circles people often talk about "Jewish-American princesses"—girls whose every whim was indulged in their childhood, who then expected the same indulgence from husbands and friends. Surely I didn't fit that mold, I have told myself, focusing on our poverty and years of separation, but yet...my self-image of being center stage and my self-indulgent behavior must come from this special feeling I had from my father in whose eyes I was a doll (Puppele), if not a princess.

6

SUMMERS IN POLAND

The small river Opur – much larger in my memory

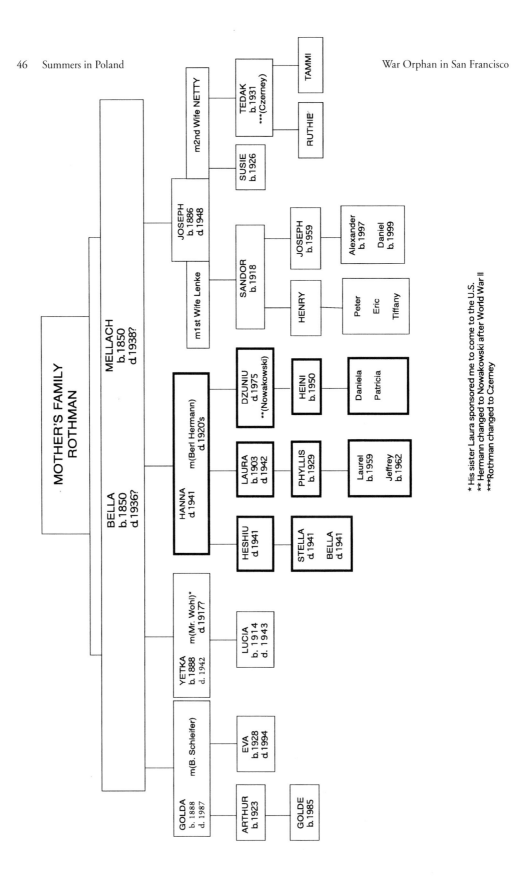

MOTHER'S FAMILY
ROTHMAN

MELLACH
b.1850
d.1938?

BELLA
b.1850
d.1936?

JOSEPH
b.1886
d 1948

m1st Wife Lenke

m2nd Wife NETTY

SUSIE
b.1926

TEDAK
b.1931
***(Czerney)

RUTHIE

TAMMI

SANDOR
b.1918

HENRY

JOSEPH
b.1959

Peter
Eric
Tiffany

Alexander
b.1997

Daniel
b.1999

HANNA
d 1941

m(Berl Hermann)
d 1920's

HESHIU
d 1941

STELLA
d 1941

BELLA
d 1941

LAURA
b.1903
d.1942

PHYLLIS
b.1929

Laurel
b.1959

Jeffrey
b.1962

DZUNIU
d 1975
**(Nowakowski)

HEINI
b.1950

Daniela

Patricia

YETKA
b.1888
d. 1942

m(Mr. Wohl)*
d.1917?

LUCIA
b. 1914
d. 1943

GOLDA
b. 1888
d. 1987

m(B. Schleifer)

ARTHUR
b.1923

EVA
b.1928
d.1994

GOLDE
b.1985

* His sister Laura sponsored me to come to the U.S.
** Hermann changed to Nowakowski after World War II
***Rothman changed to Czerney

Since my parent's homeland was Galicia, an area then in southwestern Poland, it was only natural that my parents would make visits to their families, probably every year. My father's family lived in L'vov (today called L'viv) and I recall visiting his parents, but aside from remembering that my grandpa was a small man and grandma a large woman, I cannot recall anything else. We probably visited my father's parents in L'vov each time we went to Poland. My father's older brother, Max, lived in Leipzig, Germany, and we visited him, at least once that I recall, when he bought me a pair of red shoes that I loved and that he never let me forget. Hannah, my father's sister, I can't remember at all. Max survived the war, but had no progeny. My grandparents and sister Hannah and her family perished in the Holocaust in 1941. Max and Tillie escaped from Germany to Tangier and then Portugal, ultimately settling in Canada. My children and I are the only survivors of the Finkel side of the family.

My mother's family members I know better because I spent more time with them and quite a few members, still living, gave me some information about that era of our history. The family's domicile was in Lawoczne, a village in a rural province in the Carpathean Mountains, not far from L'vov, but close to the Hungarian border. Reading the history of Jews in Eastern Europe informs me that poverty was widespread, but according to one cousin, ours was a large family, perhaps 150 members, some of them well-to-do. I don't remember many relatives; I have memory of only a few. As a child I didn't notice any signs of prosperity or poverty, and what I remember was simply a farm, different from home in Vienna.

My great grandparents were physically active and worked into their 90's until their natural deaths in the late 1930's. I remember when great-grandpa Mellach had a broken rib after an encounter with a bull in his late 80's, and was kept from his usual activities. Mellach Rothman had a dark beard and always wore a big black hat and black clothes, a typical costume for Jews in Eastern Europe. Great-grandma Bella wore a scarf around her shaved head, another Jewish custom of that area. I can't recall any conversations with these people because if I spoke with them at all, I would have spoken Polish with them, and I have no recollection of that language. Bella was married twice times; she had two daughters from her first marriage, and her husband died young. The second marriage was brief and ended by her switching partners with another woman, her new partner being my great-grandfather. She had four more living children, and with the exception of my grandmother Hannah, they all continued to live on the Rothman homestead in Lawoczne. Despite my lack of specific interactions with these relatives, I do have memories of my times there.

This is where I spent summers when I was a child. I am not sure how often I actually went to Poland, but my memories are mainly from when I was six or seven, the last possible time would have been in 1937 when I would have been eight. I think my parents took me to Poland, and then left me there for a while, and then came back to get me. I remember waiting at stations, going on long train rides that had hard wooden benches and getting train sick. Once our luggage was stolen even while we were standing right by it. My parents talked about it often, leaving me to remember the loss, but not the actual incident. In my later travels in poor countries, I have always identified with the people carrying many bundles and suitcases—bringing city goods to the country and country goods to the city—it felt like I knew that routine. I think my family must have done that too.

I don't know how long they left me at the farm, but I suspect it was a considerable time, because Uncle Dzuniu told me "every summer you would come to Lawoczne knowing only German, and then leave knowing only Polish." I don't recall my parents speaking Polish in Vienna; perhaps they wanted me to learn proper German. If I couldn't speak Polish, then I must have spent a lot of time in Poland in my own little world, amusing myself and not communicating with people. I know nothing of the Polish language now. This annual long absence from my parents, culture and language could explain why I later adapted so easily to American customs for I had had much experience in adapting to new places, learning languages and being on my own. However, I have a good feeling about my time in Poland, although I don't remember how I felt about it at the time.

When I spent summers in Poland, I lived in Bella and Mellach's house, a wooden structure that looked large to my young eyes, but was really very simple. It was close to the river that also looked large, but in fact was just a small, but fast moving stream. I had recalled it as two-story house, but later my cousins explained that it was only one story, and that the animals lived under the house. In front of my great-grandparent's house were several other houses occupied by their children—my mother's aunts and uncles and their families. Yetka Wohl, lived in one house with her family, and it was her husband's sister, Laura, already living in the United States, who would provide me with my first home in San Francisco. Yetka's twin sister, Golda lived next door with her husband, Bernard Schleifer and their two children, Eva, about my age and Arthur, a bit older. There was yet another house and it had a little grocery store attached to it, belonging to the son, Joseph Rothman and his family including three children, Shoniu (Sandor), Suzy and Tedak. These five children—my mother's cousins—but all closer to my age, all survived the Holocaust.

This farm was for household purposes with farm animals, chickens, cats, dogs and possibly some tenant farmers, but trade in timber was the main business of my great-grandfather and his children. Being a city girl I found the farm an interesting place to be, but I think I must have been very lonely for my parents and somebody to speak to. Left to my own devices I used to play with the smaller animals. My meager memories have me trying to give a cat a bath in the river, but it refused, instead scratching me all over my bare chest. I enjoyed the geese that wandered around, and found it interesting to see them being force-fed with corn to fatten them up. Another activity was to play with the little chicks—I threw them in the air to see them fly. They didn't—they dropped dead instead and I did not understand why. I heard some of the grown-ups wondering what had happened to the little chicks. I never confessed to my crime, but I did stop it. For years I chose to absolve my guilt about these murderous acts by telling myself that, after all, it was only childish curiosity. Only recently did I realize that I was probably acting out my anger at having been abandoned by my parents.

Eva later told me that when we were little she used to take me to the mountains looking for mushrooms and flowers. I don't remember this at all. There must have been a dog in my life on the farm named Rex because when it came to naming a dog, many years later, Rex was the only possible choice for my dog's name. To my surprise, later Eva told me that she, too, named her dog Rex.

One time when my father was there on the farm, he became ill with scarlet fever. He was confined to one of the houses and I was not allowed to go near him, and could only see him through a window. It was a scary time for me because I loved him so; he was very ill and nearly died in the age before antibiotics.

One of my favorite activities was doing crossword puzzles. I must have learned to do them in Vienna; perhaps my father showed me how. He used to send me bundles of newspapers from Vienna that had the crossword puzzles in them, and I looked forward to receiving them. Then, using the next day's paper, the one with the answers, I filled in the puzzles. My relatives, not observing my methods, but only the results, falsely accused me of being brilliant. I am not sure I was able to set them straight, or that I even wanted to, but looking back at that activity, I think it was still pretty smart for a 7- or 8- year old to copy the puzzles.

My grandmother, Hannah, the oldest of Bella's children, had left Lawoczne, I assume for marriage, to live in Stryj, a small provincial town on the main rail-line from Hungary to L'vov and points north. My grandfather, Berl Hermann, ended his life because of blindness before I was born. His sister (Aunt Laufer) was the link between my parents meeting since my father was a boarder at her house in Vienna when my mother visited her aunt.

I remember visiting my grandmother Hannah in Stryj though I don't remember anything about her except living in her house. There was an outhouse across the yard which I hated since I was used to flush toilets in Vienna. Once, I am ashamed to confess, I did my business on the grassy courtyard. I recall my grandmother talking to someone about this awful deed, but I did not confess nor was I accused, but I felt ashamed.

Hannah had three children: My mother, Laura, was the middle child, and she had a younger brother Dzuniu (Polish rendition of David) and one older, Heshiu (Henry). My uncles, each married with children, lived near my grandma, but often visited the farm that was just a short train ride away. The family was close, and Hannah's nephews from Lawoczne, Arthur and Shoniu, stayed with her when going to high school, the closest high school to Lawoczne.

Uncle Dzuniu had been my favorite uncle when I was young, though I can't say what endeared him to me. Perhaps he had been kind to me when I was visiting my grandmother as a small girl. Heshu's daughter, Stella, was about my age and I did not like her—but why is very dim. My recollection had to do with some jewelry we children were given, and I gave mine to a servant—and then I was accused of stealing Stella's and reprimanded.

My grandmother and Heshu owned a candy store in Stryj, while Dziuniu was working in the timber business. My father later told me that Dziuniu had a reputation for having a Midas touch—everything he did turned out profitably. During one of the difficult years in the depression, when my father couldn't find work, he left Vienna to work in the candy store. My cousins speak fondly of my father, "everybody liked him, he was charming and pleasant," they said, but the family was disappointed that he didn't make a good living, especially since he was so well educated. Since they were not so well schooled, they found it hard to understand why he couldn't find work and yet they did.

I cherish those few memories of my experiences at the farm so long ago, though I'm not sure exactly why they are so important to me. It should have been fun to be with my cousins, but I have no memories of interacting with them. I am sure it must have been lonely for me for lack of a common language, yet when I think about those summers, it is not with anger or regret, but more with pleasure. I believe that it was the closeness to nature, so different from the cosmopolitan Vienna that became deeply embedded with pleasure in my soul. Though short on details of that era, deep sentimental feelings well up inside me each time I am in the mountains, each time I see a river running by, each time I hear a rooster crowing—or see little chicks flitting about.

Today, I am fortunate to live in a hilly area above a creek with beautiful vistas of mountains. Having this view daily refreshes my spiritual need for quiet country, even though I live in the midst of a metropolitan area.

7

HITLER COMES TO AUSTRIA

March 11, 1938

As I looked out the window onto Nussdorferstrasse late on this day, I saw endless lines of soldiers marching, followed by and interspersed with trucks, and crowds of people on the street shouting "Heil Hitler." There was no end to this parade. I could feel that something important was happening because my parents were nervous, but I didn't understand this drama. Though there had been much political maneuvering in recent months and masses of people had demonstrated in the streets for some time, I was only eight and half years old then, too young to comprehend the political unrest in Europe that preceded Hitler's reign of terror. History tells me that Hitler had forced the Chancellor of Austria to resign, appointed one of his own men to the post who then welcomed the Anschluss—the Joining—to Germany. Thus, the German troops parading on my street. A fifteen-year old boy who had been looking out the window on the same street described it like this:

> I rushed to the window and looked out into Nussdorferstrasse. It was still quite empty. A few moments. The first lorry came into sight. It was packed with shouting screaming men. A huge swastika flag fluttered over their heads. Most of them had swastika armlets on the their sleeves, some wore S.A. caps, some even steel helmets.
>
> Now we could hear clearly what they were shouting: '*Ein volk, ein Reich, ein Fuhrer*' [one people, one country, one leader]. They were chanting in chorus, followed by '*Ju-da verr-rrecke, Ju-da verr-rrecke*' ('Perish Judah'). In English this sounds softer, less threatening, but in German, coming from a thousand throats, screaming it out in the full fury of their hate, as lorry after lorry with frenzied Nazis passed below our window, it is a sound one can never forget.[1]

In the next few days there was pandemonium and panic. In a wild display of anti-Semitism, Jews were rounded up in the streets and made to wash the recent

---

[1] George Clare: *The Last Waltz in Vienna.* Holt, Rinehart & Winston, NY,1980, p177
   Perish is not enough of a translation of verrecke: it can be translated as "to die like a beast"—there are other German verbs that differentiate between animals and people, as in eating: fressen for animals, denoting no manners, essen for people, denoting civil manners.

pro-Austrian slogans off the streets; Jewish businesses were defiled with red anti-Jewish slogans; their windows were broken, and property simply taken. Jews were told not to walk on the sidewalks, only in the gutters, "where they belonged." I did not experience these, but I heard my parents and Anny talking about these horrible events with fear and anger, and I've seen many pictures of these degradations. Perhaps they occurred in the more densely settled Jewish districts. I think my parents were spared these attacks, for surely I would have remembered them.

The history of the take-over has been well documented, so I leave the facts to the historians. Because I've seen so many pictures and read so many books about this period, sometimes I can't distinguish what I saw then and what I saw later—each vision deeply imbedded in my memory. In fact, although I was conscious of being Jewish, I had not personally experienced anti-Semitism before—or I don't remember. I had not known that anti-Semitism and xenophobia had been brewing in Austria for hundreds of years, felt even deeper than in Germany.[1]

Soon enough I would begin to experience the meaning of Hitler's invasion, but truly, compared to what happened to millions of other people, my personal experiences were mild. A cloud of fear and uncertainty covered our lives, and so I learned what it means to live in fear.[2] I was told to stay home, for safety. It is one thing to live in bad times, always hoping that thing would change for the better, but in Hitler's time, daily events let people know that conditions would only get worse for Jews.

---

[1] Bukey, Evan Burr: *Hitler's Austria: Popular Sentiment in the Nazi Era,* 1938-1945. Univ. of North Carolina, Chapel Hill & London, 1999, Chapter 1

[2] The fear I learned after Hitler came to Austria stayed with me until I came to the United States, but even here, on two separate occasions I had the same dread. In my last year at University of California, Berkeley, in 1952, the State of California demanded a loyalty oath from all of its employees including students. There was much protest to this action, but nothing came of it; some of my friends as well as many professors would not sign such an oath because they thought it was unconstitutional. Those who didn't sign lost their jobs and left Berkeley. I agreed with them, but I was a coward and signed the oath so that I could continue working and thus stay in school. A year later, while attending the University of Wisconsin, their Senator McCarthy began his tirade against communists. His methods reminded me of Hitler, too. Support of McCarthy was especially strong in Wisconsin and some of my acquaintances, fellow students and co-workers, were gleefully looking for suspects. Though I was not a communist, but a liberal—to McCarthyites there was no difference—the feelings of oppression frightened me. Theoretically, under the Hatch Act, it would have been possible for me, a naturalized citizen, to be deported had my fellow worker, a rabid supporter of McCarthy, chosen to accuse me for my liberal views, by calling me a communist. Today I can see that my fear was exaggerated, but then, it reminded me too much of those times in Vienna as I understood how easy it is for people to be led in the despotic direction. Although we lived with fear during our many years of confrontation with Russia, it was a less personalized fear—against the whole country, and not just one group as we Jews were singled out in Europe. However, when another minority group gets picked on, I feel it very personally.

Here, I try to describe events I remember actually happened to me as a result of the take-over. Almost immediately after the Anschluss, I was not allowed to go to the school I had attended around the corner, but needed to go quite a distance to a school just for Jewish children from all over the city. At the same time, the young boys of the Hitler youth groups were empowered by the authorities to harass the helpless Jews and to inform about any activity that might be directed against Hitler—included telling on their parents and neighbors. The youth-groups, wearing brown uniforms and proudly displaying swastikas on their arms were endorsed by the Nazis, and encouraged in their violent way all for love of the Fatherland. One day on my way home from this more distant school, a group of boys in Hitler Youth uniforms surrounded me. "Dirty Jew, Christkiller," they shouted as they threw small stones and spat on me. I stood frozen with fear in the middle, unable to move or to say anything, not even to cry; finally, their fun over, they let me go home. I still feel terror when I am surrounded and I dread parades, recalling the endless parade on that March day.

One night when I was asleep, I was awakened by hard pounding on the door. Loud voices shouted "Open the door, be quick." When my father answered the door, SS men, big men in uniforms, in high boots (the Special Service Police, Hitler's private army) shouted at him, "Jew, get your things together, you must leave right away." They would not tell us how long we would have to be away, just to hurry. Fear was in my parents' eyes, so I knew to be careful and obedient, and I was also afraid. The SS sent us to the apartment of another family a few blocks away, strangers to us, equally frightened to be awakened in the middle of the night and to accommodate another family! This probably occurred in November following *Kristallnacht* (Crystalnight) in November 1938. Hitler had ordered a giant retribution against the Jews all over his empire—windows were broken, (hence the name), synagogues burned, Jews were rounded up and various tortures and sufferings were brought about, all because a French Jew killed a policeman when he heard his father had been taken away. Hitler claimed it was a spontaneous reaction of the people against the Jews, but records show it was an orchestrated event. We were chosen to leave, I have read, because our apartment faced a big street, and Jews were not to have such "view" locations.

I don't know how long we stayed with this family, and I have no recollections of how we adjusted to this situation. We were allowed to return to our own apartment after a while, our meager belongings still there. One good thing came out of that experience was that the apartment had been fumigated and the disgusting bedbugs were gone.

◆ ◆ ◆

My parents probably represented the widely different feelings and interpretations of these events then prevalent: many people, like my father, could not believe that this chaos would last, sure that it was just a passing disruption soon to be quelled by the government. Others, like my mother, were worried and anxious and tried to make plans for escape. From stories my father later told of his childhood, he had experienced anti-Semitism in Lemberg when he was a teenager, and once had even organized some boys to fight the antagonists. But in 1938, he did not seem to be moved to take any action; he did not participate in political activity, not even in the personal actions such as applying for exit visas or getting a quota number for emigration. My parents did not share their concerns with me, but I did know from the talk between them that serious things were happening.

Our lives changed economically. Some of my mother's customers decided that they did not need to pay a Jew for their work, thus creating immense hardship for my family. There was great excitement at home: Anny and my father wanted to demand payment from these people, my mother did not want to cause any trouble. Gossip about what was happening to acquaintances and friends was the only subject of talk. (Although I remember the anxiety of the time, I do not remember the words spoken in German) People who had any means at all, found ways to leave the country, and my parents spoke of who had left and who was trying this or that means. At that time Hitler's aim was just to get rid of the Jews—to purify Germany, which now included Austria—to get these unwanted people out of the country. Although some Jews had been sent to camps, not yet called "concentration," I believe at this time they were deported for political reasons, for having been against the Anschluss, and for being outspoken.

My mother nagged at my father to get us quota numbers—which meant standing in line for hours. My father, like many others, did not believe that it was possible for the terror to last much longer, so he didn't, at least at first. Getting a quota number for the United States was very difficult since there were only limited numbers who could come in each year. The United States policy was not favorable to having immigrants. People got quota numbers just in case they were lucky and would have a chance to leave.

Getting an affidavit to emigrate was another process altogether. It was necessary to find somebody, usually a relative, to vouch that they had the means to support the immigrant. It helped if one already had many relatives abroad to beg for such papers. My mother wrote to the only relative she had, "Aunt Laura," the sister of my mother's uncle by marriage who lived in San Francisco. Perhaps because they had the same name, and because my mother had known Aunt Laura when my mother was a young girl, Aunt Laura sent us an affidavit, but it was too weak—meaning she didn't have the money required—to support the whole family. Besides getting affidavits, quota numbers, people would then have to get exit visas to leave, entry visas to enter the other country, and transit visas to pass through other countries, and finally get ship passage. If people had money, connections and /or generous relatives, there was hope that some escape would be possible.

One anonymous Austrian woman wrote about those times: (From an exhibition about the Holocaust in San Francisco)

> Visas!
> We began to live visas day and night. When we were awake, we were obsessed by visas. We talked about them all the time. Exit visas, transit visas, entrance

visas. Where could we go? During the day, we tried to get the proper documents, approvals, stamps. At night, in bed, we tossed about and dreamed about long lines, officials, visas and more visas.

✦ ✦ ✦

My afternoons with friends ceased for the most part; my best friend, Lizzi, left Vienna on a *Kindertransport* for France. In fact, Jews stayed off the streets as much as possible to avoid possible confrontations. One night when my parents and I had been visiting a friend, walking in the 1st district in town, I needed to go to the bathroom desperately. My parents encouraged me to go inside a public toilet and plead that I was alone, without money, while they walked away and waited for me around the corner. The matron let me use the facilities, after much questioning, but as I left, she followed me out the door. When she saw me joining my parents she yelled after us, and we hurried away frightened that she might call the police. Later, a curfew was imposed so that Jews could not be out after dark.

✦ ✦ ✦

My father, among many other men and women, went to the Jewish Community Center to learn trades which might help them find gainful employment in other countries. My father enthusiastically learned how to make jams and jellies—a rather inappropriate trade for him considering he was so gifted in languages and figures. Among his papers I found a small notebook—87 pages full of recipes for jams and jellies! To my knowledge, he never used this skill.

In May of 1939, fourteen months after the Anschluss when I was nearly ten, 2,000 Jewish men, my father among them, were rounded-up, put in prison; their crime was being Jewish and "stateless." The statelessness came from the fact that my parents had Polish passports that the government had declared invalid in October 1938, thus making our family stateless. It would not have been possible for them to seek citizenship in Austria after 1921[1]. As I think about the idea of citizenship, I believe that it must be a fairly new idea in history, considering how long people have been on the move. I have been told that in Austria before Hitler, citizenship was sometimes granted when a man joined the political party then in power or was in the military. At any rate, when Hitler came to Austria and started his tirade against Jews, he wanted their wealth, and then he wanted them out of the country.

In prison, my father was given some administrative work, so he did not suffer physically, such as beatings. Mentally, I can only imagine how outrageous it must feel to be in prison for no crime, with no recourse to justice, to have no knowledge what was in store for the future, and be crowded into small spaces because of the numbers. My mother and I went to visit him, but I have no recollection of the prison. I missed him terribly. The men were given the option of leaving prison, providing they left the country within ten days. They were probably stripped of most of their assets since often they were required to pay the Nazis in order to leave. Since we were poor, it made no difference because we had no assets to give up. Of course, most of the men had no place to go, and most countries were not willing to accept the men without the required papers. It took two months to find a way to leave.

Fortunately, Britain allowed these imprisoned men to immigrate without special papers of support or quotas. My father was released from prison, and made plans to go to England. He hoped he would be able to find a fosterhome for me, and a job for my mother enabling her emigration, a plan to which probably every family clung. Hopefully, our separation would be short, and we would be reunited soon. To say that I hated to see my father go is a great understatement since we were so close and I loved him so. He assured me in his optimistic way that we would soon be together, and he himself believed it. On August 3, 1939, these emigrants went together on a special transport train to the ship that would cross the channel to England.

My mother and I moved to a room in Gusti's apartment. I assume she was a

---

[1]Bukey, personal communication: According to Article 80 of the Treaty of St. Germain, residents of the former Austro-Hungarian Monarchy had until 15 January 1921 to "opt" for Austrian citizenship. My father might have been eligible, but probably not as he was a student at that time.

friend of my mother's, and maybe took us into her home out of kindness. I don't think I liked Gusti very much. In a poem she wrote to me when I left Vienna, she signed it "Your Strict Gusti"—perhaps indicating that I had objected to her rules. I probably did not take to all of these changes too easily, and was crushed by father's departure. My mother wouldn't have been able to support us living in our old apartment, I guess now, but I really don't know if she was forced to leave it again, or chose to do so because of lack of money. In fact, I don't know how she supported us. Our food supply was restricted not just by money, but also by the rationing of food for everybody, and severely for Jews. I can recall a special occasion when my mother said "I have a surprise for you, can you guess?" and then she presented me with an orange, a fruit I had not seen for a long time. It was a real treat. We usually ate potatoes and noodles, but I never went hungry; in fact, due to lack of activity, I actually became a little chubby.

We got letters from my father and our anticipation continued to grow that our separation would soon be over, but in fact, our dreams were shattered a month later when England declared war on Germany on September 3, 1939, just after Hitler invaded Poland on September 1. The invasion lasted seven days; then, in a pact with Russia, most of Poland was ceded to Russian domination, including Galicia where my extended family lived. Declaration of war meant that my mother and I would not be able to go to England, nor would there be direct communication—our mail to my father went the circuitous route via the Red Cross. My mother was able to keep in some contact with the family in Galicia.

My mother began to explore other avenues of exit. She had previously written to Aunt Laura in San Francisco. Now, my mother asked her to consider just having me, and Aunt Laura agreed, thus opening the opportunity for me to go to America with some *Kindertransport*. From my mother's later letters, I think she must have begged Aunt Laura to take me, so that it would improve her own application not to be burdened by a child. Many children had already left Vienna on *Kindertransports* to Britain and France before; I do not know why I had not been among them earlier. Perhaps, at the time, it had seemed possible that we could emigrate as a family. At any rate, the Kindertransports to England and France stopped when Britain declared war.

Somehow, I was selected to be one of the Jewish children who emigrated to the United States. We were co-sponsored by the German Jewish Childrens Association in New York if we had a relative to take us. It is now known that roughly one thousand children were allowed to enter the United States during that time, and then only a few at a time since each child had to secure a quota as well as having an affidavit.[1] I don't know how I was chosen, but I assume that my mother's close friendship with the Rabbi might have had something to do with it.

Parents had to write applications for their children to show that they were wonderful children—all well behaved, smart and lovable. I have read these heart-breaking applications.[2] I can picture each parent writing these biographies, reminding them how precious their child was, making the separation unbearably sad, but necessary to save their lives. My mother also had hopes that Anny, her helper, already in the United States, would send my father and her an affidavit. I must assume that my mother's efforts to get us both out of Austria had not worked, and what must have been an incredible hard choice for a mother, she aimed at freeing me, dreaming that a solution would be found for her own escape. As I write about this now, I am in tears thinking of her sacrifice and her dilemma. But at the time, I do not recall any tears at the separation from her. I dreamed about my reunion with my father.

As we approached the time of my leaving, an indefinite "sometime soon," my mother prepared my suitcase with the best clothes I had, clothes that I was already outgrowing and she prepared me with information about Aunt Laura, and the wonderful life possible in America. One morning she woke me with joy and enthusiasm because she had just finished writing me a poem to guide me on my journey. It didn't mean much to me then, but I treasure it now, not only for the good advice, but also for the beauty of the poem (at the beginning of the book) and her effort to make it so. In translation the rhyming is lost.

---

[1] Baumel, Judith: UNFULFILLED PROMISE, Denali Press
[2] These records are part of the GJCA files at the YIVO archives in New York.

I do not remember our parting, but my mother reminisced about that day in her letter of Oct. 7, 1941:

> *Can you still remember the day of your departure, how cute you helped me in the kitchen? Then you baked a Strudel* [German cake] *that was so cute that I have kept it until it crumbled.*

And in a letter to my father on Nov. 11, 1943, I wrote about our parting:

> *I'll never forget the day I left her. Before I had to keep her spirit up and then in the last minute, I broke down. We both cried, but her face and words made me feel so good, as she had the courage of a thousand men in her. And then again comes the old saying, I never did appreciate her, or love her, as I do now. I have a picture of her and when I see it, I think of all the fun, loving care and everything I had when living with her and you.*

I do not remember these details. In fact, not remembering how we parted has nagged me all my life.

MY FATHER'S PLIGHT

8

JOURNEY TO AUSTRALIA

August 4, 1939 to September 6, 1940

S.S. Dunera

Kitchener Camp

REFUGE IN ENGLAND

On August 4, 1939, two thousand Jewish men, recently released from a Viennese prison, departed for England. The Nazis had ordered the Jewish prisoners, my father among them, to leave Vienna within a week. Most had no visas or affidavits but, luckily, were offered refuge in England.

The refugees were sent to Kitchener Camp in Richborough, Kent, south of London, a World War I army barracks resurrected by the Jewish congregation in Kent for use by refugees from Germany and Austria. There they would await immigration papers to other countries, or perhaps find work in England.

My father never spoke to me of these times or his later experiences, and I never asked. Information about his stay in England comes mainly from his papers and letters and from many history books.[1] In 1985, fifteen years after his death, when I started to write my memoirs, I finally looked into his papers. I was surprised, shocked, sad, as well as angry; angry that we had never talked about his experiences, sad because I was deprived of a closeness with him; shocked because of the brutality that was in those papers. I was also curious to find out more.

---

[1] Bartrop, Paul R. and Gabrielle Eisen: *THE DUNERA AFFAIR: A Documentary Resource Book*, Jewish Museum of Australia, 1990, among many others.

Among the papers I found a booklet, *Some Victims of the Nazi Terror* subtitled, "The Reward of the Salvors,"[1] with many pictures depicting life in this camp. It was published by The Kitchener Camp Committee, and it looks like propaganda to show England that the refugees are a healthy, industrious group, "seeking refuge from the Nazi terror, men seeking sanctuary in a peaceful democratic state." The camp held over 3,500 men, some from Germany, not all Jews, but also Christians who had chosen to leave Germany. Pictures depict the men at many tasks, such as shaving, getting haircuts, but also mowing lawns, driving tractors, tailoring, repairing watches, etc. "until they are fitted for a trade." In fact, among the men "were doctors, architects, engineers, dentists, clerks, bricklayers and business men." The booklet shows numerous pictures of them working in different trades and gardening, and in the evening learning to speak English. Considering the climate of England, the pictures are uncharacteristic for showing so many shirtless chests, or short sleeves as if to show how vigorous these men were. In other pictures the men are wearing shirts, ties and jackets. One picture shows men sitting opposite each other at a very long table, one side taking notes, apparently interviewing, the other talking. I

My Father?

---

[1] Salvors, according to dictionary, are people who salvage ship-wreckage, cargo, etc.

think I spot my father as a writer, for he could read and write English. In fact, he was given a commendation for his work in the Registration Department for:

> ...dealing with numerous Records and Lists which required particular care. He was made foreman of this department, and having to deal with the passports of over 3500 men in Camp he became the Liason (sic) Officer to the Police.

A month later, on September 3, 1939, England declared war on Germany; everything changed. Now there would be no possibility that my mother or I would be able to immigrate to England. Germany began its bombing of Britain. By spring of 1940, Britain was fighting for survival, stretched beyond capacity, and security became an issue. After the outbreak of these hostilities the government worried about the roughly 75,000 men who spoke German living in England who could be considered potential spies. Probably 60,000 were recent Jewish immigrants escaping Hitler. A decree was issued to set up tribunals to distinguish between enemy aliens living in England before the war and current refugees from Germany and Austria. Three categories were established, but in the end, in June 1940, all were declared prisoners of war. Churchill pronounced the edict: "Collar the lot" which meant all "enemy alien" men over sixteen and under sixty throughout the eastern and southern coastal regions of England would be interned. That included many non-Jews who had fled in opposition to Hitler's racist policies in the early 1930's. Most were of high academic status—doctors and scientists who were now working in Universities and other professional jobs. Included in the enemy status were many Italians, part of a service colony working in restaurants, shops and in manufacturing, who were also interned.

The refugee group from Kitchener camp, including my father, was sent to an internment camp on the Isle of Man, off the west coast of England, previously a summer resort. Now the men became "prisoners of war," living under barbed wire.[1]

◆ ◆ ◆

---

[1] Chappell, Connery: ISLAND OF BARBED WIRE, Corgy Books, 1986

THE DUNERA

Not only did the British government imprison the aliens, soon the government wanted them out of the country, but only Canada agreed to take them. The Andora Star, a ship loaded with more than a thousand men, including captured German and Italian military POWs as well as refugees, was torpedoed on its way to Canada and more than half perished. The 444 survivors of the Andora Star were put on the next transport—the HMT Dunera. Meanwhile, refugees from internment camps were requested to join this next transport, being assured that immigration to the U.S. from Canada would be easier. When not enough volunteered, the rest were forced. My father went on the Dunera, but I doubt that he volunteered since he was expecting a visa from our friends, the Bicks, to arrive any day. Unfortunately, an affidavit for his entry to the U.S. came to England a few days after he left, but it was useless in Australia because his "prisoner of war" status, made him ineligible for immigration.

Consequently, by an ironic twist of fate, the Dunera held refugees as well as their hated enemies, German and Italian military prisoners of war. Although separated on the ship, all were now considered prisoners of war, the deadly enemy of Britain. The ship took off for Canada, was barely missed by German torpedoes, changed its course and went to Australia instead; it was rumored among the refugees that the submariners heard German spoken, and did not torpedo again.

In a letter from Australia, my father described his ordeal to me only as "it was the worst [time] I ever had in my life".

September, 10 1940:

> I have got so many stories to tell you, what I have lived through all the time our being separated, incredible things which unfortunately were true, and experienced by me. But that did not matter much, I always thought of you and our dear Mama, and that helped me to overcome the various unpleasant occurrences.

Knowing that he was subject to motion sickness, I naively assumed that had been his trouble. Although I knew that war had been declared by England on Germany, I did not understand what it really meant, nor could I imagine the difficulties he lived through. Of course, his letter to me was being censored so it is understandable that he did not say more. He could only write in pencil, and was limited in the number of letters he could write in a week. The voyage to Australia on the Dunera took longer than two months, leaving Liverpool on May 27, 1940, and reaching Sydney, Australia, on September 6. Later, all the refugees on ship would be known as the "Dunera Boys," and their ordeals, the "Dunera Scandal," or the "Dunera Affair."

◆ ◆ ◆

The details of the voyage, which follows, were pieced together from a *"Petition,"* dated December 2, 1940, sent to the High Commissioner for the United Kingdom in Canberra, Australia, demanding release from imprisonment, which I found among his papers. Presumably written by the refugees, the Petition report is a carbon copy many pages long, and bears no signature except "Camp Spokesman." It has been published in many books.[1]

The document gives the following details: 2,542 men were aboard the overcrowded Dunera. The English soldier-guards considered all men as prisoners of war, as enemy Germans because of their language, and treated them as such, although over 2000 were Jewish refugees. There were also some Catholics, including some priests and 251 Nazis and 200 Italian prisoners from the Andora Star. The guards on the ship were "Soldiers of the King's Pardon," petty criminals released from prisons just for this army duty, and internees attributed their brutality to their loutish background. Protests to officers, Lt. Col. Scott and Lt. O'Neill, of the rough treatment they were subjected to, only brought more rough treatment. The soldiers took the "prisoners" belongings that were valuable; others, including glasses, dentures, insulin, even toothbrushes as well as precious personal papers were thrown

---

[1] Bartrob & Eisen, p 206

overboard. The staff confiscated personal items of value, and most suitcases were forced open and contents rifled, or simply dumped on the deck.

Many men had to sleep on mess tables or on the floor. They were not allowed to leave the decks, and buckets for urine "were soon overflowing and sewage flooded the decks as the ship rolled. Neither daylight nor natural air ever reached the decks" though they were traveling in the tropics. Conditions in the latrines, besides not having enough—only 16 for 2,000 men—were horrible, causing diarrhea and nausea. Long lines formed at the latrines that had no doors, precluding any privacy. Razors and shaving utensils had been confiscated, and the unkempt beards caused rashes and itches. Personal hygiene suffered from lack of soap, ability to wash or change clothes, and only 2 salt showers a week.

The *Petition* goes on for 12 typewritten single-spaced pages, detailing the two-months-long nightmare, including several testimonials of particular brutality. I was shocked at the details, and furious at my father belatedly for never having talked about this nightmare, denying me the intimacy of sharing his misery and outrage.

So, instead I talked to my friends about this discovered document. I wondered what my father's role was in the making of this document. I knew he could type, not a common skill in 1940, and perhaps that is why he had a copy. Some letters to me were typed on the same typewriter, and I wondered why he had access to it. Was it my father who drafted this document? More probable that he was the scribe. Was his one of the testimonials that accompanies this document? Was he one of the men who had to walk over broken glass for his exercise program and got hit with a rifle-butt if he didn't walk fast enough? Or was he the one who thought of covering the brilliant light on the deck so he could sleep, only to start a fire, and get punished for an attempted coup? Was he the one who formed a delegation to the ship's captain to complain of the inhumanity, only to be told that the soldiers were empowered and legitimate in their atrocities? I can believe that he was part of the delegation, but he would not have been the leader—he was not the leader type. I will never know, but a later letter to me indicated that he was one of the men who had lost their valuable papers, which then delayed his application for a U.S. Visa.

Dunera Way, where the camps once stood

INTERNMENT IN AUSTRALIA

Finally reaching Sydney, Australia, on September 6, 1940, the men were put on trains for a 500 mile, 19 hour journey to Hay, a treeless, arid grazing country at the edge of the desolate outback to yet another abandoned army camp from World War I. A sandstorm greeted their arrival. They were still considered prisoners of war. Today there is a plaque on the side of the Sydney Maritime Museum, commemorating the arrival of the Dunera, and a picture inside shows weary men in their European woolen suits and felt hats, carrying a suitcase, leaving the ship and walking single file to the waiting trains. Even with their foreign tongues, I wonder how these men could have been mistaken for field prisoners.

Among my father's papers I found documents giving statistics of the men, leading me to assume that my father had a job at the camp as record keeper. Of the 922 men in Camp 7 (there was also a camp 8), 747 were Jews, and 239 came from Austria, 577 from Germany. 688 were single; they were also young, the majority of them being 16 years old, and part of the 10,000 children that had been sent to England in the Kindertransport. I have interviewed several of these men, and I deduce that their experience of internment felt quite different from my father's. Although they worried about their parents and perhaps younger siblings, they did not have the burden of worry about children and wives left behind. As one such "Dunera Boy" told me: "We were young and strong. Soon we were able to play soccer all day and we were very hopeful for our future."

Upon arrival at Hay, the refugees organized themselves with a system of self-government, set up a camp university by members who were scholars and academics, musicians and artists, and arranged sport leagues. They were concerned with providing education for the many 16 year olds to prepare them for graduation. Among my father's papers were programs of entertainment that the refugees had put together, as well as notebooks in which he wrote his English studies. They even printed some camp "money", so realistic that it got them in trouble with the law. They divided the workload for the housekeeping of the camp, and so were provided with some pin money for cigarettes and other personal essentials. The officer in charge of the Hay internment camp soon recognized that the "prisoners" were not what he expected and helped to accommodate them. The military POW's— Germans and Italians, captured in battle—were kept separate. In general, the refugees were treated well, even if isolated, still behind barbed wire, and having to live through the Australian summer heat. A few months later, they were moved to a more hospitable environment in Tatura, a fruit-growing area of southeastern Australia, providing labor during harvest season.

✦ ✦ ✦

In early 1941, the *Petition* to be released from the Prisoner of War status finally found its way to London where Parliament considered the "Dunera Scandal", as it was being called. Parliament offered apology and released the internees. The Dunera officers, Scott and O'Neill, were both court-martialed and one served a year in prison. The proceedings of the hearings were locked for 100 years. Churchill himself apologized. Since that time many books and articles, and even a fictionalized movie, *The Dunera Boys* have described the "Scandal." In fact, it was that late night movie seen by one of my friends that began my search for a bibliography. To my surprise, much had been written about it.

The release was conditional, however. Some of the refugees returned to

England, though tragically, one ship with 500 men was sunk. Some went to Israel, others returned to Britain to join the British Army, but weren't allowed to fight in Europe until late in the war. Some joined the Australian Army; these soldiers were always kept in Australia working on dock, and never saw military action because their loyalty was still suspect. Others, like my father, were released only when he secured a job helping the labor shortage in Australia. On December 12, 1942, my father was finally released to work in a woolen mill in Melbourne.

I have looked at most of the library materials, in London as well as in Australia, and I visited both Hay and Tatura. Both towns developed in part because the internment camps were there and needed supplies, and as a result of it, have grown, even modifying the desert environment by the development. Each town has established museums to these camps.

The story of the Dunera is very complicated and fascinating. Even after much research, I am still not sure I understand my father's experience of it, because he was older than the men I could interview. I know that he bunked with "orthodox" Jews, by choice. Sometime during his journey, he became more religiously observant than he had been in Vienna. Unfortunately, after we were reunited, his journey, his travails, or even his life in Australia during our separation were never mentioned again.

LIFE IN THE
UNITED STATES

9

THE FIRST SIX MONTHS

April 6 to November 8

* All letters have been translated as written without editing except for clarification that is indicated in [brackets], while (*brackets*) in italics were written by the letter writer. Some paragraphs breaks were added for easier reading.

What should have been a momentous and memorable meeting with my new family that day on the ferry boat dock is lost in my memory, but is partially recorded in the first letter I sent to my father.

April 24, 1940   Translated from German, sent to Kitchener Refugee Camp in England.

Dearest Papa!

I'm a <u>very</u> naughty child, I haven't written for so long, but I was always busy. I've been in school one week, and I must always do homework and then I must write to Mama, and when I begin to write to you, Auntie says it is bedtime.

I've been with Auntie since Wednesday, for ten days before I was in a Children's home. It is good with Auntie and I get along with her children. Her girl is 15 years tomorrow and is called Cecylia. Her brother is 13 and his name is Moe. They are very nice. Yesterday it has been 31 days since I left Mama. I left on March 20. Now, I hope both of you will come soon. I had a good trip, I was seasick for 3 days. I am very good in arithmetic and penmanship.

I was to the movies twice. I saw The Invisible Man Returns, The Swiss Family Robinson and Remember the Night. Today I will go again to the movies. The movies here have no intermissions. After Pessach I will go to Hebrew school. When I know a little bit more English, I'll get piano lessons. The children in school are very sweet to me. What is status of your coming here? A sister of a girl that I traveled with was in London and had registered Aug. 5, and she is already in Baltimore. Mama had big quarrels with Gusti's daughter who is awfully lazy and always complains. She cries all the time and is an awful hypochondriac. When I left Vienna in the middle of the day there was rain and by evening one could ice skate. Hopefully we will see each other soon, Amen. Now Auntie wants to write. How are you? Now many, many kisses. I must now be Phyllis and I don't like it. From your loving Lizzi.

P.S. Please be so dear and write Mutti often. Please save this letter and others and bring them with you.

Since I mention that I spent 10 days in a children's home, Homewood Terrace, a social worker from the Home would have been at my arrival and probably my aunt's family, but I remember little of those days. The only memory I have is my first meeting with Mr. Bonapart, the director, as a group of us children—probably all new admissions—were standing on a terrace adjacent to a big building being introduced to him by a lady, probably the social worker. He was tall, had thin brown hair and a Hitler-like mustache that bothered me. He looked us all over and had things to say, most of which I didn't understand because of my lack of English. By his frown, lack of smile, tone of voice and his pointing finger, I understood that my clothes (my precious maroon velvet dress that I wore for important occasions, but may have worn for a month on my journey) as well as my name, Felicitas, were not OK—and that somehow I wasn't OK. He pointed at me and said "Phyllis"— my new name—I guessed. I remember thinking to myself that I would somehow become acceptable to and approved of by all—a decision that was to be a driving force for most of my life.

Through an arrangement worked out with immigration officials and the German Jewish Children's Aid Society in New York, Homewood Terrace, officially the Pacific Hebrew Orphan Asylum, but commonly called The Home, became and remained my legal guardian. Since I didn't know anything of these arrangements, I was surprised not to have gone to Aunt Laura's directly. At the orphanage I was probably given medical examinations and psychological tests along with some new clothes. I don't know what took ten days to process me; perhaps a home study of my aunt's home had to done.

✦ ✦ ✦

Auntie was Aunt Laura, (also my mother's name) who had given me support papers, the required affidavit for joining the Kindertransport. She was a woman about 55, and her husband, a little man who always wore a hat, seemed to me to be much older, but wasn't. She had emigrated from Galicia where my great-grandparents and their children lived and the area where I had spent summers in my earlier years; he had come from Russia, and perhaps spoke little German, so that I had few conversations with him. Aunt Laura's brother was married to my mother's aunt. My mother and Aunt Laura had met when my mother was a young girl living in Poland, at that time was part of Austria, and German was the official language, so Aunt Laura knew German. She was nice, and so was the family. It was nice to be able to speak with someone who understood me after weeks of muteness.

I felt comfortable in this household. My new home would be in the lower flat of a wooden, Victorian house on 24th Street on the corner of an alley between Mission and Valencia. The house was small compared to our large stone apartment house in Vienna, but in my eyes the interior was deluxe since it had a bathroom with a bathtub and a toilet within the apartment. There was one big bedroom used by my aunt and uncle, and the living and dining rooms also served as bedrooms when the wall beds were lowered. There was even a piano, played beautifully by Cecylia.

I shared a room with her. She was pretty with long black hair, and was very good to me. I will always be deeply grateful to Cecylia for helping me to learn English so fast. She never tired of correcting my pronunciation and helped to make the subtler distinctions in language clearer to me. We had a lot of trouble with the word "become" since in German it means to receive or get; it took me a long time not to "become" an artichoke or a piece of bread when I simply was asking for them. She always corrected the "th" sound, unknown in German and difficult to master. Moe, 13, was very interested in science and did some experiments at home that were fascinating to me. He didn't pay much attention to me, although later would tease me.

✦ ✦ ✦

The Mission district in 1940 was a working class neighborhood of mostly Irish people, but also Italians. Mission Street itself was a bustling street with many shops and many people. My aunt had a millinery shop on this street, and Uncle a cap factory a few blocks away.

I started Hawthorne Elementary School immediately despite my lack of English. The school was a stucco, two-story building, instead of the massive stone structure that I had known in Vienna. The area around it, and the playground activities were altogether new to me since in Vienna there was no playground, physical education nor recess. I was placed in the low 5th grade, although by my age I should have been in the high 5th. In order to help me learn English, I was sent to the 1st grade class twice a day to work on reading. Of course, I could read very well, only not English. However, my deficits in language skills were compensated by my math skills, and I was quite advanced compared to my classmates; I already knew fractions, while they were studying long division.

There aren't too many other memories of my school days; I could just as well write school <u>daze</u>, since that must have been my experience there. Still, I must have enjoyed school, since I liked learning, even though I was isolated by my lack of language. One day, I heard a girl calling me a Nazi which insulted me so much that I wrote my mother about it who told me in a letter to ignore such things: "Don't worry if others make fun of you because you can't speak English yet. People who like you will point out your mistakes to you, the other kind don't matter." I wanted to learn English quickly so that I would not be mistaken again.

Fortunately for me, the public library was across the street and that helped me learn English even quicker. Cecylia, an avid reader and excellent student, spent a lot of time at the library, and introduced me to this great institution. I did not go to a library in Vienna, perhaps there weren't any, or perhaps one had to pay; at any rate, I had not known of libraries in Vienna. To my delight, I found my favorite books there—*the Dr. Doolittle series*—and I began to read those that I had already read in German. Any problems I had with words, Cecylia was always willing to help clarify and explain. Most of all, she talked to me, was helpful in all ways and in a very short time, I became fluent in the language. Unlike his wonderful sister who took such good care of me, Moe constantly teased me and bullied me, even as he annoyed his sister. She knew how to cope with his constant harassment, but it was upsetting to me since I had never shared a household with siblings before.

Because of the war in Europe, letters were slow in arriving. It often took more than a month, sometimes two or more, although I can't always tell when they came since few of the letters had a San Francisco postmark. In late May I received letters from my parents. My father wrote thanking my aunt for having me, and enclosed a letter for me. Reading it now I am astounded by his command of English.

April 27, 1940, from my father in English, from Kitchener Camp, England

Dear Mrs. Rabinowitz, [Aunt Laura]

Many many thanks for your kind lines. I am only too happy that my little child arrived there safely, and has found such charming people to protect her until our arrival there. That is a great consolation for me and facilitates my present plight. Now I have the only wish to see my wife out of the German hell. In case, her emigration papers are in order, she will be able to get her Visa in about 2-3 months. I am very grateful to you for sending the cable on behalf of my wife to the American Consulate, and I hope it will accelerate her case.

...I should thank you for informing me from time to time about my little girl, and I think she will get accustomed to [America], *very soon.*

Trusting, you and your dear family are getting on well, I remain,

Very sincerely yours,   Samuel Finkel

Enclosed a letter for my daughter.

My dear, little, Fratz   (Translated from German)

Now I am finally in the possession of a message from you, you Naughty. I have received your postcard from New York as well as the letter from San Francisco and I was enormously happy. Mutti wrote me you told her that you have written me sometimes on your way, but I haven't received anything yet. Would you do something like that? You know that I am thinking of you a lot over here and you let me wait. Now for today I forgive you.

You can't imagine how very, very happy I was to hear that you have already left Germany. Now you have to forget all the ugly and unpleasant things you have experienced; be cheerful and happy again, because the worst you have already behind you.

You have to start studying hard again, and though your lovely Muttily and I can momentarily not be with you, you mustn't neglect your lessons, you have to be even more hard-working. I am convinced that you will be even more diligent. Soon you will have learnt the English language completely, and if it goes pretty fast we will write each other only in English. I can imagine that you left Mutti only with a heavy heart, but this is just temporary, soon our lovely Muttily will come to you, and later I will come, too. That will be a happy reunion. I am just afraid that when we come that your English knowledge has so much improved that you will laugh at our English. Isn't that true?

Now my lovely, little frog, write me detailed and often. When you write to Mutti you have to be careful, you know that every careless word could harm Mutti. Write me exactly what you are doing the whole day, what you study, actually everything. Your letters would make me really happy, I have by the way no other diversion than the letters from you.

I am all right over here, I just wish to get together with you soon. I already yearn so much for you my little Fratz, but you probably don't long for me a lot! Isn't that true? No, don't sulk my baby, I know that you love your Pappi a little bit, but not like you used to. Am I maybe mistaken? We will see when I come to you.

Now many, many kisses from your "bad" Pappi

April 21, 1940   Translated from German, from my mother, still in Vienna. Her main concern was getting the necessary affidavit to come to the U.S., a concern that was repeated in each letter with mounting anxiety and frustration, along with her gratitude. She enclosed a separate letter for me.

Dearest Aunt,

Now you have met my darling daughter. I do hope you will come to love each other. A cousin of your cousin's (at least I think so) Herr Weissman visited me a few days ago and told me that Herr Weissman will send official papers for me. However, the letter took four months to reach me, and two weeks ago the Consulate informed me that additional papers would be required [for entry to US.] *Please, Auntie, thank him a thousand times in my name. I hope to be able to thank him in person soon, it is already the turn of the 3rd of June* [the quotas that enabled emigration].

May God reward you for your good deeds, I have no words for such goodness. Please write soon, I am waiting impatiently. My best wishes for you and your loved ones, also Herr Weissman. …Your Laura

My precious darling little girl,

I have received your sweet letter—a thousand kisses for it. It gave me great joy and was read in the K.G. [Jewish Community Center]. *You write in an informative and detailed way. Every day I wait with great longing for the Post. I am so curious to know how you have found our Auntie, is she as sweet as I told you? I only hope you don't give her any trouble, are pleasant to her and make yourself useful. How are the children and Uncle? Do write about it in great detail. What are the children's names? If it is possible, please send me a group photo. Have you heard from Papa? I have not heard from him in the last six weeks since your departure. If you get mail from him, please let me know. Gusti,* [a friend with whom my mother lived] *poor thing is in hospital again, I am worried about her, as you can imagine. Have you got all your things? I am so delighted that you have it so nice and yet long for my sweet Puppshen* [dolly]. *I am so alone, but please don't worry about me, be happy and cheerful, your mother is brave. Now, Pupperl, you promised to write every week, do keep your promise! I kiss you from the bottom of my heart,   …Your Mutz*

My mother's letter was not as upbeat as father's, but had some of the same sentiments. Neither of my parents used my name—they had nicknames for me. I don't know how I reacted to the statement that she was "so alone," but now I can really feel her loneliness.

Vienna May 11, 1940 Translated from German, from my mother. I can't explain why she received my letters from Budapest; I have to assume I had been told to send them there as Budapest was not part of Germany, so mail could move faster.

Today I received your second letter from Budapest, much longed for. I am so happy that you are well and happy. May the good Lord protect you always and repay our relatives' kindness a thousand fold. May they always be well and happy too. This is the third letter I am writing to you. I have nothing new to report, everything is as before. I am longing for the moment I can embrace you again....

I was so glad to hear that you were able to get shoes, I hope you wear your supports. I am glad that you are going to school; do be a good student, my darling, you have a lot to catch up on and you must work hard. ... Can you make yourself understood by Cecylia and Moe? I should so like to have a picture of them all. Have you had any mail from Papa? Frau Treister is hurt because you have not written to her. Did you receive the postcard? Send regards to Dr. and Frau Murmelstein when next you write, they always send their regards to you. Has your dear aunt a maid? If you feel homesick, just think of "Reserl" and you will feel better. Please continue to write in this way. I keep all your letters as my most precious possession and they can help you to remember your adventures later on. Enough for today, there is no more news.

I kiss and embrace you most tenderly, your Mutz

P.S. Thank God dear Gusti has returned from the hospital. She was delighted to get your letter. Do write her a few lines sometime. Write directly to my address, that way is quicker. Have you written to Anny and Rosl? ...

Dearest Aunt,

Thank you so much for your letter. May the good Lord bring you and your dear ones the happiness I felt when reading my daughter's letter. Thank God she is happy, that makes me happy too. The consulate wrote to that the Affidavit is weak again. I pointed out to them that all their regulations had been followed and asked them to say what else they require. That was three weeks ago and I have not heard from them again, so I hope that everything is in order that they will probably invited me to appear for an examination. I shall let you know. I do so want to live long enough. Kiss your children from me, may they thrive! Amen! Did you get my letters? With many kisses, Laura

Getting a visa was difficult due to the complicated bureaucracy. First, there had to be a sponsor in the U.S. with enough capital to assure the consulate that the applicant would not be a burden to the U.S. After that, there would be the wait for the applicant's quota number to be called up for examination. Later still would be other problems, but in any case, her letters convey great urgency and frustration. A few days later, another, more urgent letter.

Vienna May 15, 1940 Translated from German

Dearest Aunt,

Today I received an answer to my questions from the Consulate, as follows: "The sponsor has already agreed in writing to your traveling alone. However, the Rabinowitz Affidavit is too weak. [Not enough money] *It would be advisable to get another Affidavit from another sponsor, a Weissmann affidavit has not been received so far." This news for which I waited for three weeks, hit me like a thunderbolt; to think one had achieved what they asked for and then, shortly before one had hoped to be called for the examination, to have all one's hopes dashed by such news! I have to send you another telegram, as letters take too long...According to your cousin, Herr Weissmann on Dec.19, he intended (says Frl. Grossfeld) to send me an affidavit in February.*

However, as you had received information from me that a declaration by telegram or letter would suffice, your cousin did not send the affidavit. I beg you, therefore, to ask your cousin or his wife to be so kind and send me an affidavit immediately, I only hope it will still be possible, if not, please get in touch with...If I were to write from here, it would take too long, that is why I ask this further favor from you, after all the sacrifices you have already made which I appreciate very much and trust you to take these steps on my behalf also. Hopefully, we shall at last see some results.

Please don't hold it against me, dear Auntie, that I cause you these worries on top of the duty which I had to burden you with—whether I wanted to or not. I kiss your hands and feet for your kindnesses and will be loyal and grateful to you for the rest of my life. You are our real angel. Family Grossfeld send their regards to Herr Weissmann and please add my regards, even though I do not know them personally. In anticipation of a speedy undertaking and in the hope of having your reply soon, I kiss you from the bottom of my heart,   Your grateful Laura.

Kindest regards to your dear husband, Cecilia and Moe,

My darling girl,

Please don't let this letter worry you, you know how difficult everything has become. But I am not losing my courage, am full of trust in the dear God that he will help me this time again, as always before when we were discouraged, don't you agree, my little doll? How are you doing in school? A few days ago I answered your letter from Budapest, did you receive my answer? I am convinced that you are fine with Auntie and the family and also that you are fulfilling your duties faithfully, that you are happy and cheerful and don't make unnecessary work for anybody. What do you hear from Papa? Best regards from Frau Menkes, Weinberg, Dr. Treisler and Lucy, Fr. Fischer, Fr. Malajka, Fr. Schubert, little Otto who always is so sweet. Your letter has pleased us very much I kiss and embrace you devotedly, Your Mutti.

P.S. Do return the regards, always remember Gusti, also Dr.Murm., and Fr. Pisk.

It is German custom to include remembrances from other people at the end of letters, and I chuckle now when she reminds me to mention other people in my letters. I suppose it is nice to be remembered, but I found it a chore and it took up much space on our letters. When she asks if my aunt had a maid, that also makes me smile today—so many Europeans thought all Americans had maids. In fact, maids were much more common in Vienna, although we didn't have one, neither did my aunt, here. This letter of frustration and disappointment was the harbinger of many more during the next year in my mother's desperate effort to join me in the United States. Now I also think of the trouble my aunt and others had to go to in trying to help her: filing papers, going to consulates, wires, document fee expenses, writing to others, etc.—these all were big sacrifices for working people such as my aunt and the Bicks, my parent's friends, also trying to help my parents. Now I am also aware of my mother's religiosity, her prayers and dependence on God.

The next letter is remarkable in that I started writing in English, just two months after arriving in San Francisco.

June 4, 1940 in English, with Cecylia's help, (sent to Kitchener Camp in Kent, England)

Dear Daddy,

Please excuse me that I couldn't write you. Last Sunday we went to the fair. It was very nice out there. I had a wonderful time. We saw Billy Rose's Aquacade. I liked very much. Today we will go again, (Cecylia a. I.). Really it is beautiful at the fair. Tomorrow I will mail the letter. I will continue tomorrow. I am glad that we have only 10 days school. Last Wed. I had a letter from Mama. We will eat now lunch.

Hello Daddy: Jesterday I couldn't write you because it was too late. That way I wrote today. I am a very good pupil in Hebrew. In one week I will go to the third grade. That's fine! Isn't it?

I hope that we will go soon all together, Mama, you and I.

Now much...much 100000000 kisses your loving Lizzy.

Dear Mr. Finkel, (translated from German)

The dear Lizzi is already a total American. She learns well and speaks good English already. How are you? I am sorry I can't give you a good report about the dear Laura. I feel bad that I can't get a sufficient affidavit, but I don't lose hope.

L. Rabinowitz

The World's Fair on Treasure Island was THE big event of 1940 in San Francisco. I experienced another sense of wonderment—to think that there would actually be a World's Fair in San Francisco, and that I would be able to go to it. As it happened I went to the fair many times, always filling me with awe and delight. Luckily, Cecylia and her friends were willing to take me along. Looking back, I wonder if Cecylia did not resent having that funny little girl tagging along with her all the time, but if she did, I was never made conscious of it. We took a streetcar to the Ferry Building, then one of those wonderful ferryboats for 10 cents brought us to Treasure Island. Week by week we explored new facets of that wonderland. The brilliant lights of the main promenade, the exotic atmosphere of the whole island of palm trees and vegetation, the throngs of people, the amusements for children, all were a wonderful part of the experience. Especially memorable was Billy Rose's Aquacade as I watched wide-eyed the thrilling performance of Esther Williams diving into a pool through a ring of fire.

We also went to the movies every Saturday afternoon, mostly to the El Capitan Theater that was on Mission and 22nd. I loved going to the movies, but I was surprised that we saw pictures other than Shirley Temple, nearly the only type of film that was allowed for children in Vienna. Some of the films I saw here, such as Dr. Cyclops, a one-eyed monster who reduced people to ant-size, were especially terrifying and gave me nightmares.

Everything was new and strange to me, but what struck me most was the freedom from fear. For instance, I actually saw girls and women wearing a Star of David around their necks. At first, I cringed with fear for them, worried that someone might attack them, but eventually, I realized with relief, that to be Jewish was not a crime in America. Wearing such an ornament in Hitler's Austria was asking for trouble. To many Americans, that kind of fear is unimaginable, although Blacks in the South must have felt that way. Another thing that was liberating for me was that it was possible to walk on the grass in the parks, something that is clearly forbidden in Austria (and many other parts of Europe) still today. It was also a great comfort for me was that men didn't urinate in the streets, and I lost the fear of being molested by lurking men, giving me freedom when walking on the streets.

The free public library was the biggest miracle of all. The building was full of shelves filled with books! I could peruse the shelves to decide what to read, and then borrow books for a week or two without cost. Between those wonderful visits to the Fair, the movies and the library, my English improved rapidly while the German faded from my memory, much to my mother's disapproval.

I spent many hours at my Aunt's millinery shop. Hats were an important item of clothing in those days, usually worn by adults outside the home. The store was close to 24th Street on Mission, close to our house so I am guessing that I was asked to go there if Cecylia had other things to do. I loved the time at the shop. I liked trying on all those wonderful hats, and I liked the ladies who came in to buy them, but I especially liked "Johnny", the other saleslady in the shop. Johnny was a big fat mamma but fashionably dressed, her blond hair carefully coifed. She was abundant in every way, sweet to the customers and especially wonderful to me because she worked at breaking the language barrier with patience. Johnny was not a young woman, perhaps also in her 50s, and her boyfriend was also pleasant to me when he came to the store. Johnny would often bring me little favors, but most of all she just talked to me in a way that felt good, and I knew she liked me. I especially liked Saturday nights, a big shopping night because some customers would come in with their husbands, and Johnny would become more solicitous: "This color becomes you, Madam," or "it is wonderful for your face," speaking softly as she adjusted the hat slightly. It was wonderful to watch.

✦ ✦ ✦

I was sent to Camp in July, an extraordinary experience for any child, but especially one from a city in a foreign country; I assume that the orphanage had arranged it, since Cecylia and Moe didn't go. I had only been in San Francisco three months at the time, and my English was yet to be perfected. I went to a Girl Scout Camp at Bass Lake in the Sierras near Fresno. I had a wonderful time, and a picture I have of myself there shows serenity on my face that I see in the mirror after I've spent a few days in the mountains. I do wonder how well I was able to talk with my fellow campers, although my postcards home were in English; I expect that I was really an oddity, but I did not feel unwelcome.

July 22, 1940 Written in English from Camp Tahomi, Wishion, CA., on a penny postcard

> *Dear folks!* [to Aunt Laura and family] *I arrived yesterday 4:30 here an.* [German construction]. *It is hier very nice. We children 10 +11 year have 1 tent and we sleep outside. We are in a forest by a lake (Bass). We had breakfeast allready. Here are many irishe (christ) children. It is hier very hot and flies are beiting me. Enogh for today. Love and many kisses, Phyllis*

My group at Camp. I am third from right in the front row.

July 26. Same place. Postcard

I received yesterday your d.[dear] letter. Thanks a lot! I am here very happy. It is here very hot and I haven't anything to wear. Please could send me a bandana and tie ribbons on. [Small drawing to illustrate.] Maybe you send me 1 pair of shorts. I am pealing from the heat. We sleep outside the tent. How is everything? Love and kisses, Phyllis

Dear Daddy July 28, 1940 Translated from German

On Sunday luckily I came to this camp. It is here very beautiful and very hot, sunny and everything is green. Friday I went to a waterfall, and yesterday, Saturday, I went horseback riding. How are you? Next Sunday I will write again. Many 100000000000000 kisses. Your loving Phyllis

July 28, Reply from Cecylia and Aunt

Dear Phyllis,

Hope you are having a very good time. We are sending you a play suit, bandana, hair ribbons and safety pins. The pins are to pin your sunsuit with in case its too big around the waist. Love and kisses, Cecylia

Dear Honey, I am sending you a letter from Mutti and Daddy. [below] ...Hope you are having a good time, love from all of us, your Aunt Laura

Vienna, May 28, 1940   Translated from German

My loved child!

Today I have received your letters from May 2nd and May 15th. I was and I am happy about your message. I am pleased that you study well and are busy, but you shouldn't neglect your Mutti, besides you have to take care of the outer form of your letters. The letter from Budapest was delightful, but there have been some mistakes. The one from today reveals your absent-mindedness and disorder. I ask you to write your letters more tidily and where possible avoid mistakes, you shouldn't forget the German language. I haven't heard from Papa for a long time now and I am wondering that you don't have mail from him whereas he has already confirmed your letter. ... Uncle Max and Tilly are in Tangier, and also Aunt Jula [Tilly's sister] *flew there last week.*

Already, my German has suffered, and my mother complained about my handwriting and other mistakes. I wish that I had the letters I wrote to her to know how I reacted to hers. I must have asked her about the ship ticket. Her letter continues.

...As you know, you don't get the ship ticket until you have been invited to the examination. People usually don't get the tickets from here; most get them from the outside. ... If it's also impossible for her [aunt] *you two have to write to Anny. I*

hope that she could get the money for me and I would repay her from my income. I feel like I usually do but now I visit my friends more often.

Now my doll study hard, be good and useful. What dresses can you wear? I kiss you tenderly,   Your Mutti

Dearest Aunt,

Hopefully you are already in the possession of my telegram and some letters. It is nice of you that you look after the ship ticket. Lizzchen already knows the facts and if it is really necessary I will telegraph. Read the letter from Lizzi.

I am so happy that Lizzchen is with you and that you love her and she loves you. But the feeling that she gives you additional work depresses me. Maybe I will make it to replace you soon. Please send me a family picture that would make me happy.

Meanwhile I have received mail from Stryj. [My mother's family's home.] *Lucia* [Aunt Laura's real niece] *is in Lemberg and earns only what she needs whereas they withdrew the dear Yetty's* [Aunt Laura's sister-in-law] *pension, my brother also got a job and earns the half of what he needs. It distresses me that the poor Lucia didn't make it to leave to the USA. Now it is not possible. Don't you have any mail from there?*

I thank you for allowing Lizzchen to learn to play the piano. I am grateful to destiny that my child is under your care. What do your dear children learn? Please write me soon if Mr. Weissman sends me the affidavit. I greet and kiss you and your dear family.   Your Laura

She was diligent in keeping the wider family informed of each other, despite the difficulties with delivery of mail. There were long silences, then a bunch of letters came together. We nagged each other about not writing. For example, the next letter shows that she received mail from us upon my arrival in San Francisco, although she had already acknowledged later letters.

Vienna, May 30, 1940 Translated from German

Dear Aunt!

Your letter from April 6th with the message that my child is with you made me very happy, now I am calm and know that she is in safe hands...I have also received a nice letter from the committee that my darling child is sheltered in a good house with the lovely family Rabinowitz.…Still no news from the consulate…

My dear Lizzelein, I was very happy about your letter.…Are you well-behaved and good? Hopefully you are not a disgrace to me. I am longing for you so much and I am always with you in my thoughts. Right now I do not have a lot of time. The poor Gusti had a surgery and is hospitalized. Thank God she already feels better and hopefully comes home soon. …Mrs. Fischer, her little boy hasn't written her yet. You are very good by writing often, continue doing so because a letter from you is the sunshine in these lonely dark days. Papa is sad because you don't write him. Do you have mail from him? …Are you already studying? Study, study, study, now is the best time… 1,000,000 kisses. Your Mutti

✦ ✦ ✦

My father was having troubles, too. In the spring of 1940 Britain had interned 75,000 German-speaking refugees from the southeast of England and sent them to Mooragh Internment Camp, Ramsey, Isle of Man.

July 18, 1940 (Translated from German)

Dear Mrs. Rabinowitz,

I just received three letters from you and my little one, thank you for that. As you can see from my address I am now in an internment camp and with me all the other members of the previous camps have been interned. We are all right here, we are treated well, only that we are cut off the rest of the world with a barbed wire fence and we are not allowed to leave the camp. This is very unpleasant, but we still have one hope and that is as soon as somebody gets the visa and is able to emigrate, he will be dismissed out of the camp. If my papers were all right, I also would have the chance to get the visa, unfortunately this is not the case, therefore I have to wait, maybe my wife arrives there soon and can get me an affidavit. I thank you very, very much for your good care of my child, I will never forget your help. In anticipation of the good news that my wife is already with you I give you and your family my best regards.

My lovely, little darling,

Today I had another day of joy. Your three letters from 4/29, 5/6, and 5/12 have been forwarded and today I have received them at the same time. Also the picture came and I was enormously happy. Soon your Mutti will be with you, how happy I would be, you can imagine, I write Mutti very often but I haven't heard from her for eight weeks. I am really proud of you that you make great progress in school, I knew that everybody would like you. Over here it is very beautiful, I live directly by the sea, in the next letter I will describe you everything in detail, for today I have to close because we are only allowed to write 24 lines.

Many, many kisses from your loving Papa

✦ ✦ ✦

I doubt that at the time I understood what an internment camp was, nor do I recall Aunt Laura explaining it to me. The internees were not allowed to write in pen, only pencil. Anyway, he couldn't say anymore about it, and thereafter, for many years, the envelope would have a "CENSORED" stamp on it. His internment would have been the most unexpected turn of events—to leave Austria to avoid internment in Hitler's camps, only to be interned in Britain instead, even if not facing death! Both parents thought that the other one would be able to come to the United States because Anny, my mother's friend who was in Baltimore by then, was sending them affidavits. My parents were not able to communicate effectively with each other since mail did not go between England to Germany; rather letters were sent through the Red Cross. Thus, I became the messenger, but I don't think I did a very good job because I have many of my mother's letters that should have been sent to my father, and his to her. Sometimes I write in English, sometimes in German. In the next letter, I do not mention anything about the internment; instead I give news of my activities, am confident that God will help us, and I advise him not to despair.

Aug. 7, 1940 in English sent to Ramsey

Dearest Daddy,

Sunday I arrived here, from Camp. I like it very much there. We had swimming, boating and horsebackriding. I almost forgot that your birthday is coming soon. I wish you a very happy birthday and hope that we will be together soon. Last Sunday, the 4th of August made one year since I have seen you. But I hope I am going to see you soon. I know that God will help us and everybody who needs help. He has always helped and God will help us now. So don't despair! Friday is my Birthday and I will be 11 years old. I'm a big girl now. I have grown about 3 inches. The times goes so fast. I received a letter from you and one from Mama last Wednesday. Thank you very much! How are you? I am fine, Love and 1000000000000kisses,   your Phyllis

P.S. Cecyle correct me. If she wouldn't the letter would be terrible.

August 15, 1940 Translated from German sent to Ramsey

Dear Daddy!

I received a letter from Mutti! It made me very happy since I didn't have mail for 1$^1/_2$ weeks. Today is Thursday and (last) Friday was my birthday. It was very nice. I received 2 pairs of sock, a jacket, a sweater, a dog pin, hair things and candy. Auntie made me a birthday party and a cake with my name on it. Sunday I went to a downtown show, today I went swimming. Isn't that fine? I know how to swim like you. I learned in Camp. Yesterday I was at the fair. It was very beautiful. We saw many things. How are you? Are you healthy? I am. Many kisses 100000000000 Phyllis

In addition to the party, my aunt and family took me to a fancy dinner at Monaco's, a theater restaurant, in the North Beach District. The Italian menu had many courses and then entertainment on a small stage—

a magician, a lady singer in a beautiful dress, more music. The birthday cake was also new to me, and I was delighted to see my name written on it. I was well feted on the occasion of my 11th birthday, much more than I would have been in Vienna.

◆ ◆ ◆

Vienna, Aug 17, 1940 Translated from German, probably received end of September. My mother hasn't been getting mail from me, but probably from my aunt who may have been complaining about me.

> *Dearest Aunt!*
>
> *I thank you for your mail. I am not worried when I seldom receive mail from my child. I am convinced that she is in good motherly care and I feel that she is happy and satisfied in your home; she is longing a little bit, but that is understandable. Is she well behaved and aware of her duties? Please write me about it. If God wills, I will be able to take your place in a few months. Please don't be impatient, I know that it is hard for you to take care of another child besides your regular duties, but believe me I am not longing for anything more than to show you and my good friends my gratitude.*
>
> *I greet and kiss you, Your Laura*

August 20, 1940, Written in English, sent to Ramsey. Although I didn't know it, my father was on the high seas on the Dunera, on the way to Australia. My letters to him became shorter and shorter.

> *Dear Daddy!*
>
> *It has been a long time since I have received mail from you. How are you? I hope you are fine! I went swimming today! I had a lot fun. I'll go back to school in one week. How is everything. I hope you'll get a visa soon. Have you mail from mother. I was Sunday to a nice movie! My back is brown as an Indians! Love, Happy Birthday, 10000000 Kisses   Phyllis*

Vienna, September 1, 1940 Translated from German. Mother complains about my writing and forgetting German, but there is more hope of her getting an affidavit.

My dear girl!

I have received your postcard from you summer vacation. I am happy that you had the possibility to relax after the exertions of the last year. You are making bad mistakes which worry me a lot, because you are not a small child anymore and shouldn't forget your mother language, for example… You should only write in ink because pencil is almost unreadable. Also pay attention to the outer form, because friends are curious about your letters and they want to read them — then I feel embarrassed when they see the smear.…I hope you are healthy and happy. The only comfort for me is to know that you are all right. …Gusti is very ill, pray to God for her. Do you hear from Papa? I don't. I had one letter from the "Isle of Man" but since then I haven't heard anything. Oh God, if he could only be with you. Anny has sent an affidavit to your Papa and to me, hopefully it will also be granted to me to be with you soon. The time is terribly long. The good Anny, how she thinks about us, you should thank her too…

Are you obedient and attentive in school? Did you already learn how to swim? I kiss you tenderly, Your Mutti

September 9, 1940 Sent to Ramsey, and complaining about lack of mail from him. My English is quite good now, but still needs improvement. I was still having fun at the Fair.

Dearest Daddy!

It is a very long time since I have had any mail from you. From Mama I have already 15 letters and from you just four. I am writing you every week. I am going to school. I like school very much. We were yesterday at the fair. I enjoided very much. We had a lot of fun. We went on Gayway in the funhouse. We thought we'd have a lot of fun, but we didn't. We had to walk in the dark and most of the time we walked in the wall. Aunti and I didn't laugh the hole time, but suddenly we lought, because we saw the exit. The fair closes the 29th of September. I am very sorry it does, because we had a lot of fun there. Two months ago I send you a picture of the Sun tower. I think it is there beautiful. I wish you could be here. Now many...many 1000000000 kisses your treue Phyllis. Today is a holly day [California Admission day]

School resumed in the fall, but my memories of the following two months have vanished. Letters from my mother should have warned me that changes were coming, but I blocked those out, forgetting them altogether, or perhaps there were no letters for a while. Only recently, so many years after the letters were written, when they were translated, did I learn that my mother had been warned about what a burden I was. The letter below would have told me that my aunt was unhappy with me, but I do not remember feeling it at the time. I stopped getting letters from my father, and my mother's letters became progressively more anxious. Gusti, the lady with whom she had lived, died, and my mother had to move. Things are not good for her, and she pleads for me to be good.

Vienna, September 8, 1940 Translated from German

I had a lot to do at her home and now that is over, too. I have to leave the apartment and right now I do not know where to go, now it is very hard, but something will happen eventually...I hope you are good, well-behaved and tidy and do not make additional work for the dear aunt. Have in mind what sacrifices [she] *makes therefore be grateful and do what she asks...with joy and pleasure, this is then only a small part of what you owe her. ...Mutti*

She moved to another apartment in the same building, but I don't know the person with whom she lived, a Mr. Kogan. I don't know if I knew who he was then. Was he just a landlord? an old friend? perhaps a lover? or a kind person helping a distraught woman. I don't know how she supported herself, as I am sure that she didn't have her sewing business anymore. Those questions did not enter my mind at the time.

Vienna, September 10, 1940   Translated from German, probably received in November. Mother's problems continue and her anxiety increases.

Dear Aunt!

Thankfully, I have received your letter from August 1ˢᵗ. Like I already told you I have received an affidavit from my friend Anny, unfortunately some things are missing from this one as well, like a proof of his bank account and for how many [people] he has already issued an affidavit. I have telegraphed this to Anny last week so that there will be no delay. Believe me, my dear, if it would be within my power to come to you I would not miss a moment. Unfortunately it is not within my power, we have to have patience even if it is nerve-shattering. I believe you that it is hard for you to take care of my girl, even if you do not tell me, because I am also a working person and know for sure that a child causes a lot of trouble. I know to appreciate and acknowledge it, but there is nothing I can do and it does not help you. What should I do? I am helplessly confronted with everything and I do not know what to do. Dear Aunt, I do not have to repeat what good deed you are doing by helping us in this terrible misery, I cannot explain it with words, words fade against how grateful I am and what I feel for you. My own mother could not help me more than you did. I will be grateful to the end of my days and wish that you would never accuse me of not appreciating what you have done for me.

My mother tried to show Aunt Laura how much she appreciated her, but it didn't seem to be enough. She continues in the letter:

To make a clean sweep I have to tell you that unfortunately I will not be able to come soon; the best case would be this winter. Considering this I would suggest to put her in a children's home. Whereas I am convinced that she will not have it as good and loving there as she had it with you, but I understand that it would be unfair to ask you for more sacrifices. After all there are thousands of kids accommodated in a children's home, so she will be one of them until I will come and be able to take her to myself. I understand your situation; I am too modern not to realize that.

To your remark: the people whom you have helped are unsatisfied I will tell you the following: Yes, you are right, people forget very fast and unfortunately are soon unhappy because they are just thinking about themselves; if they would only think a little bit about others they would be endlessly happy, but in my opinion this is only the beginning until they have adopted to the new conditions. After all you have to start once more from the beginning, get used to a new way of life, and study a foreign language. These are demanding things and the human is a creature of habit. I do not think that Lizzy is unsatisfied, I hear from her letters that she is thank God happy. I am always thinking that she is still a child, and if there are some things bothering her, what happens between siblings and parents, then she can't cope with it as a grown up. You should not think like that, let her run, life is a tough school and therefore one shouldn't pamper kids, but she was not spoiled from our house either. Therefore I do not let it trouble me, I am convinced that you take care of her in a motherly way. God should make it worthwhile for you a thousand times. A propos the expenses you have because of us, I can assure you that we will repay you for it to the last penny as soon as we are there and earn money.

From her letter, I infer that Aunt Laura must have complained a lot, perhaps about me. Possibly there were fights between my cousins and me. Next there was the concern that I was forgetting German, remembering that I had once spoken Polish and had forgotten that too. The only person I could have spoken German with was Aunt Laura; otherwise, I was immersed in English in my environment and in school. I don't believe I had any inkling of her suggestion that I be put in a children's home. She continues:

Concerning the language you do not have to pay too much attention, I understand that she has to learn English but because she has already forgotten another completely learned language [Polish], *it would be a pity if she would also lose the second, now she is thank God six years older. I see in your letter that you master the Polish language completely and also your German is good. Why are you wondering, you are also an intelligent human being and know like me how important languages are these days.*

She continues, worrying about other people in Vienna.

And now my dear, I would like to ask you to call on Mr. Weissman concerning his relatives, family Grossfeld, over here. I have visited them a few days ago and I can't explain in what condition and desperation I have found these people. It was horrible! The affidavit from Weissman is too weak—which we cannot understand because he is so wealthy. Please dear Aunt, tell him from me that it is irresponsible and unprincipled to leave relatives in such a situation where they are already haunted by misfortune of the loss of a son and a brother. These are worthy women and will not become a burden for him, because they are hard working and gifted, it is an unforgivable sin to not help them. Eventually money isn't everything, even if you work hard for it. We wish to work and not need any people, that is the bitter bread. I ask him in my name not to be deaf to the desperation of his relatives, because his help is necessary.

Many kisses and greetings, Your Laura

Dear Lizzerl!

I have received your lovely postcard and next week I will write in more detail. Be good and well behaved, hopefully Papa is already with you.

1,000,000 kisses, your Mutti.

September 15, 1940   Translated from German

My dear Maederl!

I have received your letter from August 7th yesterday. I was happy to hear that my girl has spent a nice time in the camp. Now the time of heavy duties begins again and you surely have prepared yourself. Anny has already sent me the affidavit, but some supporting documents are still missing. Given this I was forced to another delay and I still don't know how long it will take, until I can take you to myself.

***I wrote this to the good aunt last week and asked her if possible to place you in a children's home...**[my emphasis] By any means you have, do what the good aunt thinks is correct without any opposition. I hope that you are aware of what good deeds the aunt did for us especially for you. You can't offer a child anything more, therefore I ask you to not give your aunt, uncle, and the nice children any reason for trouble. I have beaten it into your head over here and I remind you in every letter that you are obliged to gratefulness daily and hourly and in no case violate the hospitality. Also at home you cannot always satisfy a child, I too had to strike your lovely bottom sometimes so that you would behave, so be sensible, pay attention that you never hurt or bother anyone. Above all you have to study hard, keep your things in order, and as far as possible be not annoying. You have every-thing you need, be happy, joyful, and merry, other children would be endlessly satisfied with your situation, I suppose that your are, too.*

Our separation will not last forever, hopefully soon will come the time and we will be all together again—what we all desire so much. Do you hear from Papa? I don't know where he is right now and I am very concerned. Have you received all the letters in the right order? Also the one with the congratulation to your birthday? How did you like this day? Aunt Jula and Uncle will drive tomorrow to Berlin to visit uncle Max. So, my Murli, be good, with this you help me to bear my sorrow because I don't have it easy.

I kiss you tenderly,   Your loving Mutti

I am confused by the statement that Max is in Berlin, because a previous letter (May 28) she wrote that he was in Tangier. My mother's situation is desperate and dispairing.

Dearest Aunt!

I hope that you have received my letter from September 9th that was addressed to you to answer your letter from August 1st. I ask you, dearest aunt, not to be inpatient, you can imagine that I am helpless over here and that I cannot do anything; how would I rush to you if only I could. The situation is nothing but misery and desperation. My landlord, also my girl friend, is deathly ill, she weighs only 36 kg and is in the hospital right now. I have to endure a lot. She wants to pray but the strength is leaving her gradually. I haven't heard from Anny for a while. I am waiting impatiently for the rest of the documents. I don't hear anything from my husband either. Please write me if it is possible for you to place Lizzy in a children's home. I have heard from Stryj, my brothers haven't been home for some weeks.

How are you? I wish that you would always be happy and joyful. On the occasion of the approaching [Jewish] *New Year I wish you all the best and a lot of fortune and over all that all your wishes will come true.*

I greet and kiss you heartily,   Your Laura

I don't remember knowing of her suggestion to put me in a children's home, or that Auntie had some complaints. I don't recall any arguments, nor getting in trouble for any misbehavior. When I read the translated letter, I was completely surprised and shocked; perhaps I hadn't understood what it meant at the time. Perhaps I hadn't wanted to remember. I didn't mention the potential move in my cards to my father. The letters from September may have given Aunt Laura the courage to request placement in the orphanage, or maybe the letters didn't arrive until I had already moved. I am sure it was a difficult decision for Auntie. I don't remember what was going on in September and October at her home, or, if indeed, I was being a difficult child. I do not recall any disagreements with my aunt, although there was strife between Moe and me. His teasing was quite unpleasant, though I do not remember any reason for it, perhaps nothing more than a 13 year old boy teasing a younger sibling.

I only remember one day in November the social worker from the orphanage came and told me that I would be leaving my aunt's place to go to a foster home. I can't recall my feelings at the time, blocked out, as in shock. I would not have argued, but would have accepted my fate stoically. The social worker told me that I should not try to get in touch with my aunt or her family, although I did anyway in the following years, and did visit several times. It was not a happy moment and so I forgot the events that led up to it.

✦   ✦   ✦

These seven months had been hard on my whole family. My father had been interned by the British—made into a prisoner of war—and then shipped off to Australia, thus losing his chance to come to America to take care of me. My mother had her visa applications denied while her situation in Vienna became more precarious. And I, happily enjoying my new home, was forced to move without understanding why. When would we all move together?

10

MY FIRST FOSTER HOME

November 1940 to February 1942

November 1940 to February 1942

On November 8, a social worker from the orphanage took me and my single brown suitcase to my new home at 2214 Noriega Street. We walked up a flight of stairs to the front door. It was the home of the Reingolds, a young Jewish couple probably in their early thirties. He had a small brown mustache, she shoulder length brown hair; both of average size; other than that, I cannot remember much about them. The white stucco house was a typical San Francisco two-story row house in the Sunset district, looking much like the other houses next to it except for the design of the blue trim. The neighborhood was new to me, and it was very different from the older Mission district I had left that morning. For one thing there were few people on the streets, whereas the Mission streets were always full with pedestrians and cars. In fact, the whole neighborhood was new—the Sunset district was just emerging from the sand dunes at this time.

I don't remember what I thought as I was being moved. Was I apprehensive? even downright scared? or just stunned? I just don't remember. However, the move to a foster home proved to be a good experience, at least for a while. I experienced many new activities, found new friends and became fluent in English.

My parents were still hopeful that they would be joining me soon, but they were on the move, too. I had not had any mail from my father since the end of summer, which worried me a lot, but I still kept writing to him. They both complained of not getting mail from me, and I didn't get regular mail from them, although in 1941 I wrote 31 letters to my father and he wrote 28 to me, and I received 19 from my mother; I probably wrote at least as many to her, but I have no record of them, or how often I wrote. Since the United States was not yet at war with Germany, it was still possible to send and receive mail from my mother, but it was slow and censored. Sometimes my letters reflected my frustration about the mail.

Nov 12, 1940   From now on I would write in English.

> *Dearest Daddy,*
>
> *I am sorry that I haven't 3 month and 1/2 mail from you. Last friday I moved to a familie, one lady one gentleman, one 14 month old Baby girl and a little Boy who's name is Melvin, 4 years old. The house we live in has a children's room, bedroom, a living room, a dinning room, a bathroom, a hall and a kitchen. It is a very prettie house. I went away from* [Aunt Laura] *because Moe was very mean to me. I cried many times and I was unhappy while here I am very happy.*
>
> *How are you? I hope you are healthy! I am G.S.D.* [Gott sei Dank= God be praised] *10,000,000 kisses, your Phyllis*

My new home I described to my father was very modern; it looked new and roomier than Aunt Laura's flat. I had never seen such a modern house. Upon entering the front door that was up a flight of stairs, a short hall led to a spacious kitchen. A tile counter separated it from a built-in dining-nook with a Formica table and leather-like upholstery seats. Through the kitchen and a swinging door was a dining room with a studio couch that would be my bed. The living room could be entered from the front hall or the dining room. It had nice, modern furniture and rugs on the floors. A hall off the entry led to two bedrooms, one for the Reingolds and one for the children. In between, there was a very modern bathroom with a built-in pink tub and maroon and pink tiles on the walls and floor. Downstairs behind the garage Mr. Reingold was building a den; it led to the backyard that had grass and a few plants.

Henry Doelger had built these houses and would build thousands more in the years to come on the remaining sand dunes. When I came to live in the Sunset, Noriega Street was stopped at 30th Ave by rolling sand dunes that went to the beach at 48th Ave; our house was on the last block before the sand. All the streets sloped towards the beach, and from my corner, the ocean itself was visible. The streets in the Sunset were arranged alphabetically starting near the edge of Golden Gate Park with Irving going south. Some of the parallel streets to Noriega, such as Irving,

Judah and Taraval, had already extended their beachhead, while some other streets did not go as far as 30th. On Noriega, between 24th and 25th Avenues, there was a small shopping district with a grocery, a dry cleaner and a couple of other shops. I was often sent there to run some errands.

The Reingolds had only recently purchased the house for $4,000 with $1000 won in a raffle as down payment. Mr. Reingold was a laundry-truck driver. He and his wife had come from New York to find their fortunes in California before the post-war boom that would populate the Sunset district. These Doelger homes represented American ingenuity and creativity at its zenith, according to some magazines I read later. Although the building had begun in the 1930s, it was interrupted by the war, and resumed with fervor after the war as housing needs became great. By building good houses for the masses, the dream of home ownership was made available to the average wage earner, like Mr. Reingold. Perhaps the added income from a foster child would help them meet their bills—but I don't know for sure if they were paid something for me, the usual arrangement.

✦ ✦ ✦

For almost three months I hadn't had any mail from my father. He had left England on July 10 for Australia, arriving September 6. Although he doesn't mention the exact place, it was near Hay, a 19-hour journey from Sydney in a remote area. He wrote a letter to Aunt Laura on Sept. 9 telling her of his arrival and wondering if my mother was already in San Francisco. He couldn't write more that day because the internees were only permitted to write 150 words, and in English, although one more letter in German, below, came through.

Late Sept. 1940   Translated from German. Finally a letter from my father, now from an Internment Camp in Australia, received end of November.

My lovely, little darling,

Finally I have received mail from you, it is very old but the joy is endless. Today I have received your postcards from July 29 and August 20 which have been forwarded to this place. You see it takes a long time until I receive your mail, but nevertheless I am very happy. I thank you my love for your good wishes to my birthday, I am just wishing that we can shortly celebrate our birthdays together with our Mutti. On your birthday I have been on the high seas, I have been always with you in my mind (that is also the case right now), my wishes flew to you over the big ocean, the good spirits whom I have called shall protect you and keep you, my little darling, healthy and happy. I am happy to hear that you have it good and feel fine. It is good like this, be cheerful and happy, it will turn out well. You know that I have received a new affidavit from Anni, it says in it that a migration from here will be possible. If this is the case then you have a good chance to see your "bad" Papi soon. I am sure that this would make you happy.

How is Mutti? Until now I haven't heard from her. Hopefully she is healthy. I am all right, only that I long for you two so much. Please write me detailed and often. My best regards to the family Rabinowitz.

I kiss you many, many times, Your loving father

November 26, 1940

Dearest Daddy!

You can't imagine, how happy I was receiving two letters from you. One was from Sept. 26th, and the other was from Oct. 2nd. I am sure, that you couldn't imagine how astonished I was when I heard that you were in Australia. The last time I heard from Mama was two weeks ago. She didn't write much, but she said she was healthy. But three weeks [ago], she wrote that Gusti died and that she'd have to move. That all I heard from her. ... As I told you two weeks ago I moved to another familie, called Reingold and I like it here very much. I went to another school. ...In schoolwork I am prettie good. In fact, the teacher does not believe that I wasn't born here. I read a lot of books, and go a lot to shows. How are you? I hope you are fine 100,000,000 kisses, your loving daughter, Phyllis

Mr. Reingold, "Uncle Leo," also wrote to my father:

> *I am writing to you personally to put your mind at ease about Phyllis. She has the best of care. We like her very much and we find that she is a well-mannered and well behaved child. I must compliment you on the way you have brought her up.*
>
> *The teacher in school thinks very highly of her and has put her at the head of her class when all the children march from the schoolyard into the classroom she is the leader in charge of them. She has lost her foreign accent completely and her teachers cannot believe that she is in this country only 7 or 8 months. She speaks English like a native born. She has joined the library and every Saturday she goes down and takes out books. ...We live in a very nice and refined neighborhood where Phyllis has the opportunity to become acquainted with very nice children.*

✦ ✦ ✦

My new school, Lawton, was on the corner of Lawton and 33rd Avenue. I was placed in high 5th grade, still one-half grade below my rightful assignment according to age. By now, seven months in the United States, English had become my language, getting to be quite good; I started writing all my letters in English because German letters would not pass the Australian censors.

December 3, 1940

> *Dearest Daddy,*
>
> *...Last Saturday I went ice-skating. It was lots of fun. First, I fell but then I started to go faster and faster and I even could go round twice the arena without falling or holding on to the bars except sometimes I gave myself a little push. And the nicest thing I can tell you is that Aunt Betty and Uncle Leon promised me that they would get me a pair of roller-skates. Isn't that wonderful. We had a test in parts of a sentence. I got 3 wrong out of 28. It was very good.*
>
> *100,000,000,000,000 kisses and...love....Phyllis*

I made friends at school rather quickly and soon I was walking to school with Betty, a girl who lived around the corner. She was quick to accept me as her friend, and with that came membership in a still larger, quite popular group at school. If they took me in because I was an oddity and spoke a little funny, I never felt it—I felt accepted. We often played after school as well. I liked school, the teacher, the class work, recess and especially the friends. I don't recall friends when I think of Aunt Laura's house, but the memory of friends at Lawton is quite vivid. We often played in the sand dunes, probably my favorite pastime. Some dunes were six feet high or even more and when it rained, big puddles of water formed at their base, enough to wade in them or to make mud-pies or sand castles. Wild geraniums with their pungent smell popped out in the dunes after rain, and when I see geraniums today, I am always reminded of the ones in the dunes. We also played hide-and-seek among them. These were all new experiences for me since I had never even seen the ocean or a beach before my journey to San Francisco.

The Saturday afternoon movie continued to be an important part of my life especially since a group of friends from school went there together. The neighborhood movie wasn't far away and for a thin dime, part of my 25-cent weekly allowance, we spent four hours there. For an additional nickel, we could have a sweet; "Milk Duds" was my favorite item. The fullness of the offering—two movies, a serial, newsreel and some cartoons, and occasionally even live entertainment—amazed me since in Vienna, there was just a single movie, and children our age were often not permitted to go, even with adult chaperones.

I loved the movies and in letters to my father told him the titles and how much I liked them. The serials were most exciting as we followed the adventures of Superman, Batman and Robin, and my favorite, Captain Marvel. Bette Davis, Rita Hayworth, Kathryn Hepburn and Spencer Tracy, Joan Crawford and Humphrey Bogart were the superstars of the day, and even though I'm sure that I didn't really understand the intricacies of many of the romantic dramas, I still loved them, and still enjoy them at late night reruns. Aunt Betty, which is what I called Mrs. Reingold, used to go to the same movies on the following Monday night—Ladies Night—in order to receive a free piece of china dinnerware, and in the course of a year, she accumulated a new set of dishes.

Another one of my activities was going to the library at 18th and Judah, a classical two-story building, still standing today. It seemed far away, but perhaps only one mile. I recall walking on 19th Avenue, observing the busy car traffic, walking past the then very modern Shriner's Crippled Children's Hospital and wondering what went on in there. The low brick buildings did not resemble the big hospital in Vienna where I had my tonsils removed; that had been a big, massive building with much people traffic, but I never saw a soul at the Shriner's hospital. Sometimes, a friend would join me in my walks, but mostly I went alone, probably every other week when books became due. I considered the Judah branch a treasure house, and I am grateful today for having had the opportunity to use it so much. My reading fare included books on horses and dogs such as Black Beauty and Lassie Come Home.

December 10, 1940   I've anglicized Mutti to Mami—that is what the Reingold children called their mother.

Dearest Daddy,

Guess what? I received a letter from dear Mami. She writes that she thinks that she can come here soon. Anni sent her a Affidavit. I am pretty good in school. Friday I got my report card. I got:

Oral and Silent Reading	*B= above average*
Spelling and arithmetic	*A*
Oral expression and Science	*A*
Written expression and Handwriting, Social studies,	*B*
Industrial Art and Physical Activities, C, Behavior,	*A*

Saturday, I went to see the Great Dictator. [Charlie Chaplin's famous movie] It was very good. Friday I went downtown and bought a few Chanuka presents. Last week I promised you I would tell you about the children. First the baby, Rochelle. Well, you can't imagine how cute she is. Her hair is golden just as the sun and her eyes are as light blue as the sky. Few days ago she learned to walk...

...Now the little boy, Melvin. ...He is very darling. He is four years old. He likes to play a lot with cars such as towcars and airplanes. His hair is brown and eyes are

sky blue. There both asleep now. Onkle Lee is reading the paper and so is Aunt Betty. It is a quarter after seven and I didn't write Mami yet. So after telling you so many things, I must say good-bye …lots of love, Phyllis

Dec. 17, 1940

Dearest Daddy!

Guess what? I received five letters from you and one from Momi! Momi even send me a picture of her and I'm very glad. She thinks that she can come soon. I would be just too glad. What about you? Do you think you can come? I hope so. Everything is fine here, except there is the flue going around. I had a little cold too, but is all over now, and I hope you [aren't] *worried and asking yourself foolish questions such as, is she alwright now, did the doctor come and so forth. I am alwright now and don't you worried. …*

Tomorrow I'm going to school again. Prettie soon is Chanuka and just Monday, Tuesday and Wednesday and then two weeks of vacation. Mrs. Rabinowitz send you regards and ask you not be mad at her but she has a very bad cold and no time to write. As you know already that I am not with Mrs. Rabinowitz. I am telephoning her every once in a while or at least every week [even though I wasn't supposed to]. *My progress in school is fine, I do my work good and my arithmetic and spelling is very good, also my favored subjects. Every week I go to the library and take out some books. I read lots and enjoy it.*

Where I live now it is very nice also a very nice neighborhood. The beach is about 18 blocks away and you can see from our window the rolling waves of the ocean. It is very handy because of that you can tell how the weather is. Most of the times it is fogy and cold. Today is the first day since a long time to rain. I hope it will rain now much and when [with] *it all the flu and colds will go away.*

The weather was interesting to me. Since I had come to San Francisco in April it may not have rained again until fall—all this was contrary to the muggy, rainy summers, the brisk and rainy fall, and freezing winters of Vienna. Furthermore, the Mission district of San Francisco has almost no fog, but the Sunset has much. This long letter continues:

I didn't have any mail from Fam Bick. Almost every minute I think of you and Momi, but we can't help it. Heartely I hope you and Mom will come soon to me. How are you? ... Next time maybe I'll send you pictures of the whole familie and me. I'm here very happy.

Momi lives now one floor lower on floor No.6 instead of 12. As you know already Gusti past away! And that is how Momi got to move. In one of the letters you write that you have no mail from me. But lett me tell you that I did and still do write you every week. You didn't have mail from me because all the mail came back. You were already on the ship.

100,000,000,000,000,000,000 heaps of kisses your loving Phyllis

Some elements of German still slip into my letters. It is also interesting to me now that I was allowed to go downtown by streetcar alone, to do some shopping, and that I had money to do it with. Shopping for Chanuka presents implies that the holiday was celebrated, but aside from that, religion did not enter into my everyday life, nor did we go to Temple on Saturday.

Dec. 23, 1940

Dearest Daddy,

...Well, we got our presents earlier and I received a pair of roller skates, so this afternoon I went roller-skating. Sure enough, I flopped twice, but it was the first time on roller skates. The weather is not so good as I thought. One minute there is rain and the next sunshine. Friday we had a Christmas party and everybody had to buy a present for somebody else, and... my girlfriend bought me 3 hankies and I like them very much. We had cakes, cookies, candy and soda. My progress in school is prettie good.

Tonight Melli, Uncle and I are going to a party and everybody gets a boxful of toys and fruit. How are you? I'm alwright now and please don't worry about me. I have everything my heart desires exept you and Momi. Have patience and Momi and you will come to me soon, and we'll all be happy again. You know it yourself, dear Daddy, that it can't last forever. Let's hope and God will help us. Amen!

1,000,000,000,000, heaps of kisses. Phyllis

The roller-skates were the kind that fit onto the shoes; a skate key tightened wing nuts and screws near the toes and laces went around the ankle. They were adjustable to allow for growth. For hours I would attempt to gain control of my body, especially stopping. Our house was on a slight hill, and as I reached the corner, I often ran myself into the building since I couldn't stop.

Jan. 6, 1941 Today I am amazed at the quality of the letters I wrote—despite errors they are pretty good for a 11- year old who just learned the language. I tell about my visits to the San Francisco Zoo which was not far to our house.

Dearest Daddy!

…Today is …the first day of school since two weeks of vacation. I liked the vacation very much. I spent most of my time scating on my new rollerscates I received for Chanuka. I was in the show three times and in the zoo two times. We have here a new zoo and it beautiful. The tigers and the lions have a very lovely place, it has trees and a pool and rocks where they climb and stretch their bones. And at night they go in, in little doors come into a big house in a cage. The bears have it like that too. There is no way of them breaking out, because there are rocks on one side where they can go down, but the other side [has] no rocks, but it's a steep wall and too high too jump. The elephants as you know love peanuts and one fell down just to get a peanut. Their place is big and clean, it has a big kinda hole and a wire fence on the other. It looks like this …[the letter was literally cut out by censors where I had drawn a picture]*…a place that looks like their former home. The ducks, seagulls and black swans can fly any where they want to and they have a big lake. I don't think any of those birds have ever failed to come back. Even the peacocks go around free. The parrots are very cute. We said "Hello Polly" and they answered "Hello" and "How are you" and "Hiya". The monkeys have a big island and a lot of trees. Everything looks so gorgious and the breeze is so nice and I wish from the bottom of my heart that you and Momi could see and feel it. Amen!!!!!*

I read a lot and about two days ago I finished a book called 'The Poor Little Rich Girl". It was very good. I also went to the show yesterday. …and don't you worry, God will help us and we will soon be together. Justice will win at the end! I'm fine and healthy and perfectly happy, but wish to see you soon and with God's help I will. And now "Goodbye" or rather "Goodnight" see you tomorrow! How would that be, huh?

100,000,000,000,000,000,000,000 big, big mountains of kisses, love and a Happy New Year! Phyllis

◆ ◆ ◆

I got two letters from my mother; in the one from January 9 she thought that I was still with Aunt Laura. The next day she wrote again, including a message for my aunt.

January 10, 1941 (Translated from German, received probably in February, already four months since I'd moved.)

I just received your letter in which you told me that you have moved to another family, my lovely child. I have to say that I am momentarily very upset but after you wrote me that you didn't get along with Aunt Laura's boy it is maybe better for both sides if the situation finds such a solution. First I want to know exactly who these people are and how you got to know them. I hope that you are still under the care of Aunt Laura and that you don't forget what she has done for us. Even if you are not still with your aunt, always remember that she is our best friend in our misery. She should continue to be at your side with advice and she should be your substitute mother. Don't forget that you are alone over there and that no one is closer to you than your lovely aunt.

Why don't you give me your new address and describe the good person who was so kind to take you under her care. How old is she? If possible send me a picture from the family. Are these people Americans or foreigners? My lovely Pupperl, maybe the good woman knows somebody who wants to send an affidavit. It is for Mr. Kogan … Look out my love, maybe you can do something. …have you received mail from Anny and Arnold or Mr. Fischer? Don't write him because he behaved himself badly.

Dear Aunt, please write me exactly about everything and be the substitute mother for my child until I come. I kiss and embrace you, Laura

I did not have a "motherly" relationship with Aunt Laura. She was not a sub-stitute mother for me, although we kept in touch occasionally. I usually reported our contacts in my letters. I am touched now by mother's efforts to help other people get a visa, when she didn't have one herself. However, in the next few months, I received many request to do similar things, but I didn't know what to do. I don't remember if I told the Reingolds. Since they didn't know German, even if they read my mail, they wouldn't have known unless I translated. Perhaps I didn't understand the German anymore. I was losing my German little by little, and later my mother complained about it because she couldn't read my English. It bothers me greatly that I have forgotten what if anything I did to help her, and what I thought about her despair. In my letters to my father, when I said she was "healthy and fine," did I understand her situation? Those words seem so superficial. Was that to save my father from worry? Or was I just repressing my pain?

Jan. 15, 1941

Dearest Daddy

Last Thursday I received two letters from Mami and she writes that she is worried about you but I wrote her that you are healthy and fine. I didn't get any mail from you since four weeks. I'm pretty good in school and very good in arithmetic and spelling. Next Friday January 25th I am (and everybody else) are going to get report cards and I'm going to enter the 6A on Jan. 27. We have news every morning and I think Mr. Hi [Hitler] and Mr. Mo. [Mussolini] are very sick. I have no mail from Fam. Bick and no mail from Rosel and Engel. Everybody wants me to write them once or twice a week. But they don't write me.

Last Saturday I went to the show and saw "Third finger left hand." It was very good and then the other picture was a pioneer picture. I went with to other girls. I have about ten girlfriends. Today was the first time I was skating for a long while. I mean the first time I went to the store on skates. Roller skating is real fun. ...your loving daughter, Phyllis

January 22, 1941

> *My lovely little darling!*
>
> *I have received your two lovely letters but I couldn't answer immediately, because I have already used the granted allowance from the camp leader of two letters per week. But I have written to Mr. Reingold, I suppose that the letter has already arrived there. I am very happy about your improvement in school and I am sure that you will go on to work hard to be the best in your class. Why haven't you told me mother's new address? I am so worried about our lovely Mutterl and I would be very happy to know her out of Germany. It seems like we can emigrate from here, one day my darling you will be surprised. It has been a long time (it seems like eternity for me) since I have left Vienna,...Love and many, many kisses from your Papa.*
>
> *Best regards to the family Reingold.*

January 30th he wrote:

> *I got a letter from Mummy, informing me that she received an affidavid from Annie...that letter was written August last, so it might be that the American Visa has been granted to her...There is no other thing I would desire more than to know our dearest Mama outside of Germany. ...So far the heat is unbearable, there is nothing to be done but to get used to it. Your Papa*

The problem with mail always meant miscommunication. From that last August, things have gotten much worse, as Mother's letter of Feb. 7 will show.

Jan. 28, 1941

> *Dearest Daddy!*
>
> *This Friday I received a letter from you. You can't guess how happy I was. Please when you write a letter to me please write the date. In your last letter you wrote that you received two postcards from me. On the same Friday I received my report card. It was very good and I improved a lot. This is it.*

Silent reading	*B*	*Oral*	*B*	*Spelling*	*B*
Oral Expression	*A*	*Arithmetic*	*A*	*Science*	*A*
Social Studies	*B*	*Handwriting*	*B*	*Art*	*B*
Music	*A*	*Physical Activities*	*A*	*Tries Hard*	*A*
Obeys cheerfuly	*A*	*Is careful of property*	*A*	*is courteous and polite*	*A*
		finishes whatever started A,			

and two more A which I can't remember. I improved in Art, Music and Physical Activities. How are you? Last Saturday I went to the show with three girlfriends. It was very good. Now I'm a 6A grader. I am very happy here. The weather here is very bad. Today it was very nice. We are studying about China, Japan, Russia, Alaska, Canada, Calif., Washington, Oregon, Central America, Mexico, Peru, Chilly, French Indo-China and all the states in the Pacific and those states that border the Pacific. We will also study about Australia and then it will be easier for me to know what kind of a country you live in. I'm fine. thank God. Hows everything? I hope fine. Kisses, Phyllis.

P.S. I'll send you a picture of me, it's taken in camp Tahome. [Last year's summer camp.]

February 7, 1941 Translated from German

My lovely Maederl!

I have received your lovely letter. [Presumably from December or January] *I am happy that you are all right, I thank God every day thousands of times that you my dearest don't have to share my grief and sorrow. I have cried a lot while reading your letter and prayed to God that I shall see you one more time....*

You write that Papa is worried about me, I believe this, after all he is thank God all right and I have to suffer so much; oh, if Papa would have registered us earlier I could have been already with you and now I see no opportunity and I am so desperate because of that. When will I see you my sweetheart, when can I embrace you? I am so grateful with all my heart to the family Reingold that they are so nice to you, the only light in my dark life. Tell them that I am very, very grateful and that I wish them all the best because they take care of you. I am hoping my child that you stay with them until I come, that means I am hoping that you behave yourself to their satisfaction.

You must think of that you are alone and you have to be thankful for everything that somebody cares for you. You have to be very nice to Aunt Rabinowitz because she is the only one who helped us in our misery. Mr. Kogan thanks you for your inquiry, he is all right and healthy, his son is as desperate as I am, I have already asked you several times to take care of his affidavit, but you don't answer...So my love, I kiss and hug you, give my best regard to the Fam. Reingold. Your loving mother

Her words about my father don't surprise me, for I remember their arguments about standing in line and getting quota numbers, but I don't know how it affected me as I read the letter. My father was my hero; I might not have liked his being chastised. As I read those sentences now, I cannot help being angry and sad that he didn't register us sooner. He probably harbored the guilt of his laziness and its effects on our family all his life although he never mentioned it, which may explain why we never talked of our life in Vienna.

February 18, 1941

Dearest Daddy,

...My envioronment is very good. When you last saw me I was nine, but now I'm eleven going on twelve. That time I was a shrimp and very fat but now I'm growing taller every minute and second. When I'll reach twelve I'll be a tall and slender girl. My progress in school is very good. We are studying the Pacific Area and it's very interesting. My arithmetic is also very good and I'm far ahead of the others. I have every thing my heart wants accept you and Mom. Mom and I are healthy and so are you, I hope and pray. That's all for today. Kisses from your Phyllis

February 19, 1941 Translated from German

My lovely Maederl!

I have received your lovely letters and I was very happy that you are thank God content and happy. That is my only and biggest comfort that you are away from here and that you can study undisturbed and are able to enjoy your childhood. How happy would your girlfriends like Lucy Treister be if they would have it as good as you. God bless you on all your ways and help us to see each other again soon. Don't worry too much when you don't get mail from me so often, I am now occupied, I work for a baby factory so besides the housework I have a lot of work and worries, worries without end. If I only could be with you already that would be the best day of my life. Pray to God, he always answered your prayers. He will do it now too, hopefully.

I am happy that you have received my picture, I enclose another one which I think you will like even more. Have you heard from your father? Please enclose a letter from him, don't forget about it. I am awaiting feverishly the invitation for the check-up [from the consulate for emigration]. *Four days ago it has been one year that you have been there;* [in U.S.] *do you remember how we were freezing, today it is much warmer, but instead we have a lot of worries so that our heart and brain freeze to death. God bless us! How is Aunt Laura? Is the uncle already healthy again? Don't estrange yourself from them! I am happy that you like the lovely kids so much. I would love if you would send me a picture of you and the family. Please write me in which town your father lives.*

P.S. Today I have received a letter from Uncle Max who is in Tangier. He asks about you, if possible write to his address. ... Dear child, please go to the committee, they should try hard to order the consulate by telegram to give me the visa, otherwise I don't know how I could come to you and it is so urgent. Don't wait, instead run there immediately with the letter. Ask also your aunt and Anny if they will send me the ship ticket because without it you can't get a visa. Don't rest and see to it that your desperate mother comes to you. I kiss you tenderly, Your mother

Her desperation is so great, and her request of me to help her so frantic, but I don't remember if I did anything. This letter makes me feel terrible—did I even cry? I want to cry now when I read her despairing words. What could I have done? The committee she speaks of perhaps meant an agency which concerned itself with helping in immigration, but I knew of no committee. What was a baby factory? I know that code words were used to pass the censor's cut, but I haven't found how decode that—perhaps it really was a factory where baby clothes were made.

◆ ◆ ◆

In the beginning of 6ᵗʰ grade, the teacher announced a contest. We were to make a scrapbook of another country in the Pacific Area, and because my father was in Australia, I chose it for study. I took to this project with great enthusiasm making me feel closer to him. I wrote to the Australian consulate and to travel agencies for information; I don't know how I knew to do that, perhaps our teacher told us. I worked very hard on this project, and turned in a very fine scrapbook, but not fine enough to win the prize. The teacher told me: "Phyllis, the content of your scrapbook was the best, but it was not neatly done, so the prize went to another girl whose book was also good, but especially neat."

I have never forgotten that lesson, but it didn't change me. Neatness was not a skill that I had been taught—or at least had drilled into me, although my parents were neat, and my mother scolded me in her letters for my untidy letters. I am still not neat, despite occasional great effort on my part. Organization of the task is what interests me; doing the detail is a bore. Whenever I have to perform some task that requires attention to detail, I recall my experience with the Australia scrapbook, bitterly. Despite a great deal of time thinking about neatness and the virtue of attention to detail, both of which I feel deficient in, despite resolves to overcome my sloppiness, I have never mastered the characteristic, only mitigated it.

✦ ✦ ✦

March 4, 1941   I advise my father to learn a trade.

Dearest Daddy

…I am here very very happy. I have everything my heart wants accept you and Mom and I wish from the bottom of my heart that I had you. I hope it won't be long till we'll be reunited again and live our former happy life. If you have a choice of learning any hand jobs pick mechanist. Because here a man without a hand job can't go very far. Besides you have the talent for mechanist any how and it's a good job. So try and learn it and good luck!

I'm very good in school and I'm having a chance to be skipped. I'll try my best. Yesterday I went to the show as usual. I read a lot! …Heaps of kisses your you loving daughter Phyllis

March 12, 1941

My little Darling

I have just received five letters from you all dated Nov and December last. Although I have been very glad in getting news from you, I cannot help blaming you for your carelessness. All these letters are addressed to No. 9 Camp, whereas I am staying in No. 7 Camp...causing much delay.... I asked you to let me always have the news you are getting from our dear Mama, don't forget it!...Your Papa

There it is again—my bad habit of not paying attention to detail!

March 27, 1941

My little Darling

...I received the communication from the Home Office (British Ministry) that I have just been released from Internment on condition of my emigrating to the USA. That means that as soon as I have got the American Visa I will be permitted to leave this Camp and Country....I think ...that this question will be settled within the next two months....Love and kisses, Papa

And on April 17

...before long I will be able to leave this country. ...This all depends on the American consulate and we hope all hope this questions will soon be settled...and that the separation which has already lasted for 20 month, will soon be ended. ...Your Papa

April 5, 1941 From my mother, translated from German.Questions about my education, a ship ticket for her, and scolding about my German.

My dearest Maedele!

I have received your sweet, golden letter from the 13th of February. My joy was indescribable because I was impatiently waiting to hear from you. I am also happy that you write so lovely about Lizzy. [My old friend from Vienna—I must have heard from her.] *With that you have shown me that you have a heart and feeling, I suppose that not all your girlfriends think as nice as you, my everything. You have told me in your last letter that you are in 6th grade now. Don't you go to the Gymnasium* [German=secondary school] *You have to write me about that in detail. Have you done anything concerning the ship ticket? Say a prayer that we will be together soon. It is my greatest desire to be your mother again, to take care of you and to give you whatever your little, cute heart desires.*

What does your father write about? Have we ever thought that we would be torn apart to such distances? You have already forgotten German totally, tomorrow it will be one year since you have come to San Francisco and have already forgotten your native language, like a birdbrain. If you want that I understand you, try harder to write carefully because I don't understand English.

...Kiss you tenderly thousands of times, your devoted Mother

April 15, 1941

Dearest Daddy,

This morning I received a letter from Momy. I was very happy with it. There is some hope of Momy coming here, thats if we can get her a shipcard. We are going to write Anny and Arnold and ask them if they can get a shipcard because we can't get one here. The ship card must be send from where the affidavit was send from. We'll be able to get one.

Last week was Easter vacation and we didn't have any school at all. One day it rained but the rest of the week was very nice out. I was rollerskating all the time. One time I floped when my skate flew off and boy, did I get a black and blue mark on my knee. It's as big as a small doorknob. Few days ago we got a little chicken it's white and yellow and it's so cute. Where ever we go it follows us. Its name is Cheepy....

April 21, 1941 An upbeat letter and I request details about his life.

Dearest Daddy!

This morning I received a letter from you as I expected. It's dated March 12, 1941. ...I get 25 cents a week allowance and I can do anything with it. This week I went to the show and bought a ball. When I came home from the show, my girlfriend and I picked some flowers. We had so many we hardly could carry it. The weather here is marvelous. The sun shines and it is hot here. How is it over in Australia? I hope you can get adjusted to the heat over there! Do you get out of camp? What do you do all day long. Do you ever get out and picnic? Can you send me a picture of you and maybe of some of the beautiful scenes? I would be delighted with it. And now kisses and hugs from your Phyllis

I couldn't imagine under what circumstance my father lived when I asked him about a picnic. At the time, he was living at the edge of a desert behind barbwire fences and guards with guns patrolling the perimeter, only allowed to write letters twice a week, no contact with the outside world. The men had chores to do, the rest of the time he spent studying English.

May 10, 1941

My little Darling,

...I have been really shocked reading that your weight reached now 96 lbs. I think—and you will surely agree with me—that this amount...is a little to much for a child of 11 years. You have to pull yourself together and try to avoid any further increase in weight. A stout girl is neither a beautiful sight, nor is this state a healthy one. I do not want to preach you to stop eating, but I would like you to restrict the consumption of sweets (ice creams, etc.) to a minimum. I must still add that your mama, at the age of 25 yrs had not more than 96lbs (German lbs) i.e. only some lbs more than you have already now. ...Love and kisses, Papa

I think there must have been some differences in the calculations of pounds, but by November I had lost 6 lbs and had grown some. Nevertheless, excess weight was always a problem. In his next letter he is moved to a new internment camp, Tatura, south of Hay, but in a different climate zone. The area around Tatura is a fruit-growing area, and though still hot, not like the desert the Hay camp had been. A big irrigation project was going on in the area, and from some places in the camp, but still behind barbed wire, it was possible to see the reservoir and some trees, better than the endless desert at Hay.

May 27, 1941

> *Dearest Daddy!*
>
> *This morning I received two letters from you. I can't say how happy I was. One was from April 17, and one was from March 27. You wrote that in a month or two you might come here. And two months where past and I hope you are on your way already. I hope and wish and pray that in one month we will be together again. I think of you all the time and dream about you at night. May God help you and help you come to me healthy and sound as ever…. I think I will skip a grade. …Kisses from your loving daughter Phyllis*

I was skipped to the 7th grade to join my age mates for the fall.

May 31, 1941 From Tatura, a new internment camp in Victoria

> *My little Darling,*
>
> *Yesterday I received four letters from you dated Febr., March & April. One contained the picture of Mamy. I was very delighted …during my voyage I lost all my belongings and amongst them all the photos of Mama and you….I am staying in another camp, our situation has not changed, the only improvement has been that we are living in a far better climate. We do not know anything about our emigration….As to your suggestion to learn any "hand-job" I have to inform you that although the idea is good and perfectly right, unfortunately I have no chance of doing anything…as we are not free and are compelled to live in an enclosure and have no contact with the outer world except of writing letters….Your Daddy*

June 20, 1941 Nordhausen, Germany, translated from German. Up to now, Mother had been in Vienna, but now she was in Germany, where they manufactured weapons and where there was a concentration camp; perhaps it already was such a camp when she was there. She must have been forced to go there to do some labor, but of course, she would not be able to say so.

My dearest Maederl, my dream!

I have received a letter from you that gave me a lot of joy. Your mail and the message that you are thank God all right are my only ray of light in my dark life. The only distraction I have is my work which is very hard but still calming for the shattered nerves.

I have been here for two weeks now and I have already written you twice, hopefully you have also already received my letters. What writes the dear Papa? Hopefully he is also alright, I also wrote him several times, but I hope that he will be with you before he receives my mail. May God will it that we see each other again, I am praying every hour, meanwhile there is no chance.

What are you doing my cute doll? I expect that you fulfill your duties to the best of your knowledge and belief. I am overjoyed that you are with good people—be also good to them and appreciate every good deed because there are only very few good people, believe me, I have already gotten to know them. Do you visit Aunt Rabinowitz sometimes, give my best regards to her.

Do not forget your mother and write every week, even when I am not writing you, I only have time on Sundays and often even not then. Be good and well-behaved, study well and be decent, that goes without saying.

I kiss you tenderly, Your Mutti

Recent research about my mother's last days indicates that the forced laborers, Jews, were working in asparagus fields during the summer months, a backbreaking job.

June 24, 1941

Dearest Daddy!

This week I received two letters from you where you write that you still haven't heard from the Consol, which I am very sorry to hear. I haven't gotten any mail from Momy for three weeks already and I am a little worried. Momy wrote to me a letter and she writes that she had to go in the reich [Germany] for two month. That letter was written May 15th and she left, May 16th. Since then she hasn't written to me, or maybe she can't. How are you? Momy told me to write to the same adrese as before. I am going to write to Mr. Kogan tonight [the man Momy lived with] *and find out if he knows anything...I am very happy here and I became quite attached to the Reingold famili. The weather here is lovely. How is it over there? Now kisses and hugs from your always loving daughter Phyllis*

July 5, 1941

Dearest Daddy!

I am very sorry I didn't write to you last week but you see I was very busy. We came home from our vacation Sunday and we really had a grand time. My back is all brown and I feel so good. The weather there was wonderful. I went swimming every day and one day I went on a hike. Mrs. Reingold took a picture of me and the kids in the water and as soon as they are developed I will send you one. This time I have a surprise for you. I got two letters from Momy and one from your brother. How are you? I hope you are fine and healthy. I am thank God. Two years ago on the fourth of this Month you left us but we hope that we may be together very very soon. Amen. How are your ways of coming here?

Now kisses and hugs from your loving daughter Phyllis

P.S. I will lay. [enclose] *three letters by.* [He received these Sept.1]

July 8, 1941

Dearest Daddy,

I didn't receive any mail from you or Momy this week...but I got a letter from [her] *last Monday...You know she has to go to the Reich to work. Mom has to stay there for 2 months. She does farmers work. I think, because the man she lives with wrote me a card saying that she does "landwirtshaft" there. July 16 she will return.*

...Mrs. Reingold is very nice to me. She is going to take me to a vacation for three or four weeks. I go to Hebrew school three times a week. The weather here is lovely and the more the sun shines, the more I grow (it seems). And now kisses and hugs, ...Phyllis

◆ ◆ ◆

The vacation was to go camping in Yosemite National Park. That most memorable experience was my introduction to a place that over the years became my personal sanctuary. We began a very long journey to the mountains in the Reingold's black car [a Ford?] packed with a tent, cooking and sleeping equipment and five people. A car was not to be taken for granted in 1941; neither Aunt Laura nor my family in Austria had a car. However, it was not always pleasant to be sitting in the back seat since I suffered from motion sickness and our trip to Yosemite became a nightmare because of it. Although I tried to warn Uncle Leon when I was getting sick, sometimes the road was so narrow that he could not stop; and I couldn't wait, so I made a terrible mess in the car. I knew Aunt Betty was upset, so I tried to hold it back, but I usually couldn't. My motion sickness wasn't the only thing that troubled our journey, so did the car that overheated often on the steep mountainous roads. We had to make many stops to let the car cool off like many others that were having radiator problems. Over the years, on my frequent trips to Yosemite, especially near the Priest Grade, visions of old black cars with their hoods up, people patiently waiting nearby, fanning themselves to keep cool, remind me of that first time.

We pitched our tent in one of the broad meadows of Yosemite Valley and settled in. I don't remember much else of the camping, except that I liked it, and I can't remember how long we stayed. As I recall that campground, there were no marked out campsites as is the pattern today—there was just a lot of space, and people picked a spot. I immediately loved the scenery.

I somehow got a map of the trails of the valley and decided to go on a walk. I went by myself. My plan was to go on a loop trip, and I began by heading for Happy Isles and then Vernal Falls. By the time I got to the bridge at the bottom of Vernal, I was totally exhausted, and abandoned my loop trip. (In later years, I realized that the loop trip I had planned for myself would have been about 24 miles, and several thousand feet up.) Still, what I saw thrilled me, even as it did John Muir and millions of other visitors, and I became a habitual visitor to Yosemite the rest of my life. In fact, for several years now, I have been a volunteer for a month at the Visitor Center.

While I was having the time of my life, my poor mother was in a work camp in Germany doing farm labor and knowing that she would not be able to come to me. I am sure I did not understand her dilemma. I don't remember if I read the newspapers at that time, but news of the forced labor or concentrations camps wasn't available at that time.

Nordhausen July 29, 1941 Translated from German

> *My only loved, dearest Lizzchen!*
>
> *I haven't heard from you my sunshine for a long time now, hopefully you are in good health and you are fine. What does your dear father write about? Why don't you ever send me a letter from him? Give my best wishes to him. Unfortunately there is no possibility now to get out of here, I was always hoping to be already with you at this time, the human thinks but God directs.* [German saying] *Hopefully he will help us all...*
>
> *... I haven't heard anything from our relatives in Stryj,* [the Polish town where her mother and brothers lived] *I am very unhappy about that....*
>
> *Hopefully you will be able to continue writing to me. ... I am working here in a tobacco factory but send the letters to me to the old address in Vienna.*
>
> *Thousands of kisses from your mother! Write a lot!*
>
> *I've just remembered that your birthday is within the next days, ... I wish you to grow up happily, to see your parents soon and a lot of success in school, be happy on all your ways, God bless you!!! Amen*

July 25, 1941. My father also had bad news for me.

> *My little darling,*
>
> *I have just received your letter of May 27 and was very pleased to learn that you are well. I am so sorry to have to disappoint you, but at the present moment the Entry in the United States rendered more difficult, therefore we are compelled to post-pone our plans regarding emigration. There are still tremendous obstacles to over-come, but let us hope that things will turn for the better. Maybe that the fact of*

your living there will be of some use and effect to my cause, when reapplying for the U.S. Visa. The other day I received a letter from Uncle Max, it took nearly five months to reach me. There was enclosed a letter from our dear Mama, this being the first letter I have got from her since May last year. ...Love and kisses your Papa

Nordhausen August 9, 1941 Translated from German

My dearest, sweetest Maedele!

Today is your birthday, early this morning I thought of you my only one, it is already the 2nd year that I am not lucky enough to hug you my cutie for this reason. Now, my everything, since there is no other possibility I bless you this way. Be happy, satisfied, and joyful, good angels shall be with you on all your ways and good people shall be always with you. You shall bloom and thrive to the joy of your parents, yourself, and your environment. I give you this blessing and pray to God to hear me! Amen!!

A few days ago I have received a letter from you from June and I was enormously happy that you are thank God healthy and happy. That is my only comfort ...in these hard times. Be good, obedient, well-behaved and hard-working! You have good people around you, appreciate and acknowledge this! If you are a good person people will be good to you, too. Think of that; your parents also cannot always give and offer you everything, it is not within our power. Your father is interned and I have to work. Maybe your dear father will be able to come to you, or to conclude from your letter he is maybe already with you, for me on the other hand every possibility has been taken away momentarily, but I will not give up every hope.

My mother's birthday wishes for me are lovely and practical. She continues to give me advice on living in a world of strangers, at the same time encouraging me to be truthful, self-confident and brave. The letter continues:

But I have to tell you my love, as long as you are alone and have to rely on strangers who have to replace your parents temporarily, appreciate and respect them more than your own parents, because they just have the good will but not the duties to you. Be orderly and don't let them serve you on the contrary you should help where your help is needed, don't be lazy for any help, when it concerns others always tell the truth, even if you have done something bad that you shouldn't, have the courage to confess. If you can take responsibility to your own conscience you can also do it to God and people. Be a good classmate and especially perform your duty! Get a good foundation in school for your life. What you study now and get used to will be your guide for the rest of your life! Be brave and self-confident and now I ask you not just to read this letter and then throw it away but on the contrary to read it often and learn from it.

Write me everything from your father and give my love to him. This week I have received one letter from him which took 8 months. Write him that I am thank God healthy and that I work. Good-bye and I hug you heartily, Your loving mother ...

What lovely and useful advice! Whether I read this over many times as she suggested, I don't remember, but in fact, I have lived according to her advice. I also don't remember how I reacted to her news that she wouldn't be able to come. Now both parents were unable to come to me. Perhaps I acted out my pain by becoming fresh with my foster family.

August 21, 1941 In this letter to my father, my telling him that my mother cannot come is so stiff, so lacking in emotion about these grave disappointments. Perhaps the news was so shocking that I couldn't deal with it. I must have been very let down, as I should have been. Did I cry? Did my foster parents console me? Did I even tell them?

Dearest Daddy

Last Tuesday I received a letter from you and Momy. Your letter informed me that your emigration to the U.S. wouldn't be for some time which I was very sorry to hear....Momy wrote that she works in a Tobbacco factory. There is no way of her coming here either.

Last Tuesday too, I was a very naughty girl. I aggravated Mr. and Mrs. Reingold very much. I was so ashamed of myself I don't think I'll ever forgive myself. But I promised myself never to do such a thing again. ...

Now kisses, hugs and everything good from your loving daughter Phyllis

*P.S. I just remembered today's your birthday. I wish you all the luck one can have
and a soon reunion. Phyllis*

I have no recollection of what awful thing I did. Perhaps that was my reaction
to the letters that told me that neither of my parents would be able to come to the
States. The next few letters don't mention any disagreements. Perhaps I couldn't
write without the letter being read by the Reingolds.

Sept 17, 1941

Dearest Daddy

*...Momy writes that she is very lonesome for you and me. But let us all prey to God
and surely He will help us.*

*School has begun two weeks ago. I very happy on account of that because there is
lots of fun in school besides you learn a lot too. We have Science about physyology.
Then we Social Studies, arithmetic, Literature and grammar. We had a test in
grammar and I had had highest score. I enjoy it all and I'm eager to learn. ... I
think of you and Momy very often almost always. Now kisses hugs and wishes from
loving Phyllis.*

✦ ✦ ✦

I looked forward to school to resume in the fall. My relationships with friends
had become even more important, and I was well accepted. I was invited to join a
"club", a group of ten girls meeting once week after school to talk about movie stars
and to make scrapbooks of our favorites. When it came my turn to have the girls at
my house, I never told Aunt Betty that they were coming because I was afraid that
she would not allow it; and I was afraid to tell the group that I hadn't asked. She did
let them come in, and even found some cookies for us (the other mothers went to a
lot of trouble to feed us well). Ungrateful as I was at that time, I resented her for not
having nicer refreshments, even thoughI had not given her warning.

Nordhausen October 7, 1941 Translated from German   In this letter she reminisces about out last time together.

My only loved good child!

Yesterday and today I was lucky again to receive mail from you that made me endlessly happy. My happiness is indescribable that the lovely family Reingold is so good to you and nice and I hope that your good and orderly behavior as well as your good progress in school will contribute to that. My Herzele [little heart], if you would know how worried I am and how I yearn for you and how every letter from you moves me to tears, I have no other choice as to wait and to wait even when I sometimes believe that nothing goes on. Time goes by so fast and also the years, for it has been 1¹/₂ years since you, my love, have left me. Can you still remember the day of your departure, how cute you helped me in the kitchen? Then you baked a Strudel [German cake] that was so cute that I have kept it until it crumbled.

I was hoping that your good father is already with you, but this is unfortunately not the case, why don't you send me a letter from him I already asked you several times and required that you should tell him also everything about me. A letter from Papa takes 6 months and a letter to him takes as long, so through you he will hear something from me faster.

She describes her work routine and her living conditions in Nordhausen.

I am still working in the Cigar factory, which is very strenuous. At 6 o'clock in the morning the work begins until 5:30 in the evening with one hour recess. I would be already satisfied if I could be at home. I work with 120 women who also came from Vienna, we have dormitories and one dining room together. It is not nice and nothing pleases me.

Her nightmares and complaints with the contents of my letters.

Last night I dreamt of you that you couldn't recognize me anymore and I wept bitterly, but you good girl think about your Mutti very often and you write a lot, it would please me much more if you would instead of filling the paper with, i.e. the sun is shining every day or we have good weather write me important things like if you still have your piano lessons and if you are all right in school, if you have enough clothes to wear, what work Mr. Reingold has and so on, I hope you will do it next time.

Your German is already very, very bad for that I feel sorry because it is always good to know some languages. Give my best regards and kisses to Papa. Also give my best regards to the family Reingold and I would like to get a picture of Mrs. and Mr. Reingold as well of the cute kids you love so much. Are you a good sister to little ones? ....[regards to and from relatives]

 I know my Puppele that you cannot send a ticket for the ship but and I thought that you would find some rich people who could do it.

I kiss and embrace you, Mutti

October 10, 1941   I report on my mother's condition without any sentiment.

Dearest Daddy,

This week I received two dear letters from you. I was extremely happy with them. I am glad to hear from you that you are well, but I wasn't at all pleased when you wrote that emigration to the U.S.A. for now is impossible. I had a letter from Momy this week and she is well but she has to work in a Cigar Factory from 6 in the morning till 6 $^1/_2$ at night with only 1 hour lunch break. You write that you haven't received mail from me for six weeks but that is not my fault. I write to you every week, except one week when I was on my vacation....

I am happy here but I do wish that you and Momi were here. I am progressing rapidly in school and I enjoy school. I am considered as the best writer in the class. The teacher let me write the pupils names on the report cards wich we are getting soon. On my tests I make out very good.

Now 100,000,000,000,000...kisses, hugs and good wishes from your loving daughter. Phyllis

November 4, 1941

Dearest Daddy!

This week I have received one of your dear letters... Mr. and Mrs. Reingold are very nice to me. And I [have] *grown to love their children. Nov. 8, it's going to be one year since I live with Fam. Reingold. I am very good in school and I really try hard to do my best. How is the weather over there? It must be beautiful since it is spring. Here the rainy season is just beginning. … and now kisses, hugs and good wishes from your everloving daughter Phyllis*

Dec. 2, 1941

Dearest Daddy!

I haven't received any mail from you or Momy for over two weeks. … I can hardly wait till tomorrow, when we get our report cards. I am sure I have improved! I love school now, just as much as I used to in Vienna, maybe even more, and when holidays come I don't like them so much. I have lots of girlfriends, ten in all, and there is one especially I like. To me she is just like Lizzy Menkes but not yet as good a friend. Her name is Beverly and many of her ways are like mine, so we get together swell. I hope I will receive mail soon from you. Now a 100,000,000,000,000,000,000,000,000 kisses, hugs, and good wishes from your loving daughter Phyllis, Lizzy. Regards from Mr. and Mrs. Reingold

A few days after that, December 7, Pearl Harbor was bombed and war was declared. I don't think I was happy about that, but possibly, I might have thought that the war would help my parents. I assumed that I wouldn't be able to write anymore, not to Germany nor Australia, so I didn't.

My next letter is Feb. 25 when I have already moved from the Reingolds. I cannot remember an event that triggered our disagreements, or what I did that I had to move. What I remember most was that I didn't like having to the take the children to the park or otherwise take care of them, although just in November I had written how much I "had grown to love their children." Perhaps, I was asked to assume more responsibility for them, and that would have been most noticeable over the two week Christmas vacation. Perhaps it was the war and knowing that my parents couldn't come to take care of me that triggered my misbehavior.

During Christmas vacation, I was invited to go to a night-time birthday party. I was very exited about that, but Aunt Betty had plans to go out that night, so I could stay for only a little while in order to baby-sit for her. At this party, although it was chaperoned, we played many kissing games, which thrilled me, and I didn't want to leave the party. I hated her for interfering with my social life. I had become interested in boys. I got a big crush on a boy, Johnny, who unfortunately was my friend Betty's "boyfriend;" she dropped me as a friend, but there were other girls who were quick to befriend me. While Johnny didn't care for me, there were other boys who did, and the game of girlfriend/boyfriend soon became the interest of my life. I was twelve and a half.

✦ ✦ ✦

I became quite unhappy. I did not have the guts to tell Aunt Betty how I really felt, and today I cannot recall anything in particular, but I was unhappy. I can tell it now by the letters I had written my father at this time. They were short, the handwriting scrawled big across the page, the content trivial. The social worker was called in; she lectured me on gratitude and warned me of the dire consequences—being removed from their home—if I didn't change my attitude. I think it wasn't so much that I did things outwardly bad, I am sure, it was more my omission of duties, or poor execution of them, or poor attitude that must have driven Aunt Betty to anger and frustration. I was learning passive-aggressive behavior. I didn't talk back, but I answered Aunt Betty's complaints with dialogue in my head or under my breath, like, "leave me alone" or "why don't you do it yourself," but I never had the nerve to say so out loud. Nevertheless, I am sure I conveyed my bad attitude.

When we returned to school from vacation, I asked my teacher, Miss Roof, if I could help her after school, which gave me an excuse for not coming home after school to take care of the kids. Sometimes, I deliberately talked in class, knowing that I would have to stay after school, but it was worth it not to have to go home. Miss Roof was very kind, and seemed to know that I was unhappy, and encouraged me to talk. In response for her kind attention, I knitted her a sweater. Yes, I did!— a whole sweater, out of blended maroon and white yarn, with buttonholes, and I must have done it over vacation. I had learned to knit in Austria. I must have saved money from my allowance to buy the yarn, but how I knew to follow a pattern, is a mystery. Miss Roof was astounded by my gift, and appreciative. I was invited to her house for dinner and I really unloaded my troubles. It helped to have somebody to talk to who seemed empathetic.

✦ ✦ ✦

Without much fanfare, I was moved to the orphanage at the end of the semester, the end of January 1942. I was glad to go. I was learning that I could just walk away from unpleasant situations without actually confronting my unhappiness or unacceptable behavior. Later I found this method useful in my life.

11

LIFE IN AN ORPHANAGE

HOMEWOOD TERRACE
1942 to 1947, Intermittent

The word orphanage brings to mind brutal conditions as suffered by Oliver Twist and other orphans, but Homewood Terrace was designed to change that image. We called it "The Home." Its official name was derived from its precursor, the Pacific Hebrew Orphan Asylum. The old orphanage, built in 1891, was a single, big building in the Fillmore district. Almost immediately after it was built, a committee began planning for a different kind of home that was to become Homewood Terrace, opening in 1922. It was a radical departure from the isolating monolithic institutions that were then in vogue. By placing children in buildings that more resembled private family homes, which were called "cottages" and in better neighborhoods, the founders hoped that orphans would have an equal chance at integrating into society by learning typical social and work skills.

What follows is a description of an institution that no longer exists because, fortunately, there are fewer orphans today, thanks to more healthful conditions of life and better care for pregnant women, at least in the developed world. In addition, changes in theories of social work suggested that such large institutions are not desirable for the optimum development of children. Later, in the post-war era the usual practice was to place four to six children in regular houses with a couple as surrogate parents to supervise them. These institutions did not replace regular foster home care.

Even when I lived at Homewood Terrace, there weren't too many orphans besides some of the refugee children like myself who hoped to be reunited with their parents after the war. Most of the other children were from broken homes with one or both parents living in the city. Some, perhaps from abusive homes, had been placed there by the courts, but others had only one parent, usually a mother, who could not take care of a child or children and work. It was also not uncommon for parents to place a recalcitrant child there, hoping that the institution would civilize and reform it. Sometimes a parent's illness required temporary care for a child.

✦ ✦ ✦

I have some good and some bad memories of my life at the Home, but I never felt stigmatized by living there. I have a friend who lived in such a children's home in Chicago—she called it a boarding school—but she felt isolated, outcast and stigmatized there. Other friends who spent time in such institutional orphanages in other parts of the country were severely disciplined and hated it, often running away. In many ways the experience of living at the Home could be likened to a boarding school, and for the same reasons—the camaraderie of fellow sufferers— made the negative aspects bearable.

Homewood Terrace was considered a model of progressive child-care based on what we now call "mainstreaming," a term not in use then. By making the buildings more like ordinary family homes, and placing them in middle-class neighborhoods, it was hoped that the children would mingle in public schools and thus adopt middle-class values and manners. Accordingly, the Home was located on a large parcel of wooded hill in the middle of a upper middle-class neighborhood, the Ingleside, with entrances on Ocean Avenue between Faxon and Ashton, and bordering St. Francis Woods, San Francisco's exclusive neighborhood, but separated from it by an impassable fence and more trees. Yet, across from Ocean Avenue, was a working-class neighborhood served by Balboa High school.

✦ ✦ ✦

Homewood Terrace was the first cottage-type child care facility in the U.S.

The Home was not one building, but rather a small village containing nine "cottages," plus a gym, playground, infirmary, administration building, temple, laundry, machine shop, commissary and residences for the director and his assistant. The two entrances to the Home on Ocean Avenue were marked by big, but graceful cement portals, built as memorials to people who helped found the Home. A huge playing field and two tennis courts were at the street level. The next level up held the common buildings, and still further up the hill, were three levels of cottages and the infirmary. A paved driveway serpentined its way up the hill connecting the buildings to each other, while footpaths through tall eucalyptus trees, whose pungent acorn-shaped "fruits" I liked to step on, provided quicker ascent and descent for us walkers.

What we called "cottages" were not really cottages, that is, small houses; rather to the passerby, they would have looked more like stately mansions, both by size and by the grounds surrounding each house. Children occupied only six of the cottages when I arrived as, even then, there was a decreasing need for bed space. Other cottages provided office space for social workers and counselors, or were used by "graduates" of the home who were attending college, residences for the athletic director, and one was sometimes used by servicemen, who had been former residents, on leave from military duty.

A typical cottage

I became a ward of the orphanage through arrangements with the Jewish Welfare committee that sponsored my immigration to guarantee that I would not become the ward of the State. I spent my first days in San Francisco at the Home, as I explained in my first letter to my father.

When I next came to the Home in Feb. 1942, then 12 ¹/₂ years old, I was put in Cottage #42, located on the uppermost level of the hill, between the assistant director's house and the infirmary. I arrived with a reputation of being a difficult child, having lived with my aunt for 6 months, and in a foster-home for 15 months and being removed from both homes, perhaps for uncooperative behavior. I didn't worry about my reputation, however, for I didn't think that I had done anything wrong, and I looked forward to better times.

Each cottage was a big two-story house with generous space for twenty school age boys and girls. The exterior was stucco, painted in light tones, with large windows, both up and downstairs. The front door, reserved for guests, opened into a

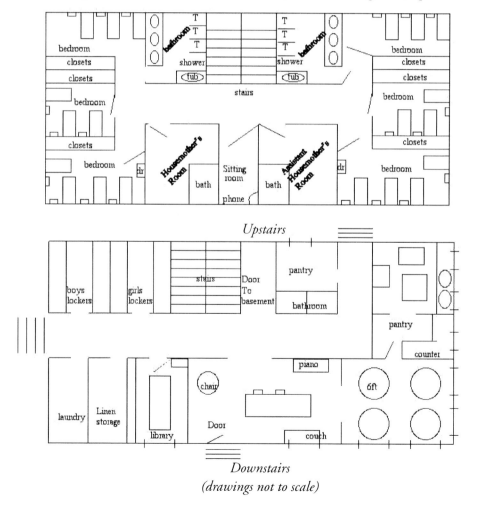

Upstairs

Downstairs
(drawings not to scale)

Living Room

large living room furnished with a sofa, chairs, piano, console-radio and library table. A large rosy-beige carpet covered most of the oak floor, and a picture hung above the piano. The daily morning newspaper, the San Francisco Chronicle, was left on the library table for our perusal, as the older kids vied for reading the funnies or the sport pages early in the day; later in the day we would use the paper to do our current events reports for school. The furniture was comfortable and functional, permitting easy socialization when we assembled there before or after dinner.

Adjacent to the living room and visible through a wall of french doors was a library with bookshelves stocked with reference works. We were each given a shelf for a personal library. I was an avid reader and collected books. When inexpensive *"Pocket Books"* were first introduced in 1942, I bought the first six books and intended to buy them all in the future, a plan that soon became impossible because the books came out at such a fast and furious pace that my meager allowance couldn't afford. Another large library table was used for doing homework, pursuing hobbies such as my scrapbooks of movie stars or playing games like Monopoly or even Ping-Pong. There was also sewing machine of which I made good use.

On the other side of the living room was the dining room, a large, light, pleasant room furnished with four circular tables, usually seating five or six people. Mealtimes were usually congenial and noisy affairs. The housemother sat at the head of one of the tables, and the three eldest children were at the head of the other tables, each with a mix of boys and girls. "Heads" admonished us to use the appropriate silverware, napkins, not to put elbows on the table, to sit properly, chew with mouth closed, etc. Sometimes, the "Heads" took great pleasure in slapping hands or otherwise punishing the littler kids for their transgressions in civility, but if there was too much strife, the housemother would rescue the offender by placing him (and it usually was a him) at the head table. One child from each table brought the food on large serving platters from the kitchen. The "Head" served the food to each child. On the whole the food was nutritious, plentiful and tasty, depending on the skill of housemother and her helpers; everybody was expected to eat some of the served fare, and seconds were sometimes available. Sometimes, we naughtily pushed the food off the table, or surreptitiously stuffed unwanted morsels into our napkins, then into pockets, then to the toilet!

Swinging doors separated the butler's pantry from the dining room and the kitchen. The pantry had spacious counters and cabinets for dishes. I spent a lot of time in this room, as one of my frequent household chores was the making of lunches. I made 30 to 40 sandwiches (sometimes 4 each for the bigger boys), individually wrapped in wax paper and placed in paper bags with some fruit or sweets. We were allowed one meat, cheese or egg sandwich and as many peanut butter and jelly as we wanted. Chopped olives mixed with mayonnaise were often another choice, but I hated the smell of the olives and the looks of the preparation. It was my pleasure to personalize the lunches by taking requests for special orders for the sandwich fixings, such as not using mustard or ketchup, putting mayonnaise or margarine on one or both sides of the bread or putting lettuce in the sandwich. The other kids praised me for my lunches. It took about an hour to fix the lunches, and I ate breakfast on the job. Once, the job was made harder when a strike prevented bread from being commercially sliced so I had to slice 60 to 70 pieces of bread for the sandwiches, a difficult task with soft white bread. Coloring the margarine was a messy, greasy job best done with bare hands, as I squeezed a capsule of coloring into a pound block of white fat and reshaped it to look like cubes of butter.

On the other side of the pantry through another set of swinging doors was the kitchen, spacious, if not functional by today's standards. A very large 6 burner, 2 oven stove dominated the room which included a large table for preparation and two sinks. Two of the biggest boys, helped by some smaller children, did the dishes. The housemother was the main cook, assisted by one of the older girls and a couple of younger girls who peeled apples, carrots and potatoes or set the tables.

Near the kitchen was yet another storage room, this one for food and cooking supplies, with many gallon sized jars and tins of beans, pickles and vegetables, and huge bowls for salads or baking. We had no refrigerator, but milk and other perishables were stored in a cooler open on one side to the fresh San Francisco air, and functional in the cool climate. Food was delivered to us from a central commissary daily. We made our own mayonnaise in gallon batches by pouring oil into an egg preparation, drop by drop. I spoiled many batches because I poured the oil too fast, causing it to curdle; we had to throw it away and start again. I don't recall being scolded for my failure.

A long L-shaped corridor connected the backdoor, near the kitchen and the usual entry for children, to the rest of the house. As we came home from school, the housemother already busy with dinner preparations greeted us in the kitchen with a snack, perhaps celery with peanut butter or some fruit slices.

Following this long cement hallway, behind the living room and library were some little rooms, including a bathroom and furnace room, and the boys' and girls' locker rooms with 5 ft. high lockers for each of us to keep personal belongings, other than clothes, such as sports equipment and games. There was also a laundry room with a giant laundry tub, although most of our clothes were washed in a central laundry. Another room was the repository for linens for bed, bath and table. The hallway ended with yet another door, called the side door, which enabled us to enter the house without being seen by the house-mother's scrutinizing eyes.

The large 2 tiered-stairway, opposite the living room led to the sleeping quarters. Directly at the top of the landing was a suite of rooms for the house-mother and her assistant, if there was one; between them was a small sitting room that held the tele-

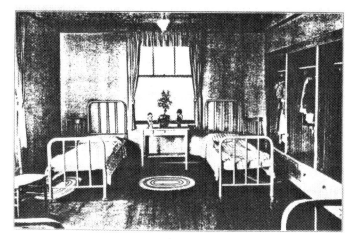

Bedroom

phone. It could be used only for special phone calls. Sleeping quarters for the boys were on one side, girls on the other. Each cottage had room for 20 children, 10 boys and 10 girls, ranging in age from 6 to 18. Spacious bedrooms with views of big eucalyptus trees, housed three or four children to a room. Each child had his or her own wardrobe (a closet without a door, revealing my untidiness instantly), with two drawers below, a chair and a bed; one chest of drawers and one table were to be shared. Typically, each room had children of all ages, so that the eldest could oversee the younger ones. The rooms were painted green, a color I came to despise as representing my prison. Pictures were prohibited but I often tacked pictures of John Payne, Perry Como or Frank Sinatra, my favorite movie star and crooners, above my bureau which

Bathroom

the housemother would periodically tear off the wall.

The bathrooms had the usual fixtures laid out so as to permit privacy, while built-in cubicles for each child held their personal objects, such as toothbrushes, toothpaste and soap. We were required to practice good hygiene. Baths and showers were typically taken before dinner, with the older children supervising the youngest.

Each cottage had a balanced age and sex distribution of children necessary to perform all the chores of running a "typical family life," although there was one Cottage that had only boys. One housemother was in charge of each house. The women were mostly older, I judge now by recalling their gray hair; some had never married, a few had even worked in the old orphanage, but most of the women were widows, forced into becoming professional mothers for lack of other salable occupations. Some were motherly figures, allowing some closeness with some of the children. Even Mrs. Goss, with whom I had many arguments, was a warm person. On their days off a relief housemother would take charge. One relief housemother, Mrs. Boughner, who came once or twice a week when the regular house mother had a day off, allowed me to talk with her after dinner with cups of coffee as we contemplated the makings of a good personality, the daily news or whether there was a God. When I was older, another housemother treated me as an adult by sharing female secrets and off-color jokes.

Lacking in this "typical" family was a live-in father figure. There were only four male staff: Mr. Bonapart and his one assistant, the "coach" in charge of the recreation program, and Mr. Otis, in charge of the maintenance and the grounds.

We all had chores to do, rotated by month and assigned somewhat by ability, as described in a letter to my father almost a year after I moved to the home (1/16/43).

I get up at 6:30 every morning except for holidays, Saturdays and Sundays. I put on my working or play clothes and go downstairs to help prepare the breakfast. Usually we have fruit or juice, mush or a cereal, toast and cocoa. Then we make our beds, and go downstairs again to do our work. Each child is assigned to a certain room, which they have to clean. We rotate every month. After we are finished with our work, we go upstairs to get dressed. Before we leave we have to see that our clothes are all hung up, and our rooms look neat.

Other work besides making breakfast or lunches included vacuuming, sweeping and dusting the public rooms, clearing tables and doing dishes. Sometime during this after-breakfast hour, the assistant director and the nurse made the rounds of each house; she to attend to health problems, checking fevers, throats and deciding if a day home from school would be in order; he, to settle any other problems.

Before we could go to public school, we assembled down the hill, in front of the gym, where Mr. Bonapart or his assistant inspected us to make sure our hair was combed, our shoes were clean, perhaps to hear about our schoolwork. This was the time when we asked permission to participate in some after-school activities, and the time when I often got scolded for my transgressions, such as dirty saddle shoes, very much in fashion then. High school kids went first, as they had farthest to go to school, usually by streetcar; then the junior highs who could walk to school, and finally, the grade school kids whose school was just a short walk away.

We also had chores after school; the boys did some of the gardening or laundry or shop work, working in the common areas of the Home while the girls usually worked in their own cottage helping to prepare the dinner. The after-school routine was described to my father (Feb. 3, 1943)

> *I get out of school at 3:10. I change my school clothes to playclothes. Then I have my afternoon lunch. As soon as I finish I help prepare the evening meal. I love to cook and bake. On Thursday I often make a cake for Friday night and they turn out good too. On Tuesdays I don't help in the kitchen since it is girl's day out. Tuesdays the boys make the dinner. On Wednesdays I work at the dentist. I now get an average of $2.50 a month which is very good pocket money. After we are finished with our kitchen work, we take our baths, or showers. When we get through its about 6:00, and then we eat dinner. After dinner is finished we have duties to perform such as setting tables for breakfast, etc. Our homework is done after that. We hit the hay, or go to bed at 9:00. ...millions of kisses, wishes, hugs and squeezes, Phyllis*

We had at least one day free to pursue our own activities, such as going to the library or for after school sports. I learned to cook here, under the tutelage of Mrs. Goss, my first housemother, and I took pride in putting together a good meal. Girls sometimes had additional tasks, such as darning boys' socks, which I hated most of all, sewing individual markings on new clothes for identification, minor mending or putting away the cleaned laundry. After dinner, we were supposed to study, but if there was no homework, we could play games, Ping-Pong, or just read. We could listen to news on the radio in the living room, but it wasn't on all evening. The housemother often sat in the living room reading the paper while keeping a watchful eye on the kids. She determined our bedtimes.

✦ ✦ ✦

On weekends we had a different routine beginning with Friday night dinner. The beginning of the Sabbath, a holy time for Jewish households, was observed with the traditional candles, white tablecloths, a meal, and our best clothes. Saturdays began with an hour of religious education, followed by going to Temple, which was on the 2nd floor of the Administration building. Mr. Bonapart usually performed the Reform services, and a tiny lady with blond braided hair wound around the top of her head provided the music on a big organ. As this was also a time when Mr. B. could address all of us at once, often there were admonishments and announcements of new regulations or routines. Nobody was excused from Temple, unless it was an older girl who had to prepare for the big meal that followed. We often had a roast or leg of lamb and special desserts such as pies. Later when I became disenchanted with religion, I volunteered to cook as often as I could.

Then came the highlight of our week—going to the movies, a Saturday afternoon institution for children in the 1940's. We went as a group, perhaps 100 children walking in twos a few blocks on Ocean Avenue, sometimes escorted by housemothers, to the El Rey theater, (a modernistic building with a big tower which is an Evangelical church today). The theater provides us with free admission for most performances. For four hours we escaped into fantasy. Along with two major features, we saw cartoons, news and one segment of a serial such as Superman, Captain Marvel or Batman and Robin. We brought our own money for the candy or popcorn. A frequent punishment was to be denied the privilege of going to the movies. The following letter to my father explained my weekends.

Dec. 18, 1942 (Not in chronological order here)

> *...We go to the show every Saturday and we go out on Sundays. I usually go to the show. Friday nights we usually have a dance and Saturday nights a basket ball game or a volley ball game. It's lots of fun. I went to one last night and I am to another tonight. We (our team) beat both times. Mostly all the girls and boys 7th grade and up have center memberships. I have one. The girls can go there swimming every other Tuesday or Thursday. There we can play ping-pong, badminton, basketball, excersize in the play room on chin bars, mats, etc. Then we go swimming for a half an hour. Tuesday is my best day in the week.*

Saturday nights meant more fun with some scheduled activity, such as basketball-games, dances or birthday parties. With 120 children, there were enough people to do all kinds of things, and the Home provided us with many recreational opportunities, hiring staff whose sole job it was to keep us wholesomely occupied. Romances were not discouraged, and typically there were no problems with "immoral" sexual behavior, or it was well hidden; of course, teenagers are very clever not to let the authorities see too much. There were romances, some going steady, and some that even ended in marriage. The Home was progressive in this area too, not focusing too much attention to this normal teenage pre-occupation with sex, nor lecturing us to avoid such behaviors. I knew of only one girl who got pregnant, and because her father was a doctor, I believe she had an abortion. That wasn't common knowledge, however.

Sunday was the day we went "out." Those children who had parents or other relatives were taken out by them, usually early in the morning, returning after dinner. The rest of us used the day as we wished. We were free of chores except to prepare our meals—usually leftovers. Sometimes we were given tickets, for movies, plays, concerts or athletic events such as the Harlem Globe Trotters or the East-West Game by Godparents. Usually there were only two or perhaps four tickets, and the housemother could parcel out the tickets at her discretion. I was often the lucky recipient because I had no place to go on a Sunday; as a result, as a teenager, I was able to see operas, plays and ballets, providing me with a cultural experience otherwise not possible for most teenagers.

Godparents were benefactors of the Home, assigned to each cottage. They visited occasionally, sometimes participated in our Holy Days dinners, and also took responsibility for giving a birthday present to each child. The child was able to request some item—say a sweater or blouse, as well as one book. I appreciated these gifts and learned to write them thank you notes. Having these special gifts was a very nice touch; otherwise, someone like me would never get a present.

◆ ◆ ◆

Love was the main thing missing from an otherwise excellent institution, per-haps the one quality that distinguishes a real family from a substitute, however progressive the latter might be. Perhaps it is not possible to love an abandoned or motherless child; perhaps the staff, themselves often abandoned in mid-life, could not give love; perhaps it wasn't good childrearing practice in those days to show affection and approval. I never thought of it much then, but now I can't recall being hugged; nobody asked how I felt, nobody brought me surprises that could demon-strate that I was being thought of lovingly; praise was rare, criticism frequent.

I was often unhappy at the Home. Many things contributed to my discon-tent—the separation from my parents, the war, and my aloneness in this country—but I think basically, the main reason was that I was a teenager. There were many occasions when I screamed outrage at the lack of liberty or the repressive atmo-sphere, but now I concede that my father would have been even stricter and more difficult. The fact that I was allowed to rebel, without cruel punishment, also speaks well for the progressive attitude of the Home. I much preferred it to the several foster homes where I had felt like a servant and not free to disagree; even if in some of my letters I said I hated the Home, overall it was better. I liked the camaraderie of the other children as we faced a common enemy—Mr. Bonapart or housemothers—and as we worked together for a common goal, the running of our cottage and finding happiness. My gregarious personality was well suited for group life, and I always had many friends. I survived my experience at the Home becoming stronger, and more competent, although I failed to learn how to negotiate with authority figures, a lesson I still need. Many children succeeded in this environment, but despite the good intentions of this liberal institution, some children were broken by the experience.

◆ ◆ ◆

In recent years proposals were made to remove children from their single parents (as a means of ending Welfare) and place them in orphanages. The public outcry was great, but I disagreed. If institutions could be as progressive as Homewood Terrace had been, I personally feel they are better than most foster homes or dysfunctional natural families.

Still, even with the big limitation of lack of love, I am grateful now that I landed at Homewood Terrace rather than some other home that might not have been so enlightened. At the Home, I had the opportunity to develop responsibility and independence, skills that served me well in my life. Furthermore, within limits, I could control my time and make my own plans for my life.

◆ ◆ ◆

The buildings and trees of Homewood Terrace no longer exist. Falling prey to bulldozers in 1970, the cottages and grounds were replaced by many streets crowded with townhouses. The playfield was filled with earth behind the wall that separated the home from the street and it now supports a supermarket and a big parking lot.

Serpentine Drive

12

COTTAGE #42

1942

My first year at Homewood Terrace went well. I was placed in Cottage #42, up on the highest level of the extensive grounds. I liked Mrs. Goss, the house-mother, and she liked me. She was in her 50's, short and round, brown hair tinged with some gray hanging straight above her shoulders, a ruddy complexion, not pretty, but warm. She was friendly and welcomed me. She taught me how to cook and appreciated my help. I liked helping her.

It was exciting to live with so many other children. We called ourselves "kids." There were about 120 in the Home altogether, of which about 30 to 40 were in my age group, so I had many companions to share activities and secrets. In my Cottage there were two girls my age, Martha and Ella (also a refugee), who became my friends. I was assigned to a room with an older girl and two younger ones. Room assignments could be changed if girls didn't get along, and as the demographics changed.

Despite many chores to do and schedules to meet, I felt free and enjoyed contributing to the whole effort and working with others. I never felt like a servant here, although in reality I did much more work than I had in the foster home, except for the responsibility of small children. At the Home I also had some responsibility for younger children, such as tending to their manners at the table, or seeing that they took their baths, but I did not have to take them places or baby-sit for them. However, when my chores were done, I could do what I wanted to do, whereas in the foster home I did not have control of my free time and this was very important to me. I had been used to having free time in Vienna and at my Aunt's house—to visit friends, go to the library, or just to play by myself. Girls had Tuesday afternoons off, and I used this time to go to the library, write letters, swim at the Jewish Community Center, or attend activities arranged by the Home's recreation director.

◆ ◆ ◆

Although the war had just started for America, and all of us in the Home were patriotic and sympathetic to the war effort, our lives were not much changed by the restrictions of the emergency. Of course, all of the windows were outfitted with dark-out shades, but for practical purposes we were not much affected. Some foods, such as meat, fats and sugar were rationed, but because there were so many of us, we could manage the rations well. We didn't feel deprived and had nutritious meals. We were all interested in the development of the war, read the San Francisco papers and discussed the news at meals, and did current event reports at school. In general, we were more interested in the battle in the Pacific, it being closer and perhaps getting bolder coverage in the San Francisco papers. Although Japanese people in California were "relocated', an action that today reminds me of the racists tactics of the Nazis, I apparently was not aware of it, or did not understand it, and have no personal recollection how I felt about it then.

Considering my personal situation—my mother in Europe and my father in Australia—I was especially anxious to have the war end soon, but I doubt that I understood what being at war really meant. Many older boys at the Home enlisted in the service, and we felt concern for them as though they were brothers. Later, I wrote to some of them while they were away, hoping to keep their spirits up.

However, my flow of mail ceased and I stopped writing, believing that mail would not go overseas any more. Mail to and from my mother ceased, although I received a couple of letters in February that she had written in October and November before the war started. These indicated that there was no possibility of her coming to me. I don't remember how I reacted to these letters—I didn't want to think of her not coming, perhaps I didn't really understand what it really meant. I think I must have blocked those dismal thoughts out of my consciousness.

Mail to and from my father was often delayed, and although he warned me of this in his next letter, yet he was often angry with me for the lack of mail. In that year he was beginning to get impatient with the sparcity of my letters. Indeed, despite my claim that I wrote every week, in fact he only had nine letters from me that year, although others may have been lost.

As I read these letters now, I find a big change in the quality of my letters between the end of 1941 and Spring, 1942—not only did my handwriting become smaller and better, but the content became more mature. It seems to have happened over the winter holidays, perhaps reflecting the change in my environment from foster home to the Home, as well as the realization that war might change my future.

✦ ✦ ✦

The public library, a converted store, was close to the Home. Since my arrival in San Francisco, I had learned to appreciate the library's treasures and I went there often. Public libraries, these wonderful institutions, in many ways were my parents. I read a variety of books, but was especially drawn to best sellers, or big, thick books that might be considered classics. Yes, I picked them if they were big, thinking that they were more important. One book, which influenced me greatly, was *Anthony Adverse*, a story of an orphan boy in New York City who rose from newspaper boy to newspaper magnate. I loved books in which the hero, or more rarely heroine, pulled himself from meager beginnings to great success. I loved mountain adventure stories because the heroes were in such danger, but usually found a solution to their problems. Both of these genres presented me with role models who championed hard work and bravery, self-reliance and a cool head. I also liked reading the writings of Thomas Payne, the revolutionary pamphleteer, having studied about him in history. His love of freedom at any cost excited me, and I made that my goal too. These readings made me more determined to be independent, an attitude that did not bring forth Mr. Bonapart's approval later.

✦ ✦ ✦

Music came into my life at this time, too. I became conscious of popular songs, in part because of the school dances. Soon, I was swooning over Frank Sinatra's *Temptation* and *Night and Day*, swaying with the Andrew Sisters, or singing along with *Mairzy Doats*, a silly jingle. I memorized songs and sang them, even though I couldn't carry a tune. When we sang in school, I was told to just mouth the words. One of my friends, Irene, was more captivated by classical music. Just then, Leonard Bernstein made his conducting debut, and Irene was excited about the turn of his career. She let me listen to some of her classical records, and thus I became interested in classical music. Sometimes I was fortunate to get tickets to the symphony, opera or ballet from the Godparents for Sunday afternoons.

✦ ✦ ✦

The letter below is the last letter from my mother that I have in my possession. There was one other letter from her about her going to Poland, "maybe I go to the nice grandma" since I mention it to my father at least two times (my letter of 5/11/42, p.159), but I cannot find it. Perhaps I sent it to him. I really didn't understand what it meant for her to go to Poland—perhaps I thought she would to go to her family as she suggested; I could not have known about concentration and death camps at that time. Although in my letters to my father I seem hopeful about her future, I am not sure I really felt that way.

November 23, 1941 Nordausen, translated from German, written before war was declared on Germany; received Jan. 26, 1942 in San Francisco, sent to my foster home, then forwarded to me at the Home, arriving sometime in February.

> *My dearly loved good child!*
>
> *Why do you write so seldom, you know how your Mutti longs for a message from you, my dearest. Unfortunately I am without your lovely letters for a long time now. I am thank God in good health and I am still working in the factory. The only luck is that I am working and find distraction in it, otherwise I would go mad, besides I earn thank God what I need for a living. How are you my sweet doll? Do you have news from your father? I am happy that you two are fine and I hope that I will live to see you again. I am longing for a picture of you and the Family Reingold, but it seems like you are not thinking about that. You have already forgotten your Mutti, haven't you? How is your studying? I hope and say a prayer to God that you are in good health and cheerful. Please write me like before every week, that is the only light in my life. I kiss you tenderly and hug you a lot, — Your mother who loves you endlessly*

Dec. 12, 1941 Received February 1942 from my father

> *My little Darling,*
>
> *In consequence of the outbreak of the war we have to give up the idea of an early reunion. Keep up your courage—…some day the war will end and then we will rejoice at the happy reunion with our darling Mama who has so much to endure. Probably, from now on, letters will take much longer…and some will be lost. …you must to avoid using figures (as you always did when conveying kisses and hugs to me) because it could be objected to by the Censors. Now my little Darling, may be that you will have to face air raids, etc. I pray to God that He shall protect you and all the other people there…you needn't worry about me, I am well and healthy and as the position is now, it is not likely to get deterriorated. Keep on writing to me…*

Dec. 25, 1941

> *My little Darling,*
>
> *I have not received any letter from you for the last two weeks… I am well though*

the climatic conditions are far from being pleasant. For the last two weeks the temperature has been 102-108 ...you can find no protection against it, even the cold shower is not much value. The worst of it is that no refreshment is available, everything, the water and other drinks are so disagreeably warm... Papa

Feb. 25, 1942

Dearest Daddy,

I'm awfully sorry I did not write to you for so long, you see, I thought no mail would go through [after Pearl Harbor and declaration of war]. *But since I received mail from you* [several letters forwarded from Reingolds]... *here it is a nice long letter that you've been waiting for. First of all, I must tell you, that I moved again, this time to a childrens home. It seems to that I'm always moving[;] sometimes, I think, it's my fault, though I don't believe it was my fault this time. I didn't think I had enough freedom. But I guess I'll just have to get along here, untill you and Mommy come here and we'll be together again.*

...I go to another school now. I did not like it in the beginning. But I'm getting to like it better everyday and I'm getting more friends everyday. ...My last report card I had 15 A and 6 B. The B's were in art, Physical Ed, Music, Self Control, Cooprates in work and play and Obeys Cheerfully. I'm fine and healthy and happy here. But very lonesome for you. ...heaps of kisses and hugs and love from your ever loving daughter, Phyllis

I did not expect my father would approve of my moving, but I didn't get his reprimand for several months.

Jan. 23, 1942, Received Mar 14, 1942

My little Darling,

... This week I have not any news from you but I am sure there are some letters of you[rs] underway which will reach me shortly. Recently I received an air mail letter from Mama, despite the airway it took three months to get here. The news transmitted is far from being pleasant, nevertheless, I have been extremely glad getting it since it has been the second letter from our darling Mama for about 1 $^3/_4$ years.

Mama wrote me the letter from Vienna where she had been on leave for 14 days. [that would have been in October] *She is very despondent because of her being compelled to stay there, she is very lonesome and longing for you. I deplore it deeply that she was not given the opportunity of immigrating into the U.S.A. Anny and Arno did their best to assist her, alas all in vain.*

Our wishes and regrets are of no use now, all we can do now is to cheer her up and to help her get through this ordeal. You, my darling, cannot write her as you used to, but you can keep correspondence going through the Int. Red Cross Society, Geneva, Switzerland.... Let us hope that all this sorrow will soon cease and give way to a brighter and happier future...I'm perfectly well and am only sorry that things have developed in such manner as to render my joining you impossible. Don't worry about it for the time being, we have to put up with it,...and I shall never stop in my efforts to achieve what I am longing for with all my heart...[reunion with you and Mama]. *Heaps of kisses and hugs. Your loving Papa.*

In his next letter of 3/14/42 he complained of not having mail from me for months or from the Bicks who were trying to get him an affidavit. He hopes to regain his freedom. He thought I was still at the Reingolds. At the beginning of the war, mail was very irregular.

May 11, 1942   I've become philosophical about our situations.

Dearest Daddy,

I received your dear letter [3/14/42] *That was the last letter since five weeks ago. ... I haven't heard from Mommy for quite a while and have not written to her since it would be useless. No mail whatsoever will go through. The last time I heard from her she said, she'd most probably have to* [go] *to Poland to work for which I'm very sorry yet there are no ways of displaying it, except for dreaming and hoping.*

I'm in H7 Grade now and in case you forgot how old I am I'll remind you I am going on thirteen. I have told you before I moved. I live in a Children's home. I don't seem to be able to get along anywhere except with you. But don't let that worry you, please, because I'm perfectly happy here. I've been taught so many lessons by different people I'm sure I could get a diploma for being able to take anything at any time and everywhere. You see, Daddy, now that I can't be with you I have to learn how to get along without you and boy does it hurt me. But I'm willing and willpower will do anything. I thought I knew a lot when I knew my lessons at school, but not until now have I realized how perfectly stupid I am. Not until now did I know what life was and what it meant to live it. And then when you come here to me with mother I'll almost be an angel and a good [one] *at that. I'm sorry I wrote all this but you are the only person I could tell this too and I just had to let it out. Please forget it now and let's be happy.*

In the next letter he "is shocked", but accepts the situation with optimism. In a still later letter, (June 19) he tries to console me. Now, I can understand his confusion and worry about me. He knew nothing of the orphanage and its responsibility for me—he had no communication with those in charge.

May 14, 1942

My little Darling,

I hope that you received letter (written to you three weeks ago, April 14) which ought to have given you a true account of what I have been feeling about the news that you had left the Reingold's family. I have been terribly shocked about these happenings and even now, though several weeks have lapsed in the meantime, I cannot put my mind at ease. The reason why I did not write in the course of the last weeks was that I have been expecting some further news and explanations from you. Now that no letter came in I won't let you wait any longer.

It is already 3 months that you're in your new home and I should like to know how you are getting on there, I only hope that you have acclimatized yourself to the surroundings and that you find the new home nice and pleasant. I am anxious to have further details and I am sure that truthful as you have always been you will provide me with a plain report on everything that concerns you. I think that life in a Children's Home is rather agreeable since you have probably got a lot of friends there and besides it provides you with everything required for learning, and this is now the most important thing for you.

Of course nothing can substitute a parent's home, but for the time being you have to put up with the new conditions, let us hope that this life of yours in the present circumstances will not last for long and that we shall soon be reunited with our darling Mama. I know it quite well how hard it is for you to go on there without your parents, my thoughts are always with you and I pray to God that he may help you to overcome easily this unfortunate time of our being separated.

Don't lose your courage my dear little girl, enjoy your being there and bear always in mind that you getting into the USA was a great luck, at least you got the chance of escaping the German hell. To know you are safe from humiliation and oppression makes me feel happy and thankful to Providence. Be kind and grateful to all those who are taking care of you, and never forget that the people you're living with are strangers and not one's parents and, and therefore, you must oblige them by exemplary conduct and amiability. In short, be so as you were when being with us, in which case I am sure everyone will be your friend and everyone will be fond of you. Let me soon know how you're doing in school. I take it for granted that it is as it used to be before, you are still one of the best in your class. Do you learn Hebrew? You should not neglect this study. It is of no minor importance than the other subjects.

I'm healthy and all right, the question of my being released is still unsolved yet I hope that this matter will soon—in one way or either—come to a head.

Let Uncle Max have some words, he complains about you not replying to his letters. Love and heaps of kisses, from your loving Papa.

June 20, 1942 I must have thrown away his letter of April 14, although I acknowledged it. I begin to stick up for myself by explaining why I left the Reingolds.

Dearest Daddy,

Today I received two of your letters dated April 21st and May 14th. I was very happy to get them though on the first letter I cried my eyes off. To think that my own Daddy doesn't believe and trust me. Daddy, I'm ashamed of you! You want me happy and I'm doing my best to be happy. When I wrote you I was happy all the time I didn't mean it. I was practically forced to write it. But you wouldn't understand that unless I proved it to you. And I will if that's what you want me to do. I wanted to leave the Reingold family after a half a year, but they urged me to stay so I did. You say my conduct is bad, so noone wants me. But that's not so. You see, other people, strangers, don't know my ways. You and Mom taught me differently than they wanted me to be.

That's why I wanted to go to this home. Here I can go around with a light heart and freedom in my lungs. Here I can get along with other children and love and be like brothers and sisters. I am perfectly happy here. I wasn't ever more happy than I am right now. When I said I didn't have enough freedom I meant only this. When I wanted to do something that was reasonable I had to do just exactly the opposite.

But now I'm happy and I am willing to stay here as long as I can or until you come here. But I doubt if it will be possible since all refugees have to be with Foster Parents. And another thing, Daddy, Don't feel sorry that I am not with Mother because I am very capable of taking care of myself and I can do a good job. When you come here you're going to find the most perfect and most wonderful girl ever to come out of Vienna. On the contrary I find this home very nice. But now lets forget about everything that happened and let's think about the future.

I got my report card and a pretty good one too: As following: English B, Social Science C, General Science A, Gym B, Cooking B, Music B, Math B. I was disappointed. But I did the best I could. I am healthy and I hope you are too. So for now, heaps & heaps of kisses, hugs and loads & loads of luck. From me with everlasting love. Phyllis

P.S.   I pray for you each night
I hope & pray that God might
Free you and Mom and
then bring you both back to me
Across the big, big sea.

What was "reasonable" to me when I was with the Reingolds was probably to go play with friends, whereas my foster mother wanted me to take care of the children by taking them to the park, or just playing with them at home. I don't know how "reasonable" I was. However, I cannot recall instances when I shirked my duties. I think it was my attitude that got me in trouble. Anyway, by now I've been in the Home for three months, and I've already stopped thinking of the Reingolds. The delay in mail caused a lot of misunderstanding, but I also didn't write that much because I was involved in my schoolwork, housework, and playing with friends.

June 19, 1942

My little Darling,

It is but now that have received your letter dated May 11th,...the first letter for about three months...the contents of your letter is not very encouraging and, surely, my Darling, you wouldn't be able to realize how it hurts me to know you there so lonely...I feel it, your lines give a true picture of your feelings and thoughts. I see how you are longing for caresses, but your parents—who as long as they had been with you had the only thought to... make you happy and gay—are now thousands of miles away from you. But all this must not discourage you, even though we are dispersed over three continents, our thoughts are always with you and I am sure that our darling Mama , though her own plight is a very hard one, has no other thoughts and desires...[but] to be reunited with us. After all, this war which has brought so much misery and sorrows upon mankind, will soon or later come to an end, making true our wishes and hopes...[to be] reunited. ...don't lose courage and don't give way to despondency.

...You must not think that your lot is hard, on the contrary, be happy and glad that you escaped the Nazi hell and that you have been given the opportunity to live in U.S.A. You just make the best of it, learn, learn and don't stop in your endeavors to get as much knowledge...

June 29, 1942 I complain about not having enough money to write more often.

Dear Daddy,

A few days ago I received an answer to one of my letters. I was very happy to get it, I assure you. As to your complaint of not getting mail from me I can explain it. You see, I can only write to you every two weeks because of my money matters. I get 50 cents a month and I must buy with that school supply, toothpaste and soap and kleenex. Put it all together I have a nickel=5 cents left which only allows me one letter, the other the home pays. I hope you will forgive me for that.

The other day I got a letter from Uncle Max. I was very happy with it as you can imagine. I awfully ashamed to say so, but I practically forgot how to write or speak German in fact I only know a couple of words and I really can't answer him without somebody's help. Inlaid in his letter was one from momy [probably the one which states she is going to Poland, but which I don't have anymore] *and I am going to lay both in to you. Your birthday is near and I wish you all the luck in the world and that we may be reunited soon.*

Things have been swell around here I mean, vacation is wonderful. In two more weeks I shall be thirteen, just imagine, I am going to in my teens. I think it's simply wonderful. ...I'll send you a picture of my self pretty soon. I have all of my bands on and most probably [will] *be able to take them off in the beginning of 1944. My teeth are going to be all straight. ...Phyllis*

P.S. The person who is in charge of the home wrote to you already and I hope you answer him. (I should get my face smacked in for being so fresh).   ...Phyllis.

Regarding my finances, the fifty cents a month didn't go far, and those children like myself who did not have parents nearby to supplement this allowance, had an opportunity to weed around the grounds, for ten cents an hour. Earned money could be used to supplement the unfashionable clothes given us from a central clothes room. I began to work first at weeding, and later that summer as a dental assistant. At this point it didn't occur to me to ask my father for money.

✦ ✦ ✦

The Home provided excellent medical and dental care for the children, and I received a lot of it. I can't recall going to a dentist while I lived in the foster home, but at the Home I began to get regular care. I had awful teeth so I went to the dentist frequently. I was given orthodontia, not a common treatment at that time, but really a luxury. My teeth were not very crooked, but my bite was not good. The upper teeth did not fit well over the lower teeth causing an overlap, and as the 12-year molars were coming in, it became obvious that there wouldn't be enough room for them. Hence, the orthodontia. The work was done at University of California-San Francisco Dental School. Since it was wartime, many dentists had gone into the Armed Services, and not many were in training; some were already in the Service, finishing their training before they moved out. As a result, I had many different dentists working on me. I was fortunate to be assigned to Dr. Wiley, then head of the department, a sweet, kind man, who took a very special interest in me, or at least in my teeth, and supervised the students' work. Years later I would learn that he was one of the leading authorities in orthodontia.

Before any treatment was begun, all my cavities needed to be filled, and I needed some teeth pulled. One of my molars was impacted, and surgery was required to remove it and three other teeth. I went to the clinic on the streetcar, roughly a 45 minute trip, requiring two transfers. I was given gas, the four teeth were removed; I spent some time waking up, and then, quite dizzy still, I went home the way I had come. Nobody helped me in this experience, and I never thought much about it until my daughter had to have her wisdom teeth removed; she not only was taken and brought home, but she spent several days, listless, on the sofa nursing her swollen cheeks. It made me realize how self-sufficient I had been.

The thing I recall the most about wearing bands, besides the embarrassment of silver teeth, was the pain. There weren't many other kids who wore braces then, and, therefore, I didn't have many friends to commiserate with. Every week or two, the dentist tightened the braces, and the pull on the rubber bands was extremely painful. The insides of my mouth were always raw from the little hooks that held the rubber bands, but the movement of the teeth was what was excruciating. For me, the pain of braces was much worse than the incessant filling of my teeth; in fact, I stopped using Novocain for fillings since that time because compared to the enduring pain of the braces, the drilling was nothing.

For four and a half years, from age 13 to 17 $^{1}/_{2}$, I made a weekly trip to UC's Dental Clinic. Usually I went after school, until I discovered in the tenth grade that

I could miss Geometry by "having to go to the dentist." Of course, it reflected in my poor grade in that subject.

✦ ✦ ✦

August 5, 1942   Three years had elapsed since I last saw my father, but I recalled the anniversary. Now I was just about 13 years old, a far different girl that he had known. In this letter, I am ashamed of my misdeeds, not explained, but I promise to reform.

> *Dearest Daddy,*
>
> *I didn't get a letter from you, but I thought I should write anyway. I know you haven't been receiving mail as you should have and I thought it all over yesterday, the 4th, when it was three years since I haven't seen you. I am really ashamed of myself. I've done so many thing that weren't nice and that were wrong I just wish somebody would punish me very strongly. I am going to change altogether. I promise on my word of honor. When you come here, I'll be a nice girl, I'll be your daughter and you'll be proud of me. Let's change the subject and turn tables. How are you, I hope fine. ... Things are swell here, and everything perfect. Even if I don't think of you during day time (every minute) I still think of you when I go to bed and say my nightly prayer.*
>
> *Your birthday is coming closer, day by day so I give you your wishes now. I wish you all the luck in the world, that you, Mommy and I be reunited again as we are praying for. That you have all the luck, happiness and health and love as God has stored away for us is my second wish. And then I wish you that all your dreams (good ones only) come true. These wishes I send to you with a million kisses, squeezes, hugs and who knows what. I think I better close now. So love and kisses (heaps) hugs and love again   Phyllis*
>
> *Aug. 8, 1942*
>
> *P.S. Before I had a chance to send this away I got your letter from July 9th and I'd like to answer a few questions. First I will be kept in school 'till I am eighteen years old. School goes up to the H 12 grade. I am now in the low eighth grade since I was promoted. The following were my marks.*

	Scholarship	Citizenship			
English	*B+*	*S*	*Gen. Science*	*A*	*E*
Math	*B*	*S*	*Music*	*B*	*S*
Social Science	*C+*	*S*	*Gym*	*B+*	*S*
Cooking	*B*	*S*			

Cue: S= Satisfactory, E=Excellent

I got on the honor roll. Tomorrow is my birthday and I got a white silk blouse. I love it. I'll try and snap a picture of my self for you. I hate to ask you but do you could get me fancy stamps. Thank you love and kisses and hugs, Phyllis ...

Friends used to ask me for the stamps from Australia, so I asked for some fancy ones to give them variety. In the next letter, my father shares his feelings about our separations. Typically, he didn't complain, but here he expresses his disappointment in the way our lives have turned out.

August 9, 1942   Received Sept. 25

My little Darling,

Today is your birthday, and now that I am going to write you, I find no words to express my present feelings. You, my darling, know how happy and gay I used to be on such occasions, but now I cannot think of your birthday without being instantly reminded of the sad fact that is already three years that I was driven away from you, three long years of living separated from you and our darling Mama. I know, my love, you feel likewise; when I left you three years ago I was thinking it would be for some months only. Oh, indeed it is a "splendid" work done by those who intended to save us from the Nazi hell, you my child are there, lonesome and abandoned, our darling Mama somewhere under Nazis' yoke and lastly, I, I have the privilege to enjoy the hospitality on an Australian Internment Camp. One cannot help think-ing that all went mad, otherwise such things could never have happened. I do not want to plunge into further meditations, nobody cares whether I find it unjust and cruel. In spite of all these unpleasant experiences we have made in the last years, we must not lose heart... Your loving Papa

Sept. 26, 1942

Dearest Daddy,

I received your dear letter from August ninght and I want to thank you a million times for your lovely thoughts. I have been a naughty girl because I haven't written to you for three weeks. But I hope you'll forgive. There are a few matters I want to straighten out with you especially the first one. In your last letter you said that I should put my mind at ease. Well, Daddy dearest, I advise the same thing for you, I think you need it more than I do, and I know I am wright. I tell you why in just a minute but first let me tell you something else.

One of your very nice thoughts was: "I wish you many happy, returns, may the future fulfil all your wishes, give you much pleasure and enjoyment and thus make you forget all the bitterness you had to experience in your past three years of your living among strange people." Indeed, 'tis a very lovely thought, but what an error. Daddy, you think I am very lonely and that I have no friends but that is wrong. Certainly, I am lonesome for you and Momy but that doesn't mean I have gone through bitterness only, in the past three years, in fact most of the years have been have been happy outside the fact that those days that weren't happy taught me some lessons of life. After I thought them over I saw my mistakes and tried to correct them and those corrected mistakes is what makes ones later life succesful. So please, Daddy, don't worry [about] me because I am perfectly happy at the home.

I have lots of friends in school and get pretty good grades. As soon as possible, I will procure a picture for you. Things are swell around here. A week ago was Yom Kippur and I fasted all day without even a drop of water. I also begged God to help you and mother to come over here. Services were very nice.

How are you? I am healthy and I have bands all over my teeth. In over a year I may be able to take them of. When you write Mom tell her hello and tell her I would write to her but absolutely no mail will go through. Heaps and heaps of kisses with love and hugs your everloving Phyllis

Oct. 15, 1942

My little Darling,

Since your last letter, which I received 30.8. no other letter came in. Six long weeks without news... It is hard enough to be so far away from you, my Darling and your letters (which I miss so badly) being the only thing that gives me pleasure should not be so scarce as they actually are. ...

Some two weeks ago I received a letter from your director, Mr. Bonapart. I am very pleased and satisfied with the information, I got about you. I am so sorry to have worried you with my letters, blaming you for your moving from one home to an-other. You see, there is one thing that never passes out of my mind and that is, the thought of you. Up to now I had no clear picture as to your position nor as the things really were. To see you happy and cheerfull is the only desire I have got now. I replied to Mr. Bonapart and thanks to his kind lines, I see that my Lizzie remained what it was; my little, sweet darling!

His apology for blaming me for moving was very welcome. Hope is rekindled!

Now, I want to tell you something which would surely please you, though you must not attach to much importance to it. As things are now there seems to be some hope that those who have their wives or children in U.S.A. would be able to proceed to them. Should this become true, I would come over to you, that would be grand. Anyhow, it would take months to get to the goal, you know 2 years ago I received the affidavits from Anny but they are now of no value. New affidavits will be required and I do not know whether Anny would be able and willing to supply me with new ones. Yet, there is a hope that I shall be able to come to you still and even during the war, and that gives me new courage and cheerful prospect.

How are you getting on? Did you enjoy your vacations? ... Papa

Oct. 28, 1942

My little Darling,

I received your letter of 29.7 and 10.8 and was really very glad. This time, for a change, I cannot complain about a scarcity of news, I see that my little darling does her best to keep me always informed. Now that you informed that you have not enough money left from your allowance to be able to write once weekly, I understand why I had to wait so long for a letter from you. I should very much like to send you some money, but I don't know whether in view of the existing restrictions it will be possible. [He is still in an internment camp.]

As I wrote you in my last letter, I received the letter from your director, Mr. Bonapart, of course, I answered him immediately, some 4-5 weeks ago. I am very glad to have got a true picture of your position, funny enough I had not the faintest idea that you were already in this home before.

...heaps of kisses and hugs, and with all my love, Your Papa

Send me your picture.

November 28, 1942

Dearest Daddy

I just received your letter from October 28. I was very happy with it. That letter put some cheerfulness in my life, because I was moody, and sulky for about a week because I had no mail from you. I also was afraid you'd bawl me out because you didn't have mail for me for quite awhile.

But I'll tell you what happened. A little girl in my house got Chicken pox and so we had to stay in the house for a week for quarantine. So after that I had a lot of makeup work to do. So I have not had any time to write you. Please forgive me. I am very glad to know that you are satisfied on behalf of my happiness in this home. Now you have a faint idea of how I live. Really, it's very pleasant....

The other night I dreamt of you. I dreamt that I ran away from the Home. (Please don't take it serious, because I wouldn't do such a thing). And as I left the gate I met you, and I was so happy, I kissed and hugged you in front of everybody in the street. Then you got a little house, and furniture and we moved in. The next day you got me a whole bunch of beautiful clothes and a lot of socks (boys). Then the next day I had to darn a lot of boys socks and I got a letter from you so really my dream came true.

My dream can have many interpretations; I like to think of it as intimate sharing with him, thus showing our love for each other, despite the gripes and complaints. I think the dream shows my real wishes. The letter continues:

About my report card, I assure you I tried my hardest to get A's more than Bs, but I find it very difficult to live up to my tries and hopes. In one week I shall get my second report card and I hope it well be better than the last one. At least I can say I tried.

I finally ask for money. Other children whose parents were in the vicinity got minor financial help for odds and ends, as well as presents for various occasions. I can't recall if I envied them, but I did get the idea that my father should help me.

Daddy, you're are darling for being so kind to me. You understand all my troubles. If it will be possible for you to send me a few dollars I would appreciate it very [much] *since my allowances is very small. I get 50 cents a month from which I have to buy soap, a toothpaste, a binder paper, and other school supplies. But please don't send any unless you're sure you can afford it. Meanwhile, how are you. I hope to goodness you're fine and healthy. I am, thank God. I'm about to go to a dance so I will close now.*

Millions of kisses,…. With heaps of love your affectionate daughter, Phyllis

✦ ✦ ✦

Quarantine was a big part of my life in the home and a frequent occurrence. In this case I was out of school for one week. If a child in our cottage came down with diseases that required quarantine— chicken pox, mumps, measles, and strep throat—those of us who had not had the disease were required to stay home from school, usually for a week. I never did get any of those diseases, or perhaps already had them in Vienna, but since I hadn't recalled if I had, and there was no record of my medical history, I often had to miss school for quarantine, perhaps several weeks in a year. Staying home wasn't much fun, as there was nothing to do except some homework that a friend would bring from school. Fortunately, I liked to read and would get a supply of books from the local library to help me endure the isolation. Sometimes, another child would be kept home for quarantine, but mostly, I was home alone.

One time, a few years later, a boy got typhoid fever, not a common disease then. We never did find out how he got it, but we all had to stay home. We were all inoculated and became sick from the shot, even the housemother. I remember many of us lying around the living room feeling feverish and nauseated and unable to lift our arms; nobody felt good enough to make meals. As an older girl then, I felt responsible for the younger children and tried to get the youngest children taken care of, though I didn't feel up to it. After a couple of days, we got over our nausea and painful arms. Then we had each other for company as we stayed home from school for another week.

Quarantine only inconvenienced us at the Home because they (Health Department or the Home's nurse?) wanted to control outbreaks in the cottages, and to limit the possible spread of the disease in the schools. Of course, other children, not living in the Home, did get these diseases, but they did not have to stay in quarantine. I never worried about getting a disease; fortunately, I was usually very healthy and full of energy.

❖ ❖ ❖

December 18, 1942

Dearest Daddy,

…Last week we got our report cards. Mine wasn't very good, but at least I tried. And then, I missed two weeks of school, one because of quarantine, the other because I had a bum stomach. So you see, I had a lot of work to make up and it wasn't as good as it would have been if I wasn't absent. It was as follows:

	Scholarship	Citizenship			
English	B+	S	Social Science	B+	S
Math	B+	S	Gym	C	S
Sewing	B+	S	Typing	C	E
Printing	A	E			

Honor points 65   Each A counts 15 pts, B= 10pts and C =5pts. Add my report card together, please. Do you think it's good?

We have Christmas vacation here now and I am positive I'll have a nice time during the days.

After living in the home nearly year, I finally gave him more details of my life in the Home, some already quoted in the previous chapter. He would not have known what the home looked liked, what kinds of children were there, how I happened to be there, etc. Mr. Bonapart's letter of September, which I don't have, may have told him of the legal arrangements.

And in a later letter (1/16/43) I wrote even more details of my school life:

...I think it is time I told you what I do all day in school. ... It is about 8:30 now. We go to school with whoever we wish to, and we don't have to go in pairs. We arrive in school about 8:50. The first bells rings. We go to our lockers, (each person has one), hang up our coats and get our books. Now I go to my first period which is English. The 9:00 bell rings and all his quiet. What we do in English and other subjects won't interest you, I'm sure. Times past, it is 9:45, and time to go to typing. I like typing because it's a lot of fun. I can do 21 words a minute. It's now 10:30 and I go to sewing. I like that too because it gives me the satisfaction of knowing I can sew my own clothes. At 11:15 we go to lunch, that is the lower division.

The same is the low and high 7th and low 8th; the others 8B, 9A-9B will eat while we are having Gym. Our lunch lasts for a half an hour and so does our Gym. We take tumbling, folk dancing and volleyball. I like tumbling best. Then I go to printing. That is my second elective, the first one is typing. I don't like printing because it's boring, we always do the same thing. We set a job and distribute and the same over again. I am the fastest person in a class of 30. So far this term I have gotten straight A -E in printing. 1:00 brings me to math. I like math. It's a lot of fun. We are studying volumes now, I have already taken Area of squares rectangles, parallelograms, triangles, trapezoids and circles. 1:45 brings a close of math and we go to social science. This is my favorite subject since we are studying about the development of the United States. I can never hear enough of this. I also like the teacher who teaches it to us. And now up 2:30 and home I go. In my next letter, I'll tell you what I do after school and at night....

I have told you of my everyday life, suppose you tell me about yours. What do you do all day; what kind of work do you do? What do you do in your free time? Please tell me about those things if possible, cause I am just dieing to know. ... When and if you write my uncle, please tell him I absolutely forgot German, and that is why I don't write to him. [Since I spoke no German with anybody, it is not surprising that I forgot it.]

How are you? I hope with all my whole heart, you are okay. I am, thank God. Goodbye for now with a million x million kisses, hugs and what have you in the manner of expressing love and gratitude. Love from your Phyllis, (Lizzy)

P.S. Please don't worry about me, as I'm O.K.

✦ ✦ ✦

1942 ended without any further mail from my mother. I do not recall how I dealt with that, but I did not think that she had died. My father was released from the interment camp in December, although I wouldn't know of it until 1943.

There had been big world changes as the Allies began fighting the Axis powers. The war was raging in many places—Africa, Europe, the Pacific Islands—and the Allies were being defeated on many fronts; however, America was just beginning to gear up to its maximum power. The country as well as the children at Homewood Terrace all wished and prayed for a quick end. I entered the world of teenagers, rushing to maturity, popularity, and Americanization. I had many new friends and was feeling very self-confident.

13

MAKING IT

Moving to the Home was a change in cultures—from an individual home to a group setting where relationships were spread out among many more people—and from a grammar school to a junior high school. Its population included children from the affluent St. Francis Woods and other upper-middle class neighborhoods, as well as children from working-class neighborhoods near the Home. The school was about 6 blocks from the Home, also on a steep hill. Aptos had good teachers and an elaborate gym and theater. Unlike Lawton, we changed classes every hour, changing teachers and classmates along the way.

I found a more sophisticated social scene at Aptos. Besides changing classrooms, some classes called "electives," boys smoking in the alley as we approached school, there were school dances. These new and exciting monthly events made me aware of popularity and affluence, things I had not noticed before, but now began to desire. As I entered this new world, I began to notice many things about my environment that I had not noticed before, including social status, personality, and prestige; adding to these changes was my personal transformation as I became a teenager, wanting to belong, to be popular and to succeed.

At the Home as at school, popularity resulted from nice clothes and boy-friends. More important was the quality of "surviving" life at the orphanage, which meant we should be as nearly normal as the non-Home world. "Making it" is how we talked about it. The staff spoke about making it as they guided us to proper behavior and careers. Housemothers spoke proudly of their former kids who had made it by becoming lawyers or doctors or businessmen. Girls who had made it had married well or had good secretarial jobs. Encouragement was given to students who excelled in scholastics, or who participated in leadership or athletics in school. These are values shared by the middle-class community at large, but are also time-honored Jewish cultural values.

The Home had its own pecking order of popularity, but there it depended on other criteria, in addition to being popular in school. For example, boys who made the school's teams were the heroes at the Home. Girls did not have as much oppor-tunity to become heroines unless they were popular with boys at school or if they held school offices. The consequences of not making it were never discussed as openly, but I inferred that it meant not becoming socially successful, a "drip," or worse yet, becoming a dropout or a delinquent. Only a few kids belonged to that last category—kids who did not do well at school, or who got into trouble with the law, mostly by skipping school. They did not stay at the Home very long while I lived there, although after the war, the Home became an institution for troubled and marginally delinquent kids. Even when I was there though, there were some troubled children, such as my bed-wetting roommate, socially shy and unhappy; some boys who had to leave for their anti-social behavior, others who had severe emotional problems, later committing suicide.

✦   ✦   ✦

For me, "making it," meant mingling with other kids at school, being invited to their activities, having boyfriends and girlfriends who were popular at school, and becoming popular myself: in other words, to be a typical teenager who wanted to be one of the gang. One old friend told me recently, "You always were more interested in being popular and with "in things." For me just surviving was never quite enough. I wanted to be popular and successful.

I had written to my father (6/29/42):

> *In two more weeks I shall be thirteen, just imagine, I am going to in my teens. I think it's simply wonderful. But I'm not going to be like other girls and wear lipstick and powder and who knows what. I am going to be really simple, so everybody will like me.*

Among friends we spent countless hours discussing how to get a better personality, how to look better and how to acquire many friends. Although looking better was on our agenda, particularly as it applied to clothes, I don't recall girls in the 1940's being as concerned with their looks as they are today, probably because the media hadn't yet set the standards; girls in their own schools did. Typically, we did not wear make-up until the last part of 9th grade, and then only lipstick, and those who did were sometimes called "cheap."

We wore our hair shoulder length and curly, not easy to do in the San Francisco fog. We tied scarves under our chins to protect our curls; sometimes we came to school with curlers under our scarf. I was concerned with my figure because I was overweight, and I and a couple of other chubby girls talked about getting thinner, but I did nothing about it. (Neither the housemothers nor the nurse ever counseled me to lose weight, although my father had earlier. Finally, when I was close to 15 years old, I was put on thyroid medication, to start my period as well as to lose weight.)

What I wasn't aware of then, but which can be documented in retrospect, is that teen-age fashions and culture were coming into their own in the 1940's, even as I was becoming a teenager. *Life,* a very popular magazine that was delivered to our Cottage, influenced me very much by giving me guidelines for how to be and how to become popular. Probably for the first time, a national magazine was devoting special attention to that demographic segment, showing the popular styles—plaid skirts, sweaters worn over blouses so as not to hug the body, loafers with pennies stuck in the ornamental design, bobby sox, worn just so, not straight up the leg, but folded specifically once or twice, white men's shirts worn open over T-shirts for casual wear along with pedal pushers, men's pajamas instead of nightgowns. Altering that uniform might earn one a stigmatic stereotype as to your school origin or even your moral character such as: "They're Mission (another high school) girls, or that's cheap." Then, *Seventeen* magazine began its publication dedicated to mold this generation. Since these magazines had national exposure, the teen culture became a national fad. I, too, was influenced by these magazines and wanted to be part of that scene. The swooning of young teenagers over crooners like Frank Sinatra was widely reported, thus making it a new phenomenon. Dancing and jitterbugging to the music of the big bands, such as Harry James, Benny Goodman and Glenn Miller, occupied our free time.

◆ ◆ ◆

My introduction to this new world began with the school dances. The school's principal (Mr. Durkee, called Mr. Turkey by the kids) was determined to teach us the social graces by having us attend a monthly, mandatory school dance beginning in 7th grade. He assigned students to several committees to decorate the gym in accordance with the seasons, to select the phonograph records, and to provide the refreshments. He was always present to make sure everybody was dancing, requiring that the boys ask the girls, though sometimes, there was girl's choice. There was some basic dance instruction in fox trot and waltz. Sometimes, boys would ask us to be their partners for the event. Sweet Jimmy, whom I had known at Lawton, asked me to go to my first school dance when I first came to Aptos. I was grateful since I was still a stranger at the school.

Some of the popular girls had a tradition of wearing a new dress to these dances, something to which I aspired, but which was quite unattainable for me because the Home issued us our clothing. The old bag (what I called her behind her back) who was in charge of that department was clearly of out of touch with teenagers' clothing requirements. I was a little overweight, but she insisted on giving me clothes meant for old, fat ladies, including girdles and corsets which no girl would or should wear. My desire to buy some nice clothes became very strong, but even when I started working around the Home, at weeding or dental assisting, I never earned enough to do very much to improve my simple wardrobe.

Another way of augmenting my wardrobe was by making clothes myself after I took the required sewing class in the eighth grade. I undertook some rather elaborate sewing projects. My first attempt, outside of class, was a pale green rayon dress with a square neckline that was trimmed in black velvet. It didn't turn out too well, but I felt a great sense of accomplishment and was proud to wear my creation. Even then, however, I knew the skirt did not hang well, and the neckline was not very neat because it is very difficult, if not impossible, to sew mitered corners to a velvet ribbon and then apply it to the dress neckline.

When I told my sewing teacher that my mother had been a seamstress, she said, "Jews make fine seamstresses—it's in their blood." That spurred me on, but I knew she was wrong. Sewing is not a gene that is passed on; it is not in the blood; it is a skill that is learned and it takes infinite patience, painstaking attention to detail (not one of my fine points), some concrete goals for one's wardrobe, and consciousness of style. I took sewing classes throughout my school years, eventually making a lined wool suit in high school. Sewing my clothes became a life-long hobby, as well as my artistic outlet, and a way for me to enhance or display my personality. I find it a relaxation and a creative endeavor.

By the ninth grade my desire for nice finery was so strong that I began stealing it. I am quite ashamed of this part of my history, but at the time my desires overpowered my morals. I toyed with the idea for a long time, until I talked myself into it, or at least talked myself out of feeling guilty about my activities; almost like making it acceptable under the circumstances. Actually, my stealing began earlier at the local dime store, where lipsticks, small ceramic animals to put on my dresser, and sometimes, candy, became the objects of my desires. Later, when I began going downtown some afternoons, I got the idea of stealing clothes. In the days before clerks counted what people took into the dressing rooms, I would take several garments in and try them all on, admiring them and coveting them. One sometimes came home with me, under all my own clothes. I did not do it too often, but for a while it was a temptation. I liked having something new to wear to school dances and to participate in the adulation that accompanied a new piece of clothing. Luckily, I never got caught, and by high school I stopped this offensive behavior, forever more conscientiously paying for my desires.

◆ ◆ ◆

Although I would never have admitted it, I was starved for love and attention. Unconsciously, I used my history of coming to America as an entry to friendships. More than two years in America now, my English matched my schoolmates' and my foreign origin wasn't discernible, making me feel very proud. However, I talked about my background because it was a way to initiate interest in me. The way I did that was to announce that I had gotten a letter from my father—then came the questions "where is he?" then "how did that happen," then "where is your mother," and so on, until my story had been told once more. I looked for compliments about my Americanization from my classmates and teachers. I liked the way people lauded me for my great adaptation to the American Way of Life; I liked their compliments on my good spirit and my efforts at becoming a good American. After all, *trying hard* is as American as can be, and I cashed in on the compliments. Of course, I was very motivated to be American. I quickly forgot all that was Austrian including its language.

I worked on developing friendships. Then, as now, I could not have too many. I read popular magazines which addressed that subject, spent a lot of time thinking about it, and I talked about friendship to anyone who was willing to discuss it. One such person was Mrs. Boughner, a housemother who would come to our cottage once a week to relieve our regular housemother. After dinner, I would join her with a cup of coffee and talk about how to make friends, how to be a good friend and how to be a likable person. I wanted very much to be such a person; I wanted everybody to love me. Although I was only thirteen, she talked to me as an adult, which flattered me. She had a good figure, nicely coifed gray hair, and unlike the other housemothers, wore fashionable clothes instead of the housedresses the others wore. I admired her wardrobe, figure and beauty shop-prepared hairdo.

According to the advice of magazines the paths to friendship were to be helpful and to be a good listener; so these behaviors became my conscious plans for becoming popular and well liked. This was particularly true of my relationships with boys. I was not popular with them, although occasionally a boy would make some overtures of interest towards me; but they would be boys I thought of as inferior—not popular, not athletic, not cute, and so I was not very interested in them. I did have some boyfriends, I guess, because I told my father about them, to his annoyance. The boys I found interesting were among the most popular at school, usually on some team, and considered "cute" by the popular girls. Since they did not find me attractive, I assumed the role of friend and confidant with them.

One such friendship was with Jerry, a boy who lived at the Home. He was popular with the girls there and at school. He was tall and good-looking, a good student and on the basketball team. When we had dances at the Home, all the girls wanted to dance with him, but he was aloof because he had a "crush" on Marian, who did not live at the Home. Her sister was a friend of mine at school. These girls came from a wealthy family, but they were not Jewish, so Jerry had some doubts about his ability to date her. I came to his aid by giving him a surprise birthday party. I asked for permission to the use the dining room in one of the empty cottages not in use as a residence, and one of the housemothers agreed to be our chaperone. I planned the party, for about 20 kids inviting Marian and several other kids from school and from the Home. I decorated the dining room with streamers of crepe paper and balloons and baked a cake, and generally arranged for the kind of party that was then common; we danced to records and played some games, such as charades and my favorite, kissing games such as "Spin the Bottle." I was the official hostess and master of ceremonies of the evening. The party was the beginning of my reputation as a hostess and organizer, and to some extent, an innovator, since children from outside had not been invited to the Home before. In my later life, I would enjoy giving parties and organizing activities.

In a letter to my Dad (1/12/44)

> *...Last Friday night I went to a birthday party and I had a lot of fun. They wanted me to be Master of Ceremonies because they think I have a swell sense of humor. This is the third party I've M.C. what fun.*

As a Master of Ceremonies I would also tell some jokes, though I doubt I was very good at it. In December 1943 I had received a book, *10,000 Jokes, Toasts and Stories* from our Godmother, (we could request a book for Chanuka) which might have supplied my jokes.

I don't remember how I financed this affair; the Home probably supplied the food and I somehow managed to scrape up some money for the decorations. Marian and Jerry's romance blossomed, and he was grateful to me for giving him the party. Although I had a big crush on him, I am not sure he knew it as I tried to maintain my "friend" role. It was a one-sided friendship, however, entitling me only to talking about him in a knowing way to my girlfriends at school, and to be recognized by him at school with a friendly hello. Still, these two favors helped me to feel more popular with the "in" crowd at school even if really made no difference.

◆ ◆ ◆

I tried many ways to become the center of attention at school. In class work, I always participated in discussions and in giving reports. One such report I remember was in an 8th grade science class, when I chose to report on syphilis, having chosen that article because syphilis looked like my name. I did not know what venereal diseases were. The newspaper article in the Sunday supplement was not specific since such subjects were not discussed openly, yet the disease was of great public health concern because of the influx of so many servicemen in San Francisco due to the war. The article warned of the seriousness of the diseases. The other students didn't know what I was talking about either since I don't recall any snickers, but the teacher was aghast and scolded me for my choice. From then on she required students to check with her before giving a report. Years later, when I had a job as sex educator for parents of children with developmental disabilities, I recalled my first venture at sex education in 8th grade with amusement, knowing how difficult it is to discuss sex freely and specifically.

✦ ✦ ✦

Still in 8th grade, I ran for office of Secretary for the 9th grade. I described the process in a letter to my father (December 3, 1943)

> *We have to get a petition and have sixteen members of our school sign it. Then we have to have a speech to pass the primaries. If I am one of the two to get elected I start my campaign. I make my speech before the school and then after about a week they vote. If I get elected, I will be secretary. Boy, what fun. Oh, I hope I get elected. My speech is going to be real funny.*

Candidates usually presented their qualifications by means of a skit or song in a school assembly during the run-off. The skit I devised was a take-off on the popular comedy radio show of Fanny Brice and her Daddy. The scenes on radio were so well done that it was easy to copy. Fanny was a spoiled little girl who knew how to get the better of her Dad. On stage during the school assembly, I sat sideways on the chair as though I was on his lap, arm around an imaginary neck and had a conversation with an invisible Daddy, telling him about my running for Secretary and why I'd be the right candidate. I might have told a joke. However, I was not good at public speaking, embarrassed, perhaps saying the wrong words, rushing through. Today, I can visualize that unpoised, clumsy girl, extending herself in a wild quest for popularity and attention—desperately trying to "make it"—but maybe making a fool of herself instead. Now, I am embarrassed for the girl, but she was not. Now, I have pity for the girl, but she had no pity for herself.

I was not elected. I wrote to my father (Jan. 13, 1944)

> *...You know, I ran for secretary. Well, I didn't pass my primaries because of one vote.*
> *We had two people to vote for in each office. Well, I voted for this girl and myself.*
> *The next day I found out she beat me by a point. So I guess that's that.*

I was very disappointed. However, failure to be elected did not dampen my quest for popularity, it made me try harder in other ways, but I did not run for office again. I strove to be better at public speaking by taking a drama class in the 9th grade, and joining the Drama club. I hoped I would learn some poise and presentation skills, though I had no illusions that I could be in a play. I did the make-up. I liked the drama club because the members were so friendly and uninhibited, and I hoped that I could learn to be that way. I felt part of the group.

✦ ✦ ✦

Sometime in the ninth grade, two of the very popular girls, Ottole and Nancy, invited me to come to their home after school. Ottole was really cute, fair, with blond curly hair, an open friendly face. Nancy was an Irish redhead with many freckles but was not as friendly. Ottole was Marian's sister and we shared gossip about Jerry and Marian. It was the first time that such an invitation had been extended to me, and I was thrilled with having "made it." I saw this invitation as a gateway to another world, one in which I wanted to participate. So, on that day, we took a streetcar from school, to Ottole's house in St. Francis Woods where I was most impressed by an electric blender, which she used to make milkshakes for us. Such luxury! Then we went to Nancy's house by streetcar, clear out in the Avenues near the beach, and spent the afternoon talking. I was unaware of it at the time, but now it seems to me that they were screening me for membership in their group. When Ottole and I were to take the streetcar home, I had no more money—I had spent all I had on the first two rides. I pretended to search in my pockets, and feigned surprise when I couldn't find any money: "Ottole, I seem to have lost the rest of my money. Can you lend me the carfare?" I felt shame and embarrassment for not having the fare. We continued to be friendly throughout school, but I did not enter her social circle, and we never were close friends.

Now I know that the social order was against me. It was too difficult to overcome the differences in social class, wealth, religion, and family in high school. Yet I never thought of obstacles of the status quo; I refused to consider them. I was sure that if I tried to become a better person, worked hard, if I improved myself, if I became more likable, someday I would make it. I'm proud that I never learned the lesson of social distinction because it's so undemocratic, and I believed in the American dream of social equality!

I was willing to aim for everything including scholarships to fancy private schools and applying for jobs over my qualifications. Thus I learned to be daring in my aspirations while taking responsibility for failures by trying harder next time. I never considered having lots of money or becoming rich as a goal, but I did want to have enough to have nice clothes.

◆ ◆ ◆

"Making It," sometimes called "survival," can take many forms and different meanings. Fortunately, at its most limited meaning—just to live another day—has never been my concern, but I am deeply moved when I read of such struggles. I am especially stirred by stories of children who were abused by parents or in foster homes and orphanages and of the homeless who often grew up in fosterhomes. That could have been my fate too. Motherless children have a bad time, even though as a society we try to find some substitutes. Our fairy tales underscore that point—has there ever been a good stepmother? Doesn't everybody hate Cinderella's stepmother for not giving Cinderella equal opportunities and some sense of worth? I often felt like a motherless, unwanted child, though at the time I would have denied that I needed a mother—I always thought I could overcome obstacles all by myself.

My big struggle with "making it" was with the sense of belonging. Overcoming obstacles requires determination, skill, desire, courage, all of which I had plenty of, enough even to encourage other people to take risks to try to overcome their barriers. However, to belong to a family, to belong to a group, to belong to a society and a culture—these require something else, something that I lost when my family was split up, and even before that when my parents left their families for Vienna. Thus, I knew that I needed friends to "make it" by creating my own group to which I could belong. My energy went into developing meaningful, deep relations that became a life-long effort. Because I had had a good beginning in my life with my parents where I belonged, felt wanted, worthy and encouraged to seek a better fortune, I was able to build an incredible web of friendship that sustains my sense of belonging.

I have "made it." I am grateful to America for the opportunity to strive at "making it" even if I don't always succeed.

14

CHOOSING A CAREER

As I read my letters to my father, I am often surprised by the pragmatic approach to life by my young self. Although I remember starting to work when I was nearly 13, I had not remembered how even at that time I was always planning for my future and trying to take charge of my life. Not only that, but I had given my father advice about learning a trade so he could get work in the United States.

My first opportunity of work came from being a frequent visitor at the Home's dentist. I can imagine myself asking a million questions about what was being done and why, so when I was given an opportunity to work there as a dental assistant, I jumped at the chance. It was more interesting and challenging than weeding the grounds, the usual work that was available. We were trained by the dentist to squirt water in the mouth, help with the cotton swabs and saliva ejectors and eventually to help prepare fillings.

I remember two of the dentists I worked for: a lady Dr. Greenwood and a man, Dr. Mordikian. She was a little bit of a woman hardly taller than I, wrinkled, with thick glasses and a rotten temper. All the children hated going to her because she was so unfriendly and yelled at them if they cried. One day I got the brunt of her temper: I wasn't paying as much attention as I should have been, and in a fit of temper, she reached across the dental chair, now occupied by a child, and slapped me hard across the face. I was stunned, not only by the pain of it, but by the insult. I was not used to being slapped; my parents never hit me that I could recall, and even in my foster home I had not been slapped. Slapping of faces sometimes occurred at the Home, but it was not common, and up to that point I hadn't been slapped. I refused to work for Dr. Greenwood again, or to go to her for treatment. It was good of the Home to give me that option.

Dr. Mordikian was much nicer; he had a pleasant disposition and encouraged me to learn more ways to help him. He also suggested I should think about the field of dentistry as a career. The only thing I didn't like about him is that he always pinched my cheeks—he said he liked the firm pink cheeks. I think I feared the recurrence of the molester of my days in Vienna, although Dr. Mordikian never did anything besides pinch my cheeks. I wrote my father of my interest in dentistry:

December 18, 1942

> *Dearest Dad*
>
> *...By the way, dad, I have decided what I want to be when I grow up. It's to be a dental assistant-secretary. That means to assist the dentist and then be his secretary and type, and do bookkeeping. It's a good job and pays from $120 to 135 from the beginning, and later 135 to 160 dollars a month. I am preparing for it in school by taking typing. I am in the low 8th grade now and when I reach the low 9, I'll take bookeeping and maybe shorthand. In that manner I can be a secretary all in itself if I can't get a job as a dental assistant.*
>
> *This home consists of several (about 10) cottages and about 20 children live in one house. One of them is the info[i]rmary. On the ground floor is a dental office. Each day, save Sunday, a dentist (a different one each day, but the same every week) comes to work on the children. A few girls (one girl to every operator) assist the dentists. I am one of them. One dentist is giving us a course on dental assisting. It's very thourough. Then we get paid 10 cents every hour. It is really worthwhile and I am*

getting good practise out of it. In case you don't know it, my teeth are having orthodonical treatment. My teeth are practically straight now.

March 16, 1943: My father is patient, but not enthusiastic about my choice. I suspect he didn't approve, but doesn't say so.

My little Darling,

...It is very interesting to hear about your plans for the future and that you already decided what you want to be when you are grown up. It is quite good when learning a lot of different things which in future life might be useful but a child of not yet fourteen cannot make up her mind in this regard, maybe some months later you will change your mind. We shall discuss this matter when I'm there, I think those few months will not make any difference for your decision.

April 15, 1943: I had to convince him of my serious, important decisions.

Dearest Daddy,

...When you said that I wasn't old enough to decide what career was to be, you where just a bit wrong. Here in America, children ten and eleven years of age decide what they want to be when they grow up. And I really must decide now because I have to choose electives. As I told before I want to be a Dental assistant. It is a good job, pays good money, it is always changing and usually meet good people. I am training for it now.

I would not mind being a surgeon but it takes too many years of college and I want to be married when I am about 21 or 22 years old. This may seem rather funny to you but, golly daddy, it's true. I don't want to waste all those years of college and money and then as soon as I finish with college be married. It is a waste of every thing and I must be thriftful. I am sure you will understand my point, you always do.

May 5, 1943: Yet I was open to new ideas.

Dearest Dad,

In your last letter (March 16) you hinted that I should not be a dental assistant. It gave me an inspiration and I am going to be a surgeon. I am almost sure that you will like that. Will you?

I had changed my mind and was sure he would approve. Perhaps he laughed at my quick switch, but he did not respond to my being a surgeon; instead

...I am glad to hear that you have given up the idea of becoming a dental assistant and that you want to go to college...I shall do everything to see you through it.

June 28, 1943: I have a problem in the workplace:

Dear Daddy,

...Thirdly, I have a big favor to ask. I am sure that I told you that I work at the Dentist as a dental assistant and that was the way I got my monthly allowance. There used to be three girls working here. One left about two months ago, which left me to be next in line for the job of senior assistant. A senior assistant gets 20c hour, while the second one in line gets 15c and the next 10c. The rest don't get paid. I worked up there for a year, and the senior assistant was leaving in two weeks. I was very happy about it because this meant I was going to get 20c an hour. About February, another girl joined up, and instead of having to work a half of a year before getting paid, she immediately got 15¢ and hour. True I was mad, but I kept my temper to myself. But last week when the main dentist said that the newcomer was to be senior—I was going to hand in my resignation. And believe me its coming in two days from today.

Now this is the favor. I don't know how much you make a month, but I do know that when you first sent me $10 you said you would do it again. Could you possibly send me $10 every three months? I hope that is not too much, but you see I am buying defense stamps and bonds, which have an interest in them, and when I am in college it won't be so hard for me to work through it. I hope with my whole heart you will send it to me, and I know I will be grateful for the rest of my life. I will be grateful without the money, but I'll be more grateful if I do get the money, because it will help me be a successful woman of tomorrow. Thanks a million.

I don't know why the other girl got the senior job, perhaps I really wasn't as good a worker. I did not turn in my resignation—perhaps I wasn't allowed to, or perhaps some other settlement was made, for I continued to assist until I left the

Home. However, it dampened my spirit about the fairness of the workplace.

I usually worked at the dentist's one afternoon and on some Saturday afternoons. Although the dentist usually did not come on Saturday mornings, when he did, it was my opportunity to avoid religious studies and services. Usually, I traded Saturday afternoons with another girl, so that we each had some Saturdays off. One time, Sylvia, the other girl, was supposed to work, but she claimed she didn't feel well so that she would not have to work. That had happened more than once, and this time, I was determined not to take her place. I was informed that I had to; the dentist would need an assistant and I was the only one who could do it.

The stubborn little kid in me said "No, I won't," and while preparing the noon meal I stuck my hands in the oven—enough to get them looking red, but not really burning them. I feigned a scream and pain, and was immediately sent to the nurse who treated me for burns by bandaging both my hands so that they were useless. "There," I said to myself, "now, I won't have to work, and I'll be able to go to the movie." However, it did not work out that way. Instead, I was told to stay in bed and rest that afternoon because of the severity of the burn! I was furious with the unexpected turn of events! Moreover, the real clincher was yet to come: The dentist called to say he could not come that afternoon, so Sylvia didn't have to work either! I spent the afternoon not resting, but lamenting my bad luck, the unfairness of life, and generally feeling sorry for myself, and she got to go to the movie!

◆ ◆ ◆

I had mentioned in the previous letter that I might want to become a surgeon instead of a dental assistant. When I was around fourteen, I decided to become a brain surgeon. My desire came from a book I had been reading, *Magnificent Obsession*, by Lloyd C. Douglas, the man who later wrote *The Robe*, a huge best seller. His books captivated my adolescent imagination and inspired my thinking about religion, God, spirituality, and service to mankind. *Magnificent Obsession* is a story of a playboy who causes the death of a prominent doctor and blindness to his widow by his reckless attitude and behavior. To compensate for his errors, he becomes a brain surgeon and restores vision to many blind patients never charging them for it and swearing them to secrecy about his good deed. The author's message suggested that in order to receive greater spiritual rewards, a person was to help people without letting others know, or at least without receiving monetary rewards. However, I read it to mean that being a brain surgeon is surely the noblest profession, one that reaps many praises and much attention. The power and accolades that came to the hero for doing heroic service through his skills, was the source of my ambition and it impressed me more than the spiritual aspect of giving.

It was my goal to become famous in some profession to receive adulation, thus I chose to become a brain surgeon, hoping that people would admire me and look to me for leadership and inspiration.

When I proudly told Mr. Bonapart of my plans, he laughed cynically: "Who do you think you are to want to be a doctor?" Your grades are not brilliant, and besides you are Jewish and have no money! You'd better think of a more practical occupation, like a secretary or a bookkeeper."

Actually, up to that point my grades had for the most part been good, which he conveniently forgot. Instead, he sent me to the psychologist to help me find a more suitable career goal. The psychologist had her own professional biases based on Freudian interpretations then in vogue.

Psychologist's Report, 7-6-43 (not known to me for decades):

> Phyllis' entire make-up suggested an aggressive, almost masculine component. This was apparent in her liking of horses, her enjoyment of scary dreams, in her independence and finally in her aggressive behavior manifestations with her cottage mother. Phyllis indicated that she had generally had been quite satisfied with Homewood Terrace, but that she found it difficult to accept authority. Thus, she has had trying times with her cottage mothers and more recently, with the dentist under whom she works. She agreed, verbally that she should make an effort to accept authority, but that she found it almost impossible to do so, especially when there was little reasoning involved in the restrictions that

were placed upon her. She related her own condition to the fight for independence that she read about. ....in summary: an extremely mature and superior girl intellectually whose personality make-up reveals an aggressive and almost sadistic trend.

The sadistic interpretation—according to Freud—comes from wanting to be a surgeon, that is, using knives. Moreover, for a girl to want to aim for the "masculine" professions made her aggressive and not quite right. I love reading her report now, because it just shows how far we've come in accepting women in all profession—not far enough, for sure, but still some progress has been made.

Since I did not know the result of this testing until many years later, it did not worry or influence me one way or another. Like children who want to be firemen or astronauts, I eventually gave up the notion of being a brain surgeon, but I still wanted to be a person that people admire for skills and knowledge. In the meantime, I took a college prep course with full intentions of becoming some kind of scientist.

15

GOOD NEWS, BAD NEWS

1943

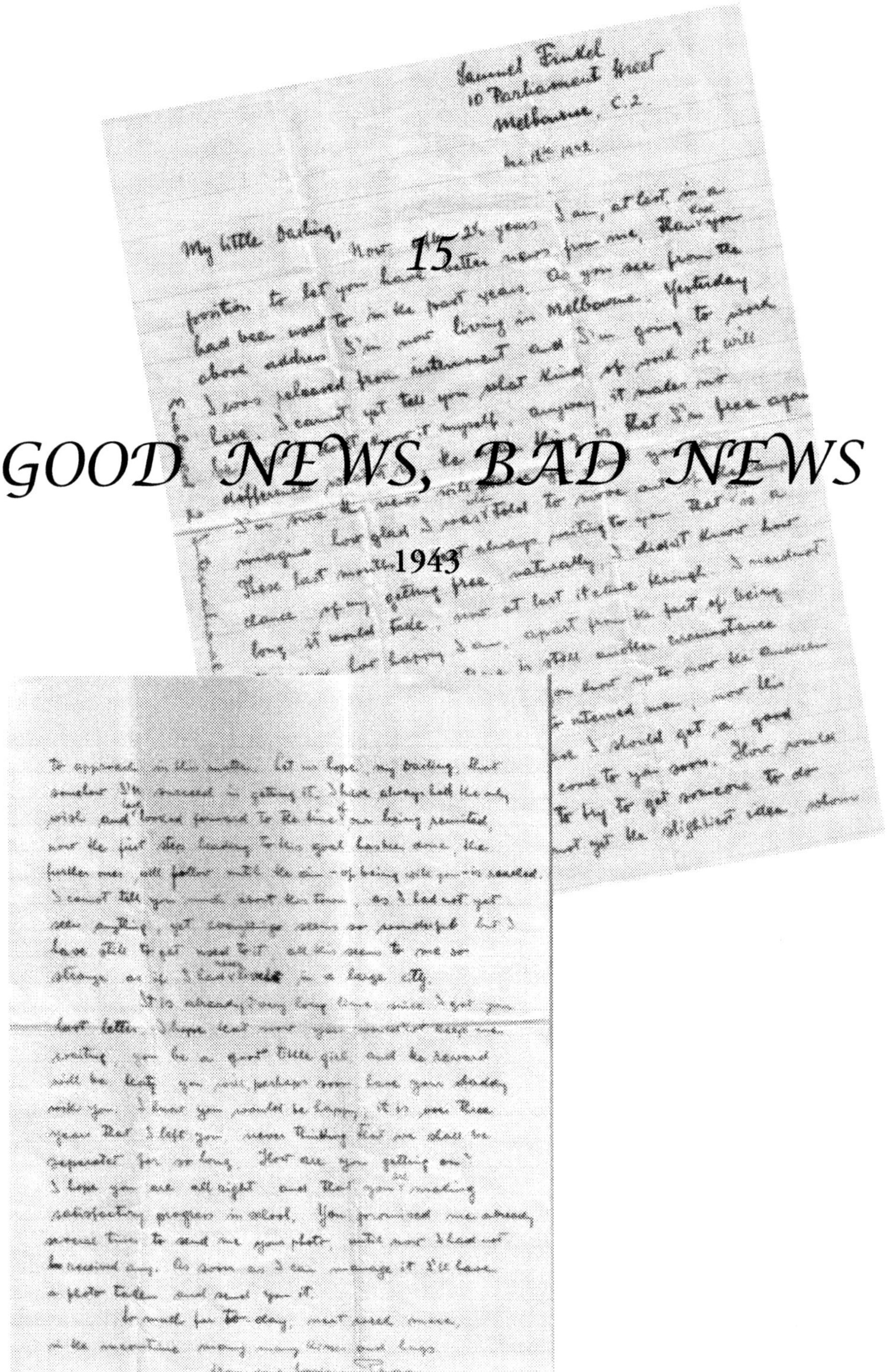
Samuel Finkel
10 Parliament Street
Melbourne, C.2.

My little Darling,
Now after 2½ years I am, at last, in a position to let you have better news from me, than you had been used to in the past years. As you see from the above address I'm now living in Melbourne.

to approach in this matter. Let us hope, my Darling, that somehow I'll succeed in getting it. I have always had the only wish and looked forward to the time of our being reunited, now the first step leading to this goal has been done, the further ones will follow until the aim – of being with you – is reached.
I cannot tell you much about the town, as I had not yet seen anything, yet everything seems so wonderful but I have still to get used to it. All this seems to me so strange as if I have never been in a large city.

It is already a very long time since I got your last letter. I hope that now you wouldn't keep me waiting, you be a good little girl and the reward will be that you will perhaps soon have your daddy with you. I know you would be happy, it is now three years that I left you never thinking that we shall be separated for so long. How are you getting on? I hope you are all right and that you are making satisfactory progress in school. You promised me already several times to send me your photo, until now I had not received any. As soon as I can manage it I'll have a photo taken and send you it.

So much for to-day, next week more, in the meantime many many kisses and hugs
from your loving Papa.

The wish and hope that we would soon be reunited was a common theme of our letters. Although my father had gotten an affidavit previously, it had not possible for him to immigrate to the U. S. because he was still considered a prisoner of war and interned. Finally, after $1^1/_2$ years of internment, he was released. Adding his time in camps in England, he had been interned for $3^1/_2$ years, but now he would be able to emigrate to the U.S., at least in theory. His joy at freedom is wonderful to read.

December 12, 1942, from Melbourne, received February 5, 1943

My little Darling,

Now, after $2^1/_2$ years I am, at last, in a position to let you have better news from me...As you see from the above address I'm now living in Melbourne. Yesterday I was released from internment and I'm going to work here. I cannot tell you what kind of work it will be as I don't know it myself, anyway, it makes no difference what it is, the main thing is that I'm free again. I'm sure this news will please you, and you can imagine how glad I was when told to move out of the Camp...

He never told me of his living circumstances in the letters. In 1999 I went to Australia to follow his footsteps. He lived in his first place only a few months, then moved sometime that summer to a modest house relatively close to his place of work where he rented a room. Also, his immigration status was changed. The letter continues:

I needn't tell you how happy I am, apart from the fact of being restored to normal life there is still another circumstance which makes it still lovelier. You know up to now the American Consul would not grant Visas to interned men, now this obstacle is removed and in case I should get a good affidavit I would be able to come to you soon. How would you like it? Well, I'll have to try to get someone to do it for me, though I have not yet the slightest idea whom to approach in this matter. Let us hope, my Darling, that somehow I'll succeed in getting it.... now the first step leading to this goal has been done, the further ones will follow...

...I cannot tell you much about this town...yet everything seems so wonderful, but I have still to get used to it, all this seems to me so strange as if I had never lived in a large city....

And from Dec. 28, 1942

...I'm now living in Melbourne, a large and beautiful city, with fine buildings, etc. It is really an excellent feeling after so long a time of loneliness to move about in streets overcrowded with people, parks and the beach etc.

Please do write often, I shall enclose an international coupon for reply stamp in every letter, thus you would not be obliged to pay for it out of your pocket money.

So much for today, all my love, heaps of hugs and kisses, your Daddy

Feb. 5, 1943   Joy at last! I have advice for his work

Dearest Daddy,

Last week I received your letter about your release from internment. You can't imagine how happy I was. I ran all around the home telling everybody the good news....Really, Dad, I am so happy about it, I can hardly believe it. Do you think you'll be able to come here soon? What kind of work do you do? I should think you'd work in a defense factory. If you need help in getting an affidavit, just say the word and I'll put my greatest effort in getting you one....

Monday was the beginning of a new term and I'm now in the High 8th grade. Since I was in quarantine the first week, I do not know how I will like it.

...Millions of kisses, wishes, hugs and squeezes. Love, Phyllis

December 28, 1942   A letter from Mr. Bonapart responding to my father's October letter, in which he apparently was concerned about my happiness sometime last summer. The long delays of mail did not make communication meaningful.

Dear Mr. Finkel,

I received your letter dated October 2nd, which was obviously delayed in transit.

Your ability to impose such sound philosophical interpretations to the unfortunate circumstances which have befallen you and your family, impels me to explain again Phyllis' actual mental and spiritual status here in America. I infer from your letter that Phyllis has given you the impression that she is down-hearted. Unquestionably she misses you and her mother, and there are moments, especially at bedtime, when her thoughts of you bring sadness to her. But she is a bright, cheerful youngster who seems to be enjoying her home life, her school life and her many friendships.

It is natural that Phyllis should want you to know how much she really misses you, and in her endeavor to convey this thought to you she is unable to tell you how much she really enjoys her life in America. It is possible that she has taken on the attitude that if she gives you the impression that she enjoys herself, that you may not believe that she really misses you and her mother. I can assure you that she misses you both a great deal, but I think that it is only fair that you know that she is in excellent health and that she is able to get the most enjoyment and the greatest benefits out of the opportunities which this life affords her.

The circumstances involving Phyllis' experiences with Mrs. Rabinowitz were of such a nature that not very much need be said about it. Mrs. Rabinowitz, with the very best of intentions, endeavored to make a home for Phyllis. However, her business has always required all of her time and most of her energies. Consequently all of the problems and difficulties which ensued and the bad feelings which grew up between Mrs. Rabinowitz and Phyllis were purely coincidental. Having failed in one home situation, it was not easy for Phyllis to adjust in another. Undoubtedly Phyllis brought with her to the Reingold family the effects of her bad experiences with Mrs. Rabinowitz.

If it were not for the fact that Phyllis is so happy at Homewood Terrace and that she is so strongly opposed to another foster home placement, I should insist that she try again to live with a private family. It is clear that the only family outside of Homewood Terrace with whom she desires to live is her own, and since she cannot yet have her mother and father with her, I shall keep her at Homewood Terrace until she is ready and willing to move.

It is contrary to the rules set down by our Federal Government controlling the care of refugee children that they live in an institution. Special circumstances up to the present has made it possible for Phyllis to remain with me. I am sure that no one in authority is this country desires to make our unfortunate young visitors unhappy. So you may rest easy in the thought that Phyllis' welfare and happiness will always be a factor in our plans for her....

Sincerely, Benjamin Bonapart

For the time being, Mr. B.'s letter made my father feel better about my behavior. However, I do not recall the bad feelings with Aunt Laura, unless my complaints about Moe's teasing were the source of the strife. Anyway, that was over two years before. Of course, I didn't read this letter until recently.

March 5, 1943

> *My Darling,*
>
> *...I received another letter from your director, and I'm mighty glad to hear all these nice things about you. I am really happy to learn how well cared for you are there, this was my main concern but now knowing how kind the people are, under whose care you have been put, I am perfectly at ease and very glad that my little darling found such a good home. ...Some weeks ago I sent you $10...which no doubt comes in handy.... The job I've got here is not in my line, but anyway I'm satisfied chiefly because...I'll be able to come over to you.... Your Daddy*

March 11, 1943   Making excuses for not writing more; but a long letter makes up for it.

> *Dearest Daddy,*
>
> *I haven't heard from you for three weeks now, but I haven't written to you for a long time. Honestly, Dad, I have a lot of homework. I am in the high eighth grade now and we are sure piled up with homework. Right now I am in Math. I hurried extra through the test so I could write to you. The test was very simple and I was finished in five minutes. In twenty minutes we go into Social Science. It is the last period of the day, and I am very fond of it. Our teacher is very intelligent and when she says something, you simply have to remember it. We discuss the war and it is very interesting. On Friday we discuss war news only. Oh, Oh, here is the bell. Well, I'll have to continue tomorrow because our house is moving to another house today, and we'll have to help move. It is going to be painted.*
>
> *Hello, Dad, this is tomorrow. I am in the library supposed to be writing a project on Democracy versus Dictatorship. I have it all planned, all I have to do now it to type it, and I can't type it now because I have to get Mr. Bonapart's permission first. He's out right now, so I'll just have to wait.*

A welcome surprise about good behavior.

I have some good news for you. Well, every year at the home there is a "prize day."
On this day the children get awarded different prizes, such as good behavior, leader-
ship, improvement and various other things. Well, I got a $5.00 prize. That will
come in very handy. I plan to add a few $s to that buy myself a best dress. Aren't you
proud of me? You should be...

How are you?...In two weeks we get report cards I expect to a very good one because
I work real hard. The subjects are hard to but, I say if there's the will, there's a way...
Love,   Phyllis

Unfortunately, the next month, my prize behavior went awry, and I got into
trouble, but I tell him the good news first.

April 15, 1943

Dearest Daddy,

I received your letter [Mar. 5] and I was exceedingly happy to receive it. I had not
gotton mail from you for about two months and I was very worried. But I am glad
it has come. I wrote to you just the same every two weeks.

Daddy, you're the sweetest man on earth, there is no one like you. You are so under-
standing and kind. I just can't express myself to tell you how much I love you. Have
you any idea when you can come here? I can hardly wait. Is there anything I can do
to help? ...

Two weeks ago, I received my report card. It was pretty good. It wasn't quite as good
as I expected it. At least I got on the Honor roll.

Typing	*C+*	*E*	*English*	*B+*	*S*
Gen. Sci	*B*	*E*	*Gym*	*B+*	*S*
Math	*B*	*S*	*Social Sci*	*A*	*E*

60 pts Honor roll

Are you satisfied? I am sure it will be better next term.

This is the first time I show my anger in a letter and explain how I got trouble with Mr. B. The letter continues:

Now, comes the bad news. I am mad. I can do anything now, swear, stamp my foot and all. About three months ago something terrible happened which I will never forget. Neither will they. I never wanted to tell you before, I had to let you know about it now, please don't worry about, because I am really not unhappy. I have lots of friends and fun and I think my boyfriend likes me and all is splendid except this.

About three months I went to the show and coming back I had an argument with a cottage mother. Naturally I stuck up for my rights and she slapped my face a few times. I went down to see Mr. Bonapart with her and she told him a bunch of lies and he naturally believed her. Ever since then he was terrible unjust: everything I did was always counted against me. I work and I receive about $4.00 or $3.50 a month. I used to have a very poor wardrobe, so I worked in order to get a nicer one. Last Tuesday a lady gave me quite a few pieces of cloth. On the same day I received your $10. I wanted to save about $5.00 and with the rest get a skirt. This is where I got mad. He (Mr. Bonapart) said I would have to put the money in the bank and leave it there. I was terribly mad that he said that. I said my father sent me that and told me to spend it the way I want not the way you do.

I want to walk away from my troubles again.

I've made up my mind to take the money out by drizzles and get the skirt after all. I've also made up my mind that I am going to try and leave the home. Damn it anyway. Excuse my language, but I am what you call mad. As I said before don't let it bother you because I know what I want and I am going to get it by hook or by crook.

Enough of that for now. Can you tell what kind of work you do? I would be most interested…I hope you are fine and healthy. I am thank God. I still go out with Mrs. Rabinowitz.

Love & kisses, & hugs from your ever-loving daughter Phyllis

P.S. Now that I have money people are jealous because they aren't as successful in attaining their want. Serves them right, the dogs (Mr. Bonapart and staff.)

March 16, 1943 This letter shows the incongruity of our correspondence: Just two months ago everything was fine, and that is what he is responding too; in the meantime, the letter above shows how things have changed. Just two weeks before, he complained about not getting mail for two months, and sternly told me that he would only write when he received a letter from me.

> *My little Darling,*
>
> *This week I cannot complain about the lack of news from you, I received two letters , Dec. 19 and Feb. 5. I have been very glad to hear all the good news of how happy you are, the fact that your are feeling fine and enjoy life there gives me more pleasure than anything else. It was really very nice of you to send me your picture, though it is very small and the features are hardly to be discerned, still it gives me some idea of how my little darling has grown up during the last four years. I think it is now out of place to address you as "little darling", but I cannot help doing so, as before my eyes is always this darling little girl who saw me off when I left her. Who thought of it that this separation meant to last a few months only would be prolonged for years....Few days ago I got a telegram from Arnold asking my particulars, this is to say that he is going to take up steps regarding my immigration. I think all this formalities will take some 5-6 months, and then the way is open to my girl.... Love, Papa*

Mr. Bonapart wrote to my father about his release from internment that had occurred almost five months before.

PACIFIC HEBREW ORPHAN ASYLUM
AND HOME SOCIETY
BENJAMIN BONAPART, EXECUT1VE DIRECTOR
San Francisco, May 8, 1943

Dear Mr. Finkel:—
I received your kind letter today and am writing to you at once inasmuch as I have to be away from San Francisco for a week or more. It is good to hear that your release has been consummated and that you are now able to plan to join Phyllis. Being able to plan, is in itself a great release from bondage. It is good to give thanks to God to know that so much has been achieved. Living in slavery one's hopes are usually in fantasy. Now you are experiencing real freedom and the progress of the War makes it possible to hope realistically.

Phyllis is in her usual good health. She was very excited and happy to receive your letter this morning which I gave to her immediately following religious services in the Synagogue. She is indeed a good child and I am sure that you will find a great deal of happiness in your reunion. Let us hope that this comes soon.

With kindest best wishes, I am
Sincerely yours, B. Bonapart

May 22, 1943 A good report card should please him

Dearest Daddy,

I did not receive any mail from you this past week, but that makes no difference. This Tuesday I received my report card, and if I say so myself, it was very good. This is what I had:

English	A	S	General Sci.	B	E
Math	A-	S	Typing	B+	S
Social Sci	A-	E	Homeroom		E
Gym	B	S			

I get a privilege pass which you get if you get 75 or more points. Each "A" gets 15 pt., "B"=10 pt., "C"=5 pt., "D"=0 pt., "F"=-5 although there were three girls in our class who get all A's mine was good.

Dinner is over now. We had combination salad fish, potatoe salad, corn, cake and milk. It was very good. For about fifteen minutes I played cards with another girl. Then I was suprised, when my cottage mother gave me a new suit. It is gray, white, yellow and I like it very much. I was so suprised. Tomorrow I am going to get another dress with the money you sent me, as a reward for a good report card....

The problem with the $10.00 in the previous letter (April 15) in which I had been so angry apparently has been resolved. I continue:

Now, about you. ... I have asked you over and over again what kind of work you do. Can you tell me this? Will you be able to send me your picture? I hope so. Oh, by the way, Daddy, last time, or the time before that, I wrote you all about a certain $10.00. Well, I was wrong. I am glad that [I] put [it] in the bank, 'cause now I can buy a dress. I hope you didn't worry yourself about it. If you did please forget about it. With love and kisses, hugs, from your ever loving daughter. Phyllis

Mrs. Goss and I had a good relationship for over a year, but it eroded. I can't recall the incident after the show (letter of April 15), yet in May I was given special clothes, but by June I was moved to another Cottage. I don't remember exactly how Mrs. Goss and I became antagonists, but I think it happened because I was asked to do more than my fair share of the work. Since I was usually quite responsible and capable, I was called upon to substitute if another girl failed in her duties. If someone was incapacitated I had to fill in. Over time, I resented losing my free time and objected vociferously. However, the one huge confrontation with Mrs. Goss that I recall most vividly developed about her procedure to wake us.

The buzzer, with bells positioned in both the girls' and boys' wings as well as downstairs, was used to wake us and to call us together for meals. In the mornings Mrs. Goss leaned on that buzzer quite a long time, and since my bed was nearly under it, it was quite unpleasant to be awakened in this manner. I requested that she be a bit gentler with the buzzer, perhaps doing it intermittently. Her response to my request was to do it even longer the next time. We continued to have some arguments about this, but it seemed to me that one time it was just too much. So one day I stepped on a chair and cut the wire to the bell. It took a day for the damage to be noticed and to be fixed, and Mrs. Goss rightly assumed that I had been the one to cut the wires, although I feigned innocence. A few days later, in response to her heavy finger on the buzzer, I cut the wires again. This happened several times; I was finally punished for the action. It was the beginning of the end of a peaceful relationship with Mrs. Goss, and I was ultimately kicked out of Cottage 42. However, I never told my father what I had done.

✦ ✦ ✦

June 10, 1943   Already in Cottage 24 which was similar to Cottage 42 in most ways. Miss Lewison was the housemother. She was an elderly spinster who had been with orphanage forever. I didn't get as close to her as I had been with Mrs. Goss until my recent troubles.

Dearest Daddy,

I received your dear letter today, after a long time of waiting. I just realized how easy it is to write every week. It doesn't even take an hour. So from now on, every Wednesday night Mr. Samuel Finkel, Esq...will get a letter mailed to him.

It's near the end of school, nine days to be exact. I am very happy about it. I hope to get a good report card. You asked me to tell you what I do during school. Well, I will commence to begin to tell you my daily routine. Here goes:

I tried a little humor. It's refreshing,—it seems my other letters are so serious.

As I told you before, I get up in the morning,...most people do. Then I either make the breakfast or lunches or maybe (every five weeks) I loaf in bed till it's time to eat breakfast. (If there is any?) After using all my strength chewing a hard, dried-out piece of bread, (with water) I make my bed, do my work, get dressed for school, and then, I make a 50 yard dash for school. If it is my lucky day, I get to school with my face all flushed, panting and looking like a mess, about a half minute before the bell rings. Then comes, my adventurous adventure. First I go to typing. There I make a dozen errors erase, strike over and get an F. Oh, well, it's all in a days work. Ah, here is English, my good friend. (I hate it, I just want to make a good impression.) The teacher is an old bag, wig, glasses and false teeth. Every time she calls on you, and you start saying your answer, she opens her mouth and makes you swallow your heart, liver, stomack, etc. Talking about heart, liver etc., it brings me to the General Science class. We are studying about electricity and a bunch of other junk. I like General Science because I have a nice time reading jokes, stories, etc. My favorite period, Gym. There we swing on the ropes, bruise ourselves, kill ourselves, who cares any how? I hope you don't. Lunch, ah, how I love it. In lunch we eat- - -gossip and maybe study for a test. (If we care enough about it.) Math is just the same as General Science, because I nearly always read. And so we come to the last period of the day: Social Science, the one period of the day were I am ambitious. Instead of reading things for fun, I invite myself to take place in an argument which is about the war. I am the nosy kind of kid, I always have to stick my two cents (in other words I always have to stick my nose into everything.) Then I go home. I work making dinner. I slop food together any old way. I don't care. I then take my bath. Then I eat dinner. Then I work. Then I go to bed. Then I do the same routine all over again.

Continued next week.

Meanwhile how are you? So am I. Millions of kisses hugs, squeezes, bla bla...Everloving Phyllis

P.S. Please don't take this seriously. I tell you the real routine next week. I was only joking to make you laugh. Love, Phyllis

June 28, 1943 (typed—a new skill revealed!) Good news always comes before the bad.

Dearest Daddy,

I wrote to you last week on Wednesday, but when I mailed it, the postage stamp came of, and a week and a half later it was returned to me. And because that happened, I am going to write you two letters; last week's and this week's.

First of all, last Friday I received my report card. It was pretty good. Here is what I got.

Subject			Final	
Gym	B+	S	B	S
Math	A	E	A	E
Social Science	A-	E	A	E
Typing	B	S	B	S
English	A	S	A	S
General Science	B-	E	B	E

In the finals, all the grades of the whole term are summarized and are recorded in the conselors Report which is used later for reference. No minuses or Pluses are alowed in the finals. Do you like my report card? I hope so.

Secondly, I was a bad girl and I was moved into another cottage. When you come to America, I will tell you what really happened. I guess by now, you must think I am the hardest thing to get along with, because I have moved three times now. Daddy, I am really telling you the truth, it is not altoghether my fault that I move so often. I believe I do something wrong, but on the whole I think it was my cottage-mother's fault. She is a very stingy woman, who cares only for herself. That is what got my guts. And she takes it out on the little kids. So I stuck my two cents in, and argued. So, naturally, being a fink as she is, and gloating when anybody is in trouble, told on me. Then when I tried to defend myself, she told a bunch of lies. Mr.Bonapart said that he could always get another Phyllis Finkel, but another Mrs. Goss is very rare.

So whether I was right or I was wrong he stuck up for her. So here I am, in Cottage 24 and truly I like it much better than 42, because the cottage Mother Miss Lewison is so much more decent....

Tell me, what do you do every day, how do you enjoy yourself, what kind of recreation you enjoy yourself with. I've told you lots of times what I do around here. Why don't you tell me? Why don't you send me your Photograph? It is vacation now, and I am going swimming every week, plus participating in a tennis tournament.

...On July 22 I am going to camp. Solong for now, with a million heaps of kisses, hugs, squeezes, and so on from your everloving daughter, Phyllis

I have no recollections of the encounter with Mr. Bonapart and Mrs. Goss, or about the little kids that started the confrontation. It was hard for me to admit to wrongdoing; did I really think nobody would find out? In retrospect, my misdeeds were not so horrible, but it seems my punishment was always to be sent away. As an adult, I find that when there are disagreements, I want to walk away from them. Speaking up for myself as a youngster did not result in good outcomes at that time, so I mainly stopped it. I did not learn to compromise or search for other solutions.

July 9, 1943   Received Sept. 16

My little Darling,

I received both your letters of May 5th and 22nd and was sorry not to be able to answer you at once because of a cold I caught last week and which confined me to bed for a few days. Now it is all over and I am perfectly healthy again. Well, I must say, at last I received two letters with nothing to worry about, on the contrary, I was really delighted when reading all this good news. I am very glad about your report card, it is really good and I hope you will always keep it on the same level.

...It is good to hear that you feel now that you were wrong in accusing your cottage mother and the others of the staff. ...By the way, some 2 weeks ago I received a letter from Mr. Bonap.[May 8] telling me nice things only, if you would read it I am sure you would say that you could not have found a better friend than him. I write you about this because I want you to appreciate his very best intentions towards you showing your gratitude and acting according to his instructions...

Heaps of kisses and hugs and all my love, Your Daddy

Friday, July 9, 1943 A joy filled summer vacation, and a bit of history of the United States

Dearest Daddy,

One week has passed, and again it is time to write to you and I am glad. Two and a half weeks have passed since school ended. Since then, I have had no mail from you. I can imagine it is because I did not write to you, (you must think) although, I wrote to you and the letter came back. I hope it does not happen again. In those two and a half weeks I have had the time of my life. I'll tell you what I did so far.

The first week I was nearly always playing tennis getting ready for a tournament. The first game I won, the second I lost in the tournament. The first week on Tuesday I went swimming as I do every week. The next week I played in various games such as ping pong, badminton, basketball and volleyball. I really had a swell time. And this week I really had fun. Monday was Independence day. On that day, 167 years ago, a declaration of Independence was written and signed, declaring the thirteen colonies in America free from the British stronghold. This day is usually celebrated with fire crackers, noise, parades, noise, parties, noise and so forth. At the home, each year on the fourth of July, we hold a track meet. It last almost all afternoon. We have races, jumps, both broad and high jumps, shot put and a few others. This year it was very exciting. The teams were almost even and at the end we had a tie. After the meet we had icecream.

When dinner was completed we went outside and I played tennis again. And I won, too. On Tuesday afternoon I did all different things. First I played basketball and then I took a sun-bath. After that I did a little shopping. Wednesday morning I worked and in the afternoon I fooled around. That night, a group of fourteen girls and boys went swimming. I had a lot of fun, diving, swimming and ducking other kids. After swimming we had something to eat. We arrived at eleven thirty at home. I went swimming again on Thursday, which brings us up to date.

I have explanations about my bad temper earlier in the year when I lost the dental assistant's job (Careers). Releasing my anger in letters dissipated the angry feelings, and I soon forgot them. The letter continues:

> *…The next time you get a letter like that, please don't believe it, I write crazy things when I am mad.*

> *But there were two things I don't remember writing. One was that of a boyfriend. It's true I have one, a very fine boy, with a lot of character, personality, brains, intelligence and looks. But I never remember writing about him. I also don't remember writing, that I wanted to leave the home. I do, if I can go home with you, otherwise not.*

I had written that I wanted to leave the home in the letter of April 15. Then in a more serious note, I praise him.

> *Now, that I've read your letter I see how selfish I've been in only thinking of my self instead of all the captives in the hands of Nazi torture. I guess I never looked at it that way. Now, after all the times I felt sorry for myself, I see how wrong I was, and how good it is to have a Daddy like you to put me to my senses. I still say you're the best man and father in the world. I read you're letter and I cried and it did me good to cry. The oldest girl in this house, whose name is Lois, read your letter and told me she thought you were a fine, refined, well-educated and intelligent man and she admired you for it. She told me to say "hello."…(I hope you don't mind her reading the letter, she doesn't usually).*

> *In two weeks I am going to camp. I'll write to you twice from there and you'll have to forgive me if they are short letters. Today is the ninth, and in one month from today I'll be fourteen years old. I am very thrilled.*

> *Now about you. I have asked so many times to tell me what you do every day and how you spend your free time, but you never did. I wish you would. Could you send me a photograph of you. What kind of work do you do. How are you. I hope you are feeling fine, and that my stupid letters don't get you down.*

> *Could you please send me Uncle Max's address and please tell me if I can write English. I would love to carry (on) correspondence with him.*

> *…love, kisses and hugs your everloving but senseless daughter. With all my love Phyllis*

Saturday, July 24, 1943   A new adventure, going to camp, but I complain.

Dearest Daddy,

…The name of this camp is Wasiata. I don't know whether you remember when I went to camp three years ago and I liked it very much, well, this camp isn't half as good. There is no horseback, no rowboating, no long hikes and a lot of other things. I don't mean to be complaining, but in comparison it really stinks. It is one great big routine. Sleep, play eat and sleep and so forth. There is no variety. Today there is Circus day. It's going to be a lot of fun I guess. They have a swimming pool here and it's very nice. We go swimming twice a day for an hour. I also take archery, which is about due now. We have camp fires without a fire. But it's fun anyhow.

Meanwhile how are you? I hope you are enjoying yourself as I am. There are lots more things to write but I haven't the time. … All my love, Phyllis

Saturday Aug. 7, 1943   Back from camp, but regreting it; I give a detailed description of activities.

Dearest Daddy,

I am home from camp already and I certainly wish I wasn't. Last week I wrote you I did not like camp, but I certainly do now. Saturday before last we had a circus day. Our cabin had to lead the parade with our tin band. Pots and pans and so forth. Then we had lunch and the regular routine. Rest and swim and then we held a sideshow. I was a fortune teller. I didn't know what I was talking about when one girl came in who really knew her business. She made a lot of fun of me. Monday we went on a hike. I had just loads of fun. At one time we had to climb a big, fat, round, slippery log which was on a steep slope. I got half way across when I started slipping, and I went almost all the way down. I got up though.

Irene, my girlfriend, really had a lot of fun. Tuesday was twin day. Irene and I were Siamese twins. We read a little poem together and got a lot of applause. Wednesday was topsy-turvey day. We wore sweaters and blouses inside out and backwards. The chairs were upside down; plates were on top of the cups; the counselors did K.P. instead of the girls and we sang evening grace in the morning. I had a good time.

There is a boys camp near our camp, which invited us to come to a camp fire. We accepted the invitation and had a joint campfire. After that we had dance. They had a bunch of nice boys there. We had refreshments and a lot of dancing. It was simply swell. The next day was a just a regular day. Swimming, Archery, craft and food. Friday was secret pal day. On Thursday night we picked names out of a box. Each person had someone else and it was a secret who they had. For instance, the girl I picked was a very swell girl who I really adored. Well, I did nice things for her all day long and at night I gave her a present and I told in a note who I was. I think it was lots of fun. Saturday we had a beauty salon. I washed faces and supposedly gave facials. This was all done for the world service, the organization of the Y.M.C.A

Monday we went on a short hike and came back in time for swimming. That day as I was on the diving board, ready to dive in without a spring, I found myself springing, then going glidingly into the air and I did the most beautiful dive. Before, you know, all I could do was to go to the edge of the diving board, pondering whether to go in or not and after about ten minutes deciding to go back and dive off the side. I am now a fairly good diver and a good swimmer. I love water. When I grow up and I am prosperous and successful I am going to own a swimming pool in my back yard.

Anyway going back to camp, on Tuesday I did the same things as on all other days. I went swimming for three hours. Wednesday afternoon I went home. I was very sorry to leave and the next year I hope I can go back for a full six weeks. Camp is really so swell. I got a beautiful tan, just the kind I always wished for, if you recall.

I am still wearing bands, although my teeth are straight; they are waiting for a tooth to come down. Then I'll get them off. Do you remember when I was a little girl I always used to get a chocolate bar when I got up? And how I used to love candy? Well, now I hardly eat any because of my bands. I hardly miss it. ...

A bit of reminiscing about our separation, and my appreciation of America.

Have you heard from Mother? I haven't, and I certainly wish I would because I am dreadfully worried about her. I haven't heard from her for almost two years. Three days ago and four years, you, very heroicly left us and as you left us we said to ourselves, assuringly, "We'll see him in one or two months and we'll be reunited again." And so, the same assuring, hopeful spirit has been in our hearts and it will remain there till we are together again. And I know I am luckiest of our family because I am in America. I don't think words can express how [I] love it. I know you and Mommy would love it as I do. It feels so wonderful to be able to go on the street without someone to stop you and ask you if you are a jew. It is really heavenly to live with people who are friendly and kind as if they were your relations. In your mind you see a country with hard-working, but laughing smiling people, it seems as though sunshine always shines on America. When I look at Europe in my subconscious mind I see a black pit with people slaving, crying and moaning and all this because one man, selfish and spoiled wanted to have his way. It's just pathetic ...

Now about you! How are you, what are you doing with yourself? I am fine. Would you please send me Uncle Max address. ...

All my love, Phyllis

Saturday eve Aug. 14, 1943

Dearest Daddy,

Another week has elapsed without me receiving any mail from you. That makes six weeks. Now, finally, I know what it feels like to be without mail from someone dear to you. I've been writing you steadily now for about four month and I do wish you would again write to me every week. I guess the old proverb, "You don't appreciate water till the well is dry," has again come true, since I really didn't miss your letters before; I knew they were coming. But now you have me worried. At night before I fall asleep I think of you waiting for a letter from me. So I write and I hope you will answer. And as I wait every day for your letter I am always disappointed. I hope within the next week I get a letter from you.

Meanwhile, I became fourteen. That is on Monday. It feels swell to be this age and I wish I could stay fourteen all the time. My God-mother gave me a white blouse which is very good looking. I had a pleasant week just passing by. I played baseball nearly always. It certainly is a good game. Then on Friday night I had a party. There were only ten boys and girls but it was one of the swellest parties I had ever been to. We danced, played games(woo woo) and ate. We had a grand time. The only people I missed were you and Mom. This week I am going to work so I can buy some school clothes with my earnings. I am working with my best girlfriend, Mildred, and we are having fun....

So I turned 14, and would go into the 9ᵗʰ grade next month. I don't know if I gave the party or somebody else honored me for my birthday. I can't remember what work Millie and I were doing, perhaps weeding again. I changed best girl-friends often.

Sept 16, 1943 I report on school, a visit to the Reingolds, and another quarantive.

Dear Daddy,

Yesterday I received your letter from July ninth. It took two month to get here and in the meantime I was worried stiff about you. For seven weeks I was without news from you. I was awfully glad I received that letter. Thanks a million for the card. I hope you are all ok. from your sickness. It seems as if every time I wrote you I hurt my hand. This time it was my thumb and took three days before it went down to regular size. It is still bruised.

School started on Tuesday and it certainly is a lot of fun. I have English, Algebra, German, Social Science, Lunch, Drama, and Gym. Today I got another letter from August 16, and boy, that certainly came at the right time.

This week I am in quarantine from mumps, but I am having fun anyway. I've quite a lot of makeup work so tonights letter won't be very long. A week and a half ago I went to Petaluma to stay with the Reingolds for ten days. Petaluma is a small town famous for eggs. I had loads of fun up there. They said as soon as you arrive here they want you to visit them so you could see how you liked it. I learned how to bikeride and it's good exercise.

Last Saturday I went downtown to get a pair of shoes, a dress and a sweater. They are all very nice. I also hope I will get a skirt and dress with the ten dollars you sent me. You asked me for a receipt for the money order, but the post office man won't give me one.

The weather here, is quite good for a change, usually it is foggy. How is the weather there? ... I hope you can come here soon, 'cause I sure miss you so much. Forever loving, Phyllis

I vaguely remember going to the Reingolds, my previous foster parents, who had moved to their Petaluma ranch, but I don't know why I was asked to visit them when I was kicked out of their home. I've said before that I'm not sure I was "kicked" out by either my aunt or the Reingolds, but I've always felt kicked out. Maybe I used the word "kicked out" because it was more dramatic in the telling, or because it felt that way. At any rate, reading about it now, makes me realize that I couldn't have been as naughty a child as I pictured myself since they invited me to spend a vacation with them.

October 12, 1943

> *Dear Daddy,*
>
> *...Meanwhile, Jewish New Years was here and Atonement day. On those two days I thought of you and Mommy, as a brief summary of how fate did things to us. I prayed, wished and hoped and I sure hope they all come true. May be my wishes to you for a happy new year are late in arriving. They still carry the same volume of meaning. And before another year is passed I hope we are united again.*

The Jewish holidays were still meaningful to me, as a time for reflection.

> *About you coming here; do you know when? I want you here so badly. For four years I haven't seen you and I yearn so much for you. ...*
>
> *I just received your letter from Sept 8, 1943. I was glad, very glad. I want to thank you very much for the money again. I just spent half of it on a dress, and it's real pretty. By the way, next time you send me money please send them to Mrs. Rabinowitz 2796 Mission Street S. Francisco, Calif.*
>
> *Next Tuesday we will receive our report cards. So I'll write you again then. Meanwhile, good luck love and kisses, Your ever loving daughter Phyllis*
>
> *P.S. I've a nice surprise for you next week.*

It looks like I was trying to circumvent Mr. Bonapart's decree—that any money from my father would have to go in the bank—by sending them to my Aunt. Tricky, but it didn't work; he continued to send it to me at the Home. Further, he had declared that he would write only to answer my letters, so there were many weeks that I didn't receive mail from him. However, from my collection of letters, I see he received 17 letters that year, but I only received 9, two of which I have lost. My next letter from him is from Dec. 6, although I mention receiving a couple of other letters. The war in the Pacific was very heavy at this time, so it is possible, that besides the longs delays, some were lost altogether, or I didn't keep some others.

November 11, 1943   Armistice day. I have a bad report card. I didn't have to tell him knowing that he'd disapprove, but I did anyway. I had excuses—quarantine, too many teachers, perhaps I was having troubles with the housemother. Something was happening during this semester because my grades were so poor compared to the A and B grades reported in June. I would surely be scolded for such a poor showing.

Dearest Daddy,

I received your letter from Sept. 14, and was very glad to receive it, as you can imagine. Meanwhile, we received our report cards, and I was terribly ashamed of mine. I got the following:

English	*C*	*S*	*Social*	*C-*	*S*
German	*B+*	*S*	*Algebra*	*C+*	*S*
Dramatics	*C*	*S*	*Gym*	*B*	*S*

Do you know algebra? I think it is a lot of fun, except that you have to start at the beginning which I didn't. You see, at the beginning of the term I was absent. Anyway, I've finally caught on, and do I like it! I guess you are disappointed that I did not get an A in German, and I easily could have if I didn't four German teachers. This term I will get a much better card.

In your letter you say that you received two letter's from me, one telling you, I hated camp, the other stating I loved it. You, as always, are right in scolding me, but this time you were especially right. The old saying 'You don't appreciate water, till the well is dry,' is so true in every respect. In every thing we do, that saying stands there and stares us right in the face. For example, I was real fresh in my old cottage of 42 and now that I am in 24, I, as well as a couple of other boys, are just as sorry as I am that we were so disgusting. How are you? I hope you are fine. Right now I have a bad cold but it will soon be over.

I hadn't mentioned my mother for a long time, but in this letter I reminisced about her and appreciate her. Today, I do not remember the day I left her. The letter continues:

How's your affidavid coming along? I hope you will be able to have it soon, 'cause I want to see you so much. I write this every week, and every week I mean it more. Four and a half yrs. are passed in which I haven't seen you. Three and a half since I have not seen Mommy. I'll never forget the day I left her. Before I had to keep her spirit up and then in the last minute, I broke down. We both cried, but her face and words made me feel so good, as she had the courage of a thousand men in her. And then again comes the old saying, I never did appreciate her, or love her, as I do now. I have a picture of her and when I see it, I think of all the fun, loving care and everything I had when living with her and you. Do you ever hear from her? Do you know where she is? I'd love to know.

I am still working at the dentist at 20 cents an hour and receive approxamately $5.00 a month. But I can not spend it as I wish. Fact is I can only spend 50 cents a week. Oh, well I am going to go along as is and wait for the day when I can live with you again.

I have a nice surprise for you for your Christmas present....millions of kisses, love, hugs and all your ever loving daughter. Phyllis

December 3, 1943 Another history lesson

Dear Daddy,

Tonight is Thanksgiving night there is no school tomorrow. I have some important news to tell you later. Meanwhile I want to tell you about Thanksgiving.

Every year, on the last Thursday of November, since 1789, is Thanksgiving. Usually it is passed up just as a regular holiday where we eat turkey and have fun, but this year we a have a lot to thank God for and pray for more good luck. As for me I've collected all the things I've enjoyed this year and they gave me plenty to think about.

I reflect on the past year, and the ups and downs of my feelings

> *At the beginning of the year I had to stay in quarantine for mumps and I was so mad. Well, I came back to school everybody was swell to me and I got popular. Last term was a lot of fun. Then I went to another house and again I was mad. But instead, I got a new girlfriend and about four boy friends. Gee, they are so swell. I can trust them with anything and visa-versa. We're just one big happy family. For that I am most grateful. When I went to camp I thought it was terrible, but when it was time to go, I missed it.*

Not liking changes, and then loving them is still one of my characteristics, although as I got older, I have become more mellow and appreciative more quickly. More of the letter:

> *Today is a big day. Tonight is the big turkey dinner. Today is also a big football game; it's between two high schools. Of course I couldn't go. I had to stay home and make the meal.*

> *(After dinner) We just got finished eating and was it good. A few other things I am thankful for is that I have parents like you and Mom. In my opinion there are no better people in the world. And I can hardly wait til you come over.*

> *Monday—I'm in German now and I have a study period. Gee, German is so boring. We learn nothing. ...I have a big surprise for you. I know you won't like it but I am going into another foster home. When you come here I want you to be able to get accustomed to the American way of life, so I have to practice. I'm sure you'll understand as you always do. And I have another reason, too. This time it shall be something nice because I am old enough to understand to be good. I'll have to say good-bye now, so with all my love, Phyllis*

I loved the idea of Thanksgiving as a holiday; the report of it was no doubt triggered by a recent review of it in Social Studies. Nevertheless, I took the essence of the holiday seriously in reflecting on things I could be thankful for; I wonder if I realized how often I was mad, and yet glad afterwards? I find myself still taking inventory on Thanksgiving Day of the year that has passed, searching for some meaning to the events that have shaped my life. Now Thanksgiving is everyday.

The word "swell" was excessive in my vocabulary, perhaps in every teenager's vocabulary, like "cool" is today. I don't remember when I stopped using it, but it amuses me to read it so often in my letters. My father didn't think it was so swell! In some letters he would put quotes around "swell" in referring to a comment I had made about parties or boyfriends. I don't think he minded the word, as much as my attaching importance to activities he preferred I would avoid. Although German was my father's first language he knew English better than I; the grammar in his letters was correct, although sometimes a bit formal, and sometimes following a German sentence structure. After his death I discovered notebooks in which he had studied English usage during his internment; the detail of that study explained why he had such a good command of the language. Still later, when we were finally reunited, he would often correct me on usage; and he always knew the definition of any word I was too lazy to look up.

✦　✦　✦

I must have known that my father wouldn't be pleased about my moving to yet another foster home, which is why I left that important message to the end of the letter. Somehow, the year, which had started so well, had not ended so well. I was escaping again—to another foster home.

Dec. 6, 1943

My little Darling

I received your letter of October 12...I am certainly glad that you had such fine vacations, now you are at school again and I hardly need to urge you to learn and learn, and to do your utmost towards achieving the best results in school. You must always bear it in mind that by being diligent and acquiring the most possible amount of knowledge you don't do any for me...but only for yourself and your future.

...Let us hope that we soon shall be reunited and our darling Mumi with us, that is

the only thing only mind and in my heart and God help us that is soon comes true...Hugs and kisses, your Daddy

December 23, 1943

Dearest Daddy, I love you

I got a letter from you last Saturday, but being I had to prepare a Chanukah Dinner I was quite I occupied. Well, last night we had a big dinner, turkey and all and what fun I had. As a present from the Godmothers I received a book, namely: 10,000 Jokes, Toasts and Stories. [I had requested it]. It is very big and I love it immensely. I started reading it and I almost split my sides. Gee, they're funny. Here's one from the American scene: Millionaire (to a beggar) ——"Be off with you, this minute"

Beggar: "Look here Mister, the only difference between you and me is that you're making your second million, while I'm still on my first.

And here's another which I thought was good.

"My poor fellow", said the lady, "here is a quarter for you. Goodness, it must be dreadful to be lame, but just think how much worse it would be if you were blind." "Yer right lady", agreed the beggar, "when I was blind, I was always getting counter-feit money."

And then I got a bandana. It is pink and blue and has large squares. It is awfully pretty. I also got a string of blue pearls. They are so dainty. And I am also getting something else, but I don't know what. It is about 8:30 p.m. now and I listening to Christmas Carols over the radio. They sound so relaxing and homy. I can remember Vienna and how it looked during X-mas season with trees brightly lit, shining through the windows. It is much prettier here. You ought to see it.

Last Tuesday we got our report cards and I improved 75% and had as follows:

	Last Time		This Time	
English	*C*	*S*	*B+*	*S*
Social Sci.	*C-*	*S*	*C-*	*S*
Gym	*B-*	*S*	*B*	*S*
Algebra	*C+*	*S*	*B+*	*E*
Drama	*C*	*S*	*A*	*E*
German	*B*	*S*	*B+*	*S*

Isn't that swell? Next time I'm going to get an A in Algebra and German and English. That will be "sweller" yet. Right now we are having Xmas vacation but so far I've had no fun. Work, work, and more work. How's the weather over there? It's supposed to be winter here, but the wheather is sure nice.

What's doing? Last night, I took out all the letters I had received from you and friends and as I read them I thought of the people and how most probably, they've changed as I did. I doubt it if you'll be able to recognize me. Therefore, I am at last sending you a good photograph of me. I am going downtown this afternoon and see my proofs. I hope they turn out good. Maybe you could send me one of you. I would really love that. So—until next time Merry Xmas and a happy New Year with all my love and heaps of kisses your everloving one, Phyllis

The holiday dinners were a big production. The girls were busy with food preparation for several days before the feast. Most often it began with canned fruit cocktail, followed by roast turkey with stuffing or roast beef, sweet and white potatoes, canned peas, fresh baked muffins, and fresh baked pies.

I was a fairly accomplished cook by this time, being the housemother's chief helper. The four circular tables in the dining room were rearranged to permit a long head table made of sawhorses and long boards, covered with white linen tablecloths. Prior to the party, the house was cleaned with great care: a janitor came and polished the wooden floors with big circular brushes until I could almost see my reflection, and I would slip as I rushed back and forth to set the tables. Our godparents sat at the head table, perhaps as many as five couples, behind nametags that bore such names as Strauss (from Levi-Strauss), Koshland, Lillienthal and Zellerbach. I guess that they were mostly older since they never brought their own children with them. I don't remember much about them, as they did not engage us in a lot of conversation. Did it make them feel benevolent to be among us poor children? or did it bore them coming to the Home for these occasions? From the children's point of view, it meant company manners, always a chore! Both guests and children were dressed in their finest clothes, while the housemother, flitting around making sure that everything was in order, probably in mortal fear that one of the children's poor manners would reflect badly on her.

The gifts I speak of in the letter were given to us by one of the Godparents handing out all the presents. I had asked for the bandanna; it was popular for girls to wear bandannas tied under the chin to protect our fashionable curls from the San Francisco fog and wind. We were taught to write nice thank-you notes to the Godparents for their gifts.

Although we were Jewish, we could not help notice the general celebrations of Christmas both in the school and in the neighborhood, as well as the music. That year, the movie, White Christmas, and its title song had just become popular. There were many other songs, like "I'll be Home for Christmas" that spoke dreamily of the war ending. I had no difficulty liking both Chanukah and Christmas, although Christmas was definitely ignored at the Home, and if I had made my liking of Christmas known, I probably would have been scolded. My father would not have enjoyed my wishing him a merry Xmas, or my dreamy reminiscence of Vienna.

My grades had improved considerably from the first quarter, but overall, I was barely a B-student. I loved Dramatics, but I did very little acting.

✦ ✦ ✦

So the year ended, but not the war, although some gains were being made and it was looking more hopeful for our side. The hope of being reunited with my father was put on hold again, and I was longing for him more than ever. I saw his coming as a release from unpleasant supervision. However, he would have been stricter, and would not have been able to provide me with as many enjoyable experiences, such as those in the summer.

16

MY NEMESIS

Benjamin Bonapart was the director of the orphanage. He was in his 40's or 50's, a tallish man, perhaps 5'10", portly, who carried himself well. He was always dressed in a suit and hat. He had a brown Hitler-like mustache; his top hair, beginning to thin over the crown, was neatly combed over the skull. He didn't smile too often. Criticism, judgment and commands were his style of communication with me. I thought of him as a dictator, and I found ironic amusement in the coincidence that he had the same name as one of the most famous dictators of history, Napoleon, and a mustache of another.

He lived on the grounds of the Home with his family—a wife whom we hardly ever saw, and a son, who was roughly my age, but did not go to the same schools as the rest of the kids, and he didn't play with us either. It must have been tough to be the son of the director!

Mr. Bonapart claimed to be fair, just and very concerned about the welfare of the children; in fact, he had many favorites, but I was never one of those. My reputation as a "difficult" child preceded me to the Home, although I was not aware of it. I thought of myself as a "good" girl, so I didn't have trouble with accepting the rules—until I saw that they were not equally applied.

In the previous chapter some of my problems with Mr. B (as we often called him) mentions some of my confrontations, but also includes some letters he wrote to my father speaking only well of me. However, my over-all memory of our relationship is not favorable, and his disapproving tone of voice is etched in my mind.

Often I evoked his negative voice by was asking for something that was not typical of the Home. Admittedly, sometimes my requests were bold, as when I wanted to buy clothes in a store instead of getting them from the Home's supply, or when I wanted to go to a night basketball game. These he found demanding, and just for asking I would get punished by having to do extra chores around the house. I would not have asked for something special had I not seen others doing so. The request would usually be made at the assembly point near the gym where the junior and high school kids gathered for inspection before going to school, a time for asking for special requests. Mr. Smith, or later, Mr. Liebhoff, the assistants, were always nice to me, but Mr. Bonapart seemed to enjoy harassing me. His foulest trick was so humiliating that I can barely describe it without wanting to scream. It usually occurred in this morning line-up:

"May I go to the basketball game tonight-our team is winning," I asked enthusiastically.

"What is it that you want?" he said sarcastically, making me repeat my request while bouncing his finger under my chin so that it would make me stutter.

"I wou-wou-would li-li-like to go to the bask-basketball ga-ga-game tonight," I stuttered, unable to finish the sentence without tears of fury.

"And why should you be allowed to go? What did you do to deserve special privileges?"

"I did all my work," I stammered to his continued chin chucking, humiliating me further, as he denied my request.

I would end up crying, he would demand an apology for my greed and selfishness. The effect of this abuse—not being able to get out a complete sentence without stuttering—was total degradation. Other children were witnesses to my humiliation, perhaps as an example, but I never saw anyone else treated this way. Soon I learned not to cry—in fact, my tears were shut off for many years as I was determined not to give him the pleasure of my emotions. In due time, I also learned not to ask, but to simply do, for which I was also punished. When permission to go to the game was denied because no one else was going, I went anyway. I sneaked out of the house after dinner. I didn't enjoy it very much, however, because I was afraid of getting caught, although nobody from the home was supposed to be there. However, one of the housemothers and a couple of her "kids" were there and they spotted me. I was punished by not being allowed to go out for a month, and verbally berated by Mr. Bonapart for taking things into my own hands. I thought it was grossly unfair that the other children had been able to go, and that I wasn't.

He made me feel that it was wrong to ask for anything. Instead of building my self-confidence, he tried to destroy it. Ungrateful, or, more often, selfish were words he used to denounce me. I was always being "selfish" in asking for things that I did not deserve. I worried about that loaded word. How could I be selfish when I did many nice things for my friends? How was I selfish when I just requested things that others got? One time, I requested a new pair of shoes—high heels. I was around fifteen at the time, and the girls were beginning to wear high heels. Some of the other girls had already gotten them, and as they were not available at the central clothing "store" at the Home, they had to be purchased with money.

"Who do you think you are," he chided me while bouncing my chin in front of everybody waiting to go to school. "You are so selfish and greedy. No, you cannot have money for a pair of high heels." To my chagrin, my roommate who was my age, a pathetically shy girl who still wet her bed, informed me the next day that Mr. Bonapart had suggested that she might want some new high heels, to be in fashion. She was surprised that he had thought of it, but I knew where he got the idea. I wanted to explode with my anger at that man, but at the time, anger was an emotion that I tried to keep under wrap, although sometimes I would release my feelings in a letter to my father. I vowed I would get back at Mr. Bonapart some day.

Ironically, it happened a few years later, when I was seventeen and my father had already come to the United States. I was living in Cottage#22 then, with Mrs. Blumgarden, a housemother I liked and who liked me. One day I was asked to go to Mr. Bonapart's office. Oh, no, I thought, what did I do this time? However, I did not fear him anymore, since I knew that my time at the Home was almost over. He greeted me very cordially, which surprised me since our habitual encounters were typically hostile. He asked me about my father and his work, my schoolwork and my plans for college. I wondered what this was all leading up to. Then he said:

> We would like you to move up to Cottage 42 againto be Ella's room-mate. As you know she has many emotional problems, and we think that you could be helpful to her to become more independent. You used to get along with her, and she has requested that you be her room-mate again. If you did that we would provide you with some special privileges, such as less work around the house, or perhaps special cloth-ing allowances.

Then he smiled graciously as if we'd always been friends. I couldn't believe what I heard—after all these years of getting punished for my independent person-ality, now I was being asked to use it to help another girl—one who had been held up to me as a model of good behavior, who was praised for her non-aggressive, quiet ways! Although I didn't dislike Ella, I did not want to be burdened with the responsibility of "caring" for her—and I did not want to sleep in her room, as I recalled with disgust waking to the stench of her urine-soaked bed.

> "No," I told him. "I don't want to leave Mrs. Blumgarden's house, I don't want to be Ella's roommate again. Besides, I will be leaving the home as soon as my father and I can find an apartment."

He asked me reconsider, and for the next week or so, he kept asking me to change my mind. "It would be a way to prove that you aren't selfish," he said. Although I felt sorry for Ella, and was flattered that finally some part of me was considered worthwhile, I gloated that I had finally gotten my revenge by denying his request.

Perhaps it was selfish not to want to help her, but I had already convinced myself that being selfish was a good idea; that unselfishness would get me nowhere-after all, nobody else tended to my needs. I had to think of myself—to be selfish—but as long as I didn't hurt anybody else by my behavior, I finally persuaded myself that it was all right. I'll admit to being self-centered, but not to selfish. It is such a loathsome word! Trying to make peace with my reputed "selfishness," I found an ally in Ayn Rand's books, especially *The Fountainhead.* Through her characters, she convinced me that selfishness, or as she called it, altruism, was the virtue of being true to oneself. Some of her other points of view in the book I didn't agree with, but at the time, it helped clarify my own values. Today, we would call such selfishness "assertiveness," now a desired trait.

◆ ◆ ◆

I hated Mr. Bonapart with a passion—I longed to find ways to irritate him, to get even with him for interfering with my life. For example, my father sent me money—usually $10.00 every three months—that I used to buy clothes. When Mr. Bonapart discovered that I received money from my father, (his letters to me were sometimes censored by Mr. B.), I had to put the money in the bank. I vented my anger in my letter of April 15, 1943 to my father. I was outraged. "It wasn't fair," I fumed to myself and to friends who listened to me in agreement. Other children received money from their parents, but only mine was confiscated because it was sent, rather than given. It was an invasion of my privacy, it was dictatorship, like Hitler. I organized a rebellion against him, making picket signs and had a bunch of us circling his house, shouting "down with Bonapart." Since I can't recall the consequence of this violent breach of proper behavior, now I think that I must have only fantasized it, but the image of the picket signs and the chanting are so vivid, that I am not really sure whether it happened or not.

The final act of his meanness came about after the war when my father would, at last, be coming to the U.S. His papers had been approved; he was now awaiting ship's passage, so it seemed imminent, although it actually took more than a year. Meanwhile, Mr. Bonapart kept telling me that I would not be able to live with my father when he came because he would not have any money and would not be able to support me. Of course, he might have been trying to prepare me for the reality of the future of an immigrant—my father might not be able to get a job, when jobs were scarce, but I recall it as another condemnation of me, of making me feel insecure, and belittling my father's abilities. He sent me to the psychiatrist because he felt that I needed counseling about my fantasy about my father's coming.

I went to the psychiatrist, even though I felt my looking forward to my father's coming was not a fantasy. I had been waiting for it for seven years. At the doctor's, I kept asking questions about immigration laws. I wanted some authority to answer my questions: Would my father be able to bring money into the U.S.? How much? Would he be allowed to work? Would I be allowed to live with him? Was there a law against it? Of course, the psychiatrist didn't know the answers; she had nothing to do with laws. It was a session of total miscommunication. At any rate, I did not believe Mr. Bonapart, nor the psychiatrist—I was sure that somehow my father and I would manage. I was working part-time at a department store at the time, so I would be able to work, despite Mr. Bonapart's negative view of our abilities.

Five years later, in 1953, when I was working on my master's degree in Anthropology, I wrote to him asking for my records, as I wanted to study the process of acculturation, and could use myself as a "case." Over the years I had had many IQ and other psychological test and visits with psychiatrists that I believed would show the process of adapting to another culture. He sent me the materials I requested, and then, in a cordial letter he said, "You see, I always had your best interest at heart. You were in your worst states of rebellion, I was the "bad guy." That helped you to put the blame on someone. And as long as it helped you, my job was better done, even though I lost your friendship." Quite the contrary, I saw how badly I had been misjudged by the professionals, especially that above mentioned psychiatrist whose report to the Home indicated that I had "neurosis with paranoid tendencies and fantasies!" That report did not enhance my already low opinion of social workers and psychologists who had listened to my words, but had never heard them. From my readings later, I found that psychiatrists support the status quo more than the patient; often, unfortunately, such misdiagnoses do damage to many people.

◆ ◆ ◆

I have never quite gotten over his question of "Who do you think you are?" a question which challenged my right to aspire, to dream and to desire. During my career, and even now sometimes, when I want to do something out of the ordinary, I come face-to-face with that question, and it sometimes defeats me. My encounters with Bonapart unfortunately served as model of my future encounters with men, and especially men of authority. I found myself either humbly asking their permission, totally unsure of myself, or boldly demanding what I wanted. Neither approach worked well, and in most cases, I used the wrong approach with the wrong man—when I should have been using my initiative, I retreated; when I should have been modest, I was bold. I have still not learned to read authority figures.

◆ ◆ ◆

I nurtured my hate for Mr. Bonapart for many years even after I left the Home. I didn't want to forgive him; I wanted to get even by showing him what I accomplished. Finally, when I did succeed in life, getting advanced degrees in Anthropology and Public Health from prestigious schools with scholarships and honors, I forgot my hate, letting his memory fade away. However, when my marriage failed, and later, when I had trouble finding work, his original judgment of me: "Who do you think are?" came back to taunt me—was I really not capable? A flawed person? Did I really have no right to happiness and success?

Eventually, I gave up hating Mr. Bonapart, but I haven't forgiven him for his abuse, which sometimes haunts me, even now. On the other hand, I am grateful now that I could hate him without fear of being thrown out on the streets. Because he was an authority figure I could hate him without guilt or ambivalence. Had it been somebody I loved, like my father, I could not have rebelled as easily. Rebelling helped me to mature out of the bad feelings, but it also gave me the power of self-determination of which I have been proud.

17

ANOTHER FOSTER HOME

1 9 4 4

This year would be my most difficult year, but it started optimistically as I contemplated going to another foster home. It was my year-end surprise in my last letter of 1943. I was now in the 9th grade, 14^1/$_2$ years old. I cannot recall specifically what prompted this move, but a later letter to my father refers to my misbehavior. Furthermore, it was a Federal regulation that refugee children should not live in institutions, so perhaps these two factors were responsible. The first letter is full of joy and patriotism, and indeed the tide was turning for the Allies in the long war.

January 12, 1944

Dearest Daddy,

How are you, Gee, I haven't heard from you for about four weeks and I guess I'm kinda worried about you; the fact is I'm very worried. What happened? Aren't you feeling well? or something? I hope nothing is wrong.

Meanwhile New Years has passed. We had a party, it was pretty good, but not long enough. I danced with my boyfriend almost all the time, and was it heavenly. He's so swell.

The next day, New Year Day, my girlfriend and I went to see the East-West football game. Each fall the colleges play this interesting sport and at the end of the season one or two men from each college, who are outstanding, play in this big game. All the profits go the hospital for crippled children. It was a swell game. It was a tie score of 13 to 13. During half-time they unfurled the world's biggest flag; an American one. It was 70ft X 120ft large and needed 150 sailors to carry it. What a sight. What beauty. Then we said the "Pledge of Allegiance" and sang our national anthem "The Stars Spangled Banner." The Stadium was filled. 75,000 people of all nations, races and religions attended. To hear all of them sing, with one thought behind it, the thought of a freer world, peace for the earth and goodwill to men, and for everlasting victory, was beautiful. I shall hope and pray that next time, when I see this, I hope you'll be with me.

My glowing description of the flag, pledge and singing of the anthem remind me that I am still very moved by such patriotic symbols, often evoking tears. Then, as now, I feel privileged and extremely lucky to be in America. The letter continues:

Well, anyway your picture will be ready in a week and I shall have it sent to you immediately.

As I told you before I am going to a foster home, and I am almost sure I'll last with them until you come.

Last Friday night I went to a birthday party and I had a lot of fun. They wanted me to be Master of Ceremonies because they think I have a swell sense of humor. That is the third party I've "(M.)(C.)'d" what fun. O'course, my boy friend was there and we danced, ate and talked. Gee, was it swell.

Now, I'm out of words, except to say swimming is starting again, and I shall strive to get to be a marvelous swimmer and diver. In school I've a lot of fun, at nights I'm always on the telephone. I'm about always on there. I have a lot of fun everywhere and I will have doubly so after I leave this place.

Now, take care of yourself and love (heaps) kisses and hugs from your everloving daughter, Phyllis

P.S. I love you

N.S. I love you very much

Through the generous donation of tickets by our Godparents, some children of the Home were privileged to participate in many of the community's cultural events. Not everybody could go to the East-West game, or to the ballet or the opera, and I can't remember how the tickets were distributed. I was often a recipient, possibly because I was not visiting my parents on Sundays as so many other children were.

I enjoyed sports very much. I followed my school's sports reports eagerly in the morning paper. I also liked to participate in sports, though I was a klutz. If I got reasonable grades in Gym it was because I tried so hard. Fortunately for me, I had the opportunity to indulge in my best sport, swimming, through the Home's membership in the Jewish Community Center.

I can't remember a time when I wasn't boy crazy, but it usually was a one-sided affair. I'm sorry I forgot the wonderful boyfriend who made my New Year's evening so heavenly, but I am sure that our romance didn't last very long.

My letters to my father were mostly optimistic and happy, as much to bolster myself as to reassure him. Although I was often unhappy because I couldn't get my way or was having confrontations with Mr. Bonapart, I was happy about my social relations, exited about my projects, such as running for office, and happy with myself that I was "adjusting" to the American way of life. I am amused by the sentence about "my swell sense of humor." I can remember being the M.C. and enjoying it immensely, but I had forgotten that I had a sense humor until I read these letters. My sense of humor was lost somewhere along the way to maturity.

✦ ✦ ✦

The following letter was received on January 23, 1944. My correspondence with my father was impaired by the long time of delivery, often more than six weeks. Of course, that they arrived at all was a miracle, as there was a huge war being fought in the Pacific. I usually received his letters one at a time, but he often got several of my letters at once, probably held up by the AustralianCensors. Although this happened often, he would be quite irritated when mail didn't come regularly.

Dec. 19, 1943 Received Jan. 23

> *My little Darling,*
> *I have just received your letter of Nov. 11th and you can well imagine how glad I have been reading the "fine" marks of your report card. So far it is the worst one I ever read, instead of improving, the marks received by you are getting worse. What is the use of telling me that you are ashamed of it, once and again I have told you that your only task and duty now is to devote most of your time to learning. If you did as I have always have asked you to do, there would certainly not arise the necessity of being "terribly ashamed." Do you remember your friend Rosenkranz? She used to be the best pupil of your class in Vienna. Well, she is now living here with her parents, and from what I heard she is now again the best in her school here.*
>
> *I would like to hear the same of my daughter, but, alas, for four years you keep promising that the "next term" would be better and as usual there is always something that prevented you from achieving these "better results." Well, after all I cannot do more than to tell you that this state of things is terribly bad and unless you pull yourself together and to work there is little hope left for you success later on at a college.*

My father has forgotten that all previous report cards were good, and I had been on the honor roll. Although in the above letter my father complains about my poor grades for four years, it was only this report session that they were so bad, C+. In the June 1943 report card I had 3 A's and 3 B's, a good report card. In that Nov. 11th letter I am ashamed of my behavior in Cottage 42, now almost a year before. He did not read my letter carefully. He continues:

> *Then you write that you are sorry for your being so disgusting at Cottage 24. You seem to have the ambition to make a nuisance of yourself wherever you come, where is this going to bring you? Well, my dear child, I wish I would not have to write about all this, if your mother whom you pretend to love so much, would know all about that it would shock her more than anything she has to endure now. This letter will give you little pleasure, but it will certainly tell you how much fun I derived from reading your news.*

> *That's all for today, perhaps are your next letters such as to give you a more cheerful answer. Did you receive $10.00 I sent two weeks ago?*

> *With all my love, hugs and heaps of kisses,   Your Daddy*

January 23, 1944

> *Dear Daddy,*

> *I received your letter from Dec. 19. I was glad to hear from you, but I certainly was not glad to read all of your complaints.*

> *First of all, I never was the smartest student in my class in Vienna and I hardly expect to be here. I do study and I don't especially care what grades I get as long as I know that I know. And I certainly am not going to be a sour-puss, a dead egg and such just so I get all A's. Some girls do that and few people like them because they are uninteresting. I know what I am supposed to know and you can be sure of that.*

> *Daddy, you know that I haven't been with you for 4 1/2 years and without mother for 3 3/4. As I grew up, my parents didn't train me as they wished. Strange people did. True, you didn't want it that way, but after all, I had to make up my mind as to the kind of a person I wanted to be when I grew up. I decided I should stand up for my rights, no matter what, if I thought I was right. I decided to lead and not follow as a meek, helpless girl. I've done just that. And if a woman, who has never had children of her own, knows nothing of child psychology, is going to hit me, sock me and call me names because I disagreed over a simple matter I am not going to stand for that.*

> *Most probably you think I am a spoiled brat and everything don't let yourself be*

fooled. Maybe this is vain, but, 90% of the people who know me, think I have a very good personality, character, intelligence and ability to look out for myself. So don't be worried over me, I'm just fine. Besides, by the time you get this letter I will be in a foster home.

Last of all what do you mean by saying: " If your mother, whom you pretend to love so much....?" I love mother and [if] I didn't, I wouldn't say I did. I do love Mother and dearly. I was shocked when you wrote that. I wished I knew where she was so I could write to her and inform her about all. I've tried to get in touch with her through the Red Cross but of no avail, since I do not know [where] she is living.

Three more days until the term ends. I will then be a high nine and in June I will be graduating from this school. I like it very much and I shall miss it. I have a lot of fun, flirting with the boys, dancing and learning. Yesterday, I sent you a photo of me and I hope you will like it.

So... don't worry about me, 'cause I'm fine and growing to be a nice little girl.

I hope you're fine as I am and that all is going fine. Write soon. Kisses, hugs and all my love,   Yours, Phyllis

My father's reference to my mother at his displeasure of my behavior was to make me feel guilty and study more, but it only made me angry. Of course, we did not know of her whereabouts at that time since I had not received letters from her since 1942 when she mentioned that she would be sent to Poland by the Nazis. I dared not think about her death and put the thought out of my head.

✦ ✦ ✦

February 7, 1944   A new semester has started and I am in my new foster home.

Dearest Daddy,

Well, I'm here. In my fosterhome; I mean. Gee, is it swell. I have my own room and everything. The name of the family is Jonah. They have two children, Stanley, 7 and Ken, nearly 3. They are very cute. I came here yesterday afternoon. I'm going to stay here until you come here. And I hope it will be soon. Right now I'm listening to a radio program. It's kind of funny.

In the fosterhome I had more chances to listen to radio shows when I was alone in the evening baby sitting for the children. Jack Benny and Fred Allen were my favorite comedians, but I liked other shows too, like The Shadow, One Man's Family, The Lone Ranger. The letter continues, showing great improvement in my grades.

> *You know that last letter I wrote you and all those bad things I said guess I meant them but don't take them too seriously 'cause I still love you. I got my report card Friday and this is what I got.*

	3rd Report	*Final*
English	*B+S*	*B S*
Gym	*A S*	*B+S*
German	*A S*	*B S*
Algebra	*B E*	*B E*
Drama	*A+S*	*A S*

> *I thought that was pretty good don't you? From 2 C's and 4 B's I got 3A's , 2 B's and a C. I am now going into my last year of Jr. High and I certainly wish you'd be here for my graduation...So until next time, Love, your everloving, Phyllis*

✦ ✦ ✦

My new foster home was in the Richmond District on 20th Avenue near California, an area characterized by two story flats, middle class families. Though my foster parents were Jewish, we did not go to Temple nor follow a kosher kitchen. Mrs. Jonah was involved in some Jewish groups, and played Mahjong with Jewish friends. Our flat was on the 2nd floor, and it consisted of six rooms; a living room, dining room, kitchen, two bedrooms at the end of a long hall, and beyond one of the bedrooms, a "sun porch" which was my room. The flat was very nicely furnished, especially the living and dining rooms; I remember most the very thick sculptured Chinese floor coverings that I struggled to vacuum properly.

Mr. Jonah was in the import business, hence the oriental carpets. He was often away from home on business. Mrs. Jonah did not work. She was a tall, heavy-set woman, while her husband was thin and rather retiring in his manner; she was definitely the head of the household.

Despite an hour's commute, I was allowed to continue to go to Aptos Jr. High

School for my last semester there. The commute involved changing buses three times, but I was rewarded by being on the same bus with my old flame, Jerry. I had a terrible crush on him while we were both living at the Home; in fact, I had given him a birthday party as a means of getting closer to him, but it hadn't worked. Now he was living with his mother in the Richmond and commuted on my bus route to his high school. It turned out that Mrs. Jonah was his aunt, and I dreamed of family gatherings where we might be together, but they never happened. Nothing developed in the relationship. On the other hand, because of the long commute I was cut off from my friends for weekend activities, and that turned out to be a cause of much unhappiness in the next few months.

February 15, 1944　His tone is so sarcastic!

My little Darling,

A few days ago I received your letters of Dec. 3rd and 23rd. I think I should extend to you my best thanks for them, after all, I had, this time, to wait only some 6-8 weeks for news from you. Actually, I could not quite make up my mind as to whether it wouldn't be advisable to keep you waiting for an equal period, because judging from your eagerness to write it is quite easy to perceive your interest in keeping up the correspondence and how "anxiously" you are looking forward to my letters. I think I shall have to reduce the number of letters to you, say to one in four months, by this means you will be under the "moral obligation" to answer three times a year only, and this, I feel, would make you happy. This, after all matters most, I do not want to bother you with anything you dislike, don't come with excuses, I had enough of them in the past four years, as to attach any importance to it.

So much regarding letter-writing. And now could you just tell me what happened again that you are moving to another home. Certainly some new disagreement with those in charge of the Home. I have always tried to influence you in a good way, asked you again and again to bear in mind that as, for the time being, you have not your parents there and have to live with others, your behavior should be exemplary so as to make friends with all those who have been so kind to care for you in our absence. Instead in the past four years you changed places 5 times, you don't want me to believe that all those were bad people and you alone were an angel? Well, my child, I'm really ashamed of it. I should have never dreamt that my daughter would turn out in such a way, so much more that being now nearly 15 years of age you should be able to realize you position and act accordingly.

There was one thing in your letter which has given me much pleasure, i.e. your report card. I am very glad indeed to learn of the good progress in school made by you during the last term. Your promise to try your best, and still improve it in the present term is satisfying and I hope you will stick to it and not disappoint me.

I'm glad to hear how well you are getting on, and I'm looking forward to you sending me your photo as promised in one of your last letters. Well, you may be quite right in assuming that I would not recognize you now, small wonder this, it is already 4¹/₂ years that I have not seen you, and you certainly changed a good deal. Anyhow, I'd love it to have at last your photo to see what you look like now.

I'm sorry, I cannot tell you anything as to when I'll be able to get over there. I had now news from Arno concerning my case, and I do not know how far things went in the State Department. It takes a terribly long time to arrange everything connected with getting a visa, and so I've to wait patiently. Someday I'll arrive there unexpectedly and take you by surprise. Up to that time don't keep me worrying, be good as I always have asked you and see to it, at least, now at your new place that the people are satisfied with you.

I'm all right, and hope to get some good news from you, in the meantime, All my love and heaps of kisses from your Daddy

April 1, 1944   I also complain about lack of letters.

Dearest Daddy,

I received your letter from Feb. 15 and you claim that I never write to you. I write you every week and if you do don't get mail from me I don't know what I can tell you. It is very seldom that I don't write every week. Before I got your last letter there was a gap of nine weeks before I had any news.

Four years ago today I arrived in New York. It was a happy day. You see I thought I'd be with you and Mom before the year was through. I didn't know any English but now there is no trace of an accent. I have achieved a lot of things in four years. I am now a lady nearly fifteen.

In your last letter you wanted to know why I was leaving the home, you think there was some conflict. There wasn't. I just wanted to get out into the world, meet people and have lots of friends when you arrived. I wanted you to be all built up when you get here so you won't have much trouble in getting accustomed to the American way of life. But you only think of this more as my fault and error. I wrote Mr. Bick....

They are swell to get you a visa.

We have Easter vacation this week. … Why don't you tell me what you do all the time?

All my love, kisses, hugs and squeezes Phyllis P.S. Please write every week…

March 21, 1944

My Darling,

After a long, long time … I received three letters from and your photo. The letters were of Jan. 12, 28 and Feb. 7. ….

Phyllis at 14: Jan.25, 1944

I am delighted to have, at last, your photo on my writing table and whenever looking at it, I have a funny feeling it is a strange person and a strange quite unknown face that I see. I still cannot get used to it, I cannot find any resemblance to what you looked when I last saw you nearly five years ago. Well times change and so do we. I simply cannot help it, but whenever I think of you there always appears before my eyes the picture of my little girl when she was 10 years at the time I left her. Anyhow, I'm mighty glad to have your picture here and I like it very much, though I would have preferred to see a smiling and more cheerful face.

I didn't have any pictures of him, either. The picture of me is not very good. Having photographs taken was expensive, and very few people I knew had cameras. More advice on my behavior. The letter continues:

And now to your letters. You are complaining about my letters which sometimes annoy you. Well my child, being your "dearest dad" you have got to put up with it, after all it is my right and duty to tell you if I find something wrong with you, or if your progress in school is not satisfactory. I'm not going to mince words, and hearing of something which to my mind is not correct, I'll tell you whether it pleases you or not. My only intention has always been to show you the right way and give you the best advice. You write that you do not want to be "a meek follower, but to lead." I'm glad to hear how self-assured you are and nobody, and I'm the last to ask of you to put up with any injustice. But there is some misconception, as you cannot expect elder people in whose care you are to follow you, their job is to teach you and bring you up and I'm sure whatever they do or say it is inspired by the best intentions. After all, grown up as you are, you are not yet fifteen and you will certainly [agree] *that your experiences are not sufficient to judge about elder people.*

You are now in a new home, it is up to you to make your foster-parents love you and be kind to you. With stubbornness this cannot be achieved. And just mind you, one's own parents have to put up with some whims of their children, strangers have not! You write that you are happy in your new home, and it is just swell, believe me my darling no one is more delighted about it than I am, and I wish I would hear the same a few months later on. I hope you will arrange things so as to stay there until I get over to you which I think is bound to take place within the next few months.

Again, there is some new hope of his getting an affidavit.

I just received two letters from Arno & Anny. They write me my papers are at the State Department and that they expect a favourable reply any day. You simply cannot imagine how much I'd like to be already with you. Arno is really a good friend, he is untiring in his efforts to get me over there, he takes so much trouble and I hope he will succeed. Anyhow, you should write to them...

March 20, 1944

Dearest Daddy,

About a week [ago] *I received some good news. Mr. Bick wrote to Mrs. Rabinowitz and said that you would be coming here within six months at the latest. When I heard that I started crying. I was so happy. Have you heard about it before? I hope it's true and sure because I've been disappointed so often. Then I will be with you again. We will be going to live in Washington I suppose. I believe they invited. Although* [they] *may have trouble finding room for us but I don't see why I talk about it now.*

Once more, there is the hope that my father would be coming to rescue me. Now there are new questions—will I have to live in Washington, D.C.?

The home I'm living in is swell. As I've told you before I have my room and it has all the sunshine in the house. A large bed, a closet, 2 chests of drawers are in it too. They are going to put a rug in too. Life is so different here. You meet the nicest people and so many. In about 6 weeks I've met about 25 people and about 7 my age.

More troubles with Mr. Bonapart; they would have been while I was still in the Home. The letter continues:

About four weeks ago I got some new clothes. A jumper, skirts, a coat, a jacket and sweaters and stuff. That damn stinker Bonapart took my sweaters away. He said I was too greedy, and too selfish and insulted you and Mom. I swore at him and told him to mind his own business. I don't think I hate anyone as much as him. I could kill him if it wasn't against the law. Enough of him.

Apologies for a previous letter January 23 where I said what I felt. …Remember that awfully disgusting letter I wrote you about eight weeks ago. I hope you'll forgive for it. I must have been out of my mind to write that kind of a letter.

I'm feeling fine and am getting a tan. The weather is awfully nice. By the way did you receive my picture yet? We are getting report cards this week so I'll tell you about my grades in the next letter.

… I have not heard from you for eight weeks. So love, hugs and kisses(the maximum) your everloving daughter Phyllis

✦ ✦ ✦

April 23, 1944   Hope dashed again by another delay in the immigration process.

Dearest Daddy,

I have just received a letter from Mr. Bick or Arno as you might call him. I was so disappointed when he told me that the State department wouldn't give you a visa. Everything was so sure and I was longing for that so much, I was practically in a daze. It's really too bad. I would have loved to be with you again. Maybe I shouldn't say this but I'm so used to being disappointed about you coming here I don't want to hope anymore as all my hopes get shattered anyway. If that's the way fate goes why can't we have a lucky break. I think four to five years is enough suffering for any one. I don't know whether I should have written this but it think it's about time somebody knew how I felt. If this makes you unhappy I'm sorry about it cause I don't want you unhappy.

Tell me, have you received my photo yet? I hope you like it.

As you know in 9 weeks I graduate from Jr. Highschool. This term sure flew by. Just imagine in two weeks we get report cards again. I am sure mine will be good.

How are you? I hope you are fine and every thing is just perfect. I wish sometimes you'd tell me what you do in your spare time as I do.

I am feeling fine but disappointed. In six months I get my bands off. Isn't that swell?

Incidently you always say why don't I write to you? In 13 weeks I have received one letter from you. And that was seven weeks ago. Who has writer's cramps now? huh? As I've said before I write every week and I'd mail it air mail except that a stamp cost $1.10. Which is more than I get for my weeks allowance.

Mrs. Jonah said hello and said she will write you soon. Write soon, with fondest love, your everloving Phyllis

May 11, 1944   Reprimand for my shocking language

My Darling,

Today I have received your letter of March 20th…much as I like reading your letters, however there is always something in it that I do not like. For instance in today's letter the language used by you when referring to Mr. Bonapart is shocking. To judge from what you are writing one might think that the people of Homewood Terr. have always tried to make you unhappy and whatever you experienced there was the worst one could think of. Well, I'm of quite a different opinion and deeply grateful to them that in a time when you were deprived of the care of your parents they took this burden upon themselves, gave you a home, brought you up and still (I'm sure) are doing their best to smooth your way in life. So much for your "hate" of Mr. Bonapart.

…I received your photo. You want to know whether I like it? Need I tell you how glad I'm to have at last your picture? Of course, I'd like it much more to be with you to see you personally…Anyhow, I placed it in such a position that whenever I'm at home there can scarcely be a minute of not having you before my eyes. There is nothing that occupies my mind more than the thought of your mother and you, and I should have never dreamt that the way to you would be so hard and full of obstacles…Just the other day I received words from Arno telling me that I shall have to wait for another 6 months until he would be able to again approach the State Department for my visa. Five years I have been waiting for it, and now again it was put off for another 6 months…

…All my love and heaps of kisses from your Daddy

May 20, 1944

Dearest Daddy,

…Sunday I came down with a temperature of 100 degree. On Monday it rose and it went up to 104 degree. Mrs. Jonah was very swell to me. She phoned Homewood

Terrace and told them to send a doctor but they said they couldn't because he was out for the day. It was his day off. Well he came the next day. But then I had developed a strep.(streptocacus?) throat. When you have strep throat you have a very hard time to swallow. Well I had to take sulfa drugs. And on Wednesday I was almost well. My temperature had gone down to normal. Thursday I got out of bed and walked around. On Friday I went outside and took a sunbath and today I'm just as fine as I could possibly be. I missed a lot of school but I'll have to make it up. We got our report cards but I didn't get mine.

I hope you are fine and swell, I am, please do not worry over me. hope to hear from you soon. I remain your everloving daughter Phyllis

April 17, 1944   Received June 11

My Darling,

I have received your letter of Feb. 24th and I'm really very glad …that you made up your mind to write to me every week. This is good news…and I hope you keep your promise….

You will certainly complain that I do always find fault with what you write or do. But as it is there are things to which I cannot and will not agree. For instance, your present attitude towards the people in charge of Homewood Terr. …considering what these people did for you during the past years,…I am ashamed of my daughter being so unmindful of all this, using bad language when referring to those in charge of the Home. I must say it is disgraceful…

…Time and again I wrote you and pointed out the importance and necessity of devoting most of your time toward studying, …the answer given in your last letter,…" I am not hunting for 'A' marks and as long as I know what I am supposed to know I'm satisfied". Well, you were satisfied but it is sure the teachers were not, and neither am I. …I very often find the grammar bad and spelling is sometimes shocking! These things have to be learnt, but if fun-making with your girl friends and flirting with boy friends is all that matters with you, so the prospects are not bright…At your age there is only one important thing, to prepare for the future by acquiring as much knowledge as possible….That doesn't mean I want you to be a "sour-puss" or "dead egg," far from it, I want you to enjoy life, to have pleasure and fun, but learning must take up the first place.

…Even having been rather harsh with you today, you know it, my darling, that my thought are always with you and I'm longing for the day of our reunion. All my love and heaps of kisses, Your Daddy

Despite my personal troubles, there were important changes in the war since the beginning of the year. In January, the Russians had invaded Poland and liberated Warsaw and German troops retreated. In February the Allies met at Yalta to discuss and agree to the shape of the world after the war. In April, Okinawa was retaken beginning the recovery of the Pacific losses. D-Day—the invasion of France by allied forces—occurred on June 6th. It marked the beginning of the ending of the war.

June 11, 1944 A rebuttal to his complaints and criticisms.

Dearest Father,

I just received your letter from April 17

No. 1. Look Dad, I've written you before and you replied that you're my father and it's up to you to put me on the right track. Well, O.K. I know it. And I'm glad you do it but I think, when you criticize everything I do, I think it's enough. You complain about my behavior, my grades which you think my boyfriend is the fault of and everything else. Look, I wish you would look at it from my point of view. Homewood Terr. and it's stinken executives own me. They can do anything they please to me. Everything I do is wrong as far as they are concerned and they never stop punishing for things which happened months ago. Don't you see how miserable it must be to be owned by somebody else. Living in Germany was sometimes better than it is here. We had no freedom there but at least I had personal freedom but here my arms and mouth is tied. Don't misunderstand me I love America, it's wonderful but it's H. Terrace I hate. I should be grateful but I can't very well be when a narrowheaded one-track minded fat bitch takes pleasure in ruining other people's lives. That's that.

No. 2. I didn't ask you for $10.00 every month. I asked you for $10.00 that month which I think was February. And please, don't send me any money unless you can absolutely spare it.

No. 3. Why the hell do you always bring boyfriends into the picture. I have written you twice about a fellow and every time you want to criticize you always bring him into it. I wish you wouldn't refer to him at all unless you want to find out about him. He has nothing to do with anything.

No. 4. Then you complain about bad language. I am not a baby and if I want to let my emotions out about those things I will. You can be sure I don't swear in Public. But when I write to you I get so involved I have to swear. And I will.

No. 5. Why do you complain about my grades. A B average is good. I am no master mind and believe me I am not going to study 90% of my time. You can be sure I'll be a success when I grow up and as for my spelling. When I write you I think of you so wholly that my pen just flies. I thought that you'd understand that. But from now I shall use the best grammar and have a dictionary by my side and look up every word.

Just refering to No. 1 why must you insist on saying they (H.T.) have good reasons for restricting me from everything? I was invited to go to a formal party and you'd think it would be O.K. but no, what if I should spill coke or something on my cousin's formal. They're sure that Mrs. Rabinowitz would sue H.T. The sweetest woman in S. Francisco who has never done anything to harm me or H.T. and they have to tell stories about her to everyone like a bunch of gossipers. Well, my aunt finally decided to give it to me. And if I don't feel like 2 cents. H.T. always has a good reason to be mean. Your letters are about the only thing I look forward to. But lately all you've made me do is cry and feel that even my own father doesn't like me any more.

I give him an ultimatum!

So, I've just decided. When you write I just want to hear how you are and what you do and stuff about you. Unless you do, and I realize I'm threatening, I am not going to write to you anymore. I just don't want to cry anymore, there are other things I have to cry about. Now, please Dad, I love and miss you an awfully lot but with everyone of those letter I get bad memories. So please let's have friendly letters, with laughter and warmth, friendship and love. I'm sure you'll like those kind too.

How are you? I am graduating a week from this Thursday on the 22nd. Wish you were here. I am going to send you a snap-shot of me next week. Until then all my love and love you very much. Love Phyllis

How about a friendly letter?

I have no recollection of going to a formal party. It must have been around winter vacation, perhaps a Christmas party before I moved to the Jonahs. Where would I get a formal? It would have been too expensive to buy one, so I must have asked Cecile (Aunt Laura's daughter) if she had one. Mr. Bonapart's objection to borrowing it must have been just to stop me from going, but it made me feel bad because I thought that my aunt felt she had to give it to me.

My life with the Jonahs was OK as long as I was in school, still at Aptos, and had my friends around me, but when summer came, I became forlorn because I had no friends in the neighborhood. Also now I was asked to take more responsibility for the children that I didn't particularly enjoy, and my time was not my own. I didn't even get to go swimming at the Community Center.

For July, plans were made to go to Boyes Hot Springs, a resort area north of San Francisco. Mr. Jonah would be away on one of his business trips and Mrs. Jonah had rented a cabin for a month. I looked forward to going away, hoping that I would be able to make some friends there. The most remarkable feature of Boyes Springs was the gigantic swimming pool under a huge glass dome that allowed the light, but filtered the searing heat of the area. There were many diving boards of different heights. Music wafted over a loudspeaker as we played in the water. *I'll Get By, You'll Never Walk Alone, Sentimental Journey* were some of the tunes played often, reminding us all that the war was separating families. In addition to the big beautiful pool, there were many other, smaller ones with varying hot temperatures for short soaks, not particularly interesting to teenagers and children. I had to watch the children in the pool and I resented it.

Mrs. Jonah made friends with many young service men who were at Sonoma Mission Inn, a swank resort that had become a R & R Center (rest and recuperation) for service men coming out of battle. Perhaps there were some at G.I.s at Boyes Hot Springs, too. They were invited for dinner or evenings and I could hear conversations about homosexuals and lesbians. Although those words were in my vocabulary, I didn't understand what it all meant. I was not included in the conversations, so I listened carefully through the thin walls hoping to get informed. I wondered how she engaged these young men to speak with her, when I, almost fifteen, might have been more fun, or so I thought. I felt like Cinderella.

✦ ✦ ✦

One night, July 17th, a very loud explosion caused me to fall out of my bed; I was sure we were being bombed! But there was only the one blast and I went back to bed. We learned the next day that the munitions warehouse at Port Chicago, perhaps fifty miles away, had exploded, and killed 320 seamen, 202 of them were African-American. Fifty of these ammunitions workers refused to go back to work and were convicted of mutiny. I might have forgotten this incident except that it culminated in a lawsuit that has been running for all these years; it is reported on every so often in the papers thus reminding me of the incident and the unhappy times when I was with the Jonahs. The sailors' families sued for wrongful imprisonment; finally in 2000 their discharges were changed to "honorable."[1]

◆ ◆ ◆

One day I was allowed to rent a bicycle to go riding with a new male acquaintance. I was very excited by the prospect of an afternoon with this young man, but almost immediately, I fell off the bike and sprained my ankle so I could hardly walk. When Mrs. Jonah realized that I wouldn't be able to baby-sit and do other chores, she was upset and we returned to the City immediately. It happened to be August 9th, my fifteenth birthday. I didn't even get a card, or even a "Happy Birthday" wish.

We arrived in San Francisco around dinnertime, and I was instructed to feed the children, since she would be going out with friends. I was furious. I hobbled around to make the dinner, made the beds, gave the boys baths, and put them to bed. Then I took one of her cigarettes that she had left behind and started to smoke. I was lucky that I didn't set the house on fire because I took the cigarette to my room, to my bed and under my covers! From then on I began to smoke her cigarettes when she was out and left them around. I was not caught.

Monday, Aug.14, 1944

Dearest Daddy, my doll,

I've received your two letters from June 20th and July 10, and also $10. Thanks a million.

I am home from my vacation but before I came I had a little accident. You see I was

---

[1] Allen, Robert L.: *The Port Chicago Mutiny,* Warner, 2000

riding a byke and I tried to turn in gravel, but I couldn't and fell off my byke. I sprained my ankle and for awhile it was awfully sore but it's O.K. now. Meanwhile I was fifteen. When I first came to America and I started getting in trouble and made vow that I would tell you everything when I was fifteen. I had hoped you'd be here but since you aren't a letter will. At any rate I don't want you to worry about me.

I think I should start by telling you that I am very unhappy. My guess is that I have no character and I can't get along with people. In some of the letters I have written you I have been very fresh and mean but that's a result from being unhappy. Mrs. Jonah told me you and she were corresponding. If you were what impression do you have of her?

Mrs. Jonah is having a pleasant holliday on me. In all the six months I've been here, I do all the work and she has a pleasant time. In the mornings I get up real early, while she sleeps and I feed the kids. They are a couple of brats, fresh and they never listen and they treat me as if I were a maid. I feed them and I do the dishes and then around 10:30 the lady gets up. Then I have to make the beds and if I'm a little slow she says: "It is about time you did them." The other day my sprained ankle was killing me and I'd have to sit down every once in a while. It was late in the afternoon and she was entertaining while I was working. She is not a good housekeeper. Then she goes out in the afternoon while I take care of the kids and if I don't do something like clean up the house or something she says: "We can't go on like this me working and you loafing." Then I get the dinner ready and do the dishes. And if she get invited out to dinner I feed the kids. She goes out almost every night. Often I have to mop the floors after dinner. On Sundays, I can [go]out. But before I go out I must give the kids breakfast and come back at 7:00. Mrs. Jonah is making a sucker of me. But Daddy, I don't care. I'm going to stick it out till you come and it better be soon. I hate it here but Homewood Terrace is worse. The State department better give you a visa.

But let us forget me. Soon it is your birthday and all I could say is happy birthday and all the luck in the world. I do hope to see you soon. I am feeling fine and I hope you are same. So until next week, I'm your everloving daughter, love Phyllis.

Monday, Aug 28 I apologize for a previous letter, and feel sorry for myself.

Dearest Daddy, Doll

Gee, I haven't had a letter from you in two weeks and I haven't a thing to write about. By now you most probably got the letter [April 21] where I told you I wouldn't listen to you but I guess you really don't believe me. But when I get mad I've got to blow of steam somewhere.

I sure hope you're going to get your visa this [year] *as I am awfully lonely for you I haven't seen you in five years and I'm missing you an awful lot.*

There is nothing new around here. I work all day and everything I do is always wrong, in fact the way I get treated around here I often wonder why I was born. Why did God or fate have to separate us? I get no news from anyone, Mom, Arnold or you once in awhile. I can't go out with my friends or even phone them. Most of the time the lady goes out and plays cards while I stay home with the kids. What fun.

Did you even hear of the classic book: David Copperfield? It is by Charles Dickens and if [you] *can read it, do. Wonderful book reminds me of myself.*

How are you feeling? I am O.K. But I have a bad cold. Went to the Dentist this A.M. Hope your fine, love always Phyllis   …Happy New Year

My letters were the only outlet for my frustrations at this time because my friends didn't live nearby. I stopped being cooperative, and started sassing back. I felt cornered; I didn't want to go back to the Home to be scolded by Mr. Bonapart, and then by my father. I felt miserable. School—Washington High School—started, and I didn't know a soul. I realized how much I missed my friends. I continued with my fresh mouth, almost demanding that I be kicked out.

Sept. 24, 1944

My little Darling,

I received three of your letters—June 30th, July 14 and 31, then two days later from Aug. 16th. Plenty to read, but still more to worry about especially the last did upset me. I would have never thought that you had to do all this kind of work you are writing about and I need not tell you how I feel about it. I fully realized how all this tells on you. I wish I could, at last, take care of you myself and not to see you dependant anymore upon other people's kindness. Unfortunately, fate decided otherwise, and keeps us separated. I want you to know that I feel and understand how unhappy and lonely my little darling must be. But now, Darling, listen to me and be sensible. Those present conditions are not going to be forever and one day I'll come over to you and relieve you from all those troubles. Arno promised to take up my case again…Put away every thought of despondency, it is of no good and does not help either.… All my love, and heaps of kisses, your Dad

Sept. 30, 1944 A letter from Mrs. Jonah

My dear Mr. Finkel,

I can't think of anything I'd rather not do than write this letter to you!

For the past seven months, Phyllis has been a member of my household. I've tried, believe me, to help her take her place in my home. I've advised her in her school studies, nursed her when she was ill and in short, I have done my best. My children have been shown no partiality and my Household has been very considerate and well-mannered with Phyllis. However, somewhere along the line, I've failed.

I'm sorry but I find that I have to send Phyllis back to Homewood Terrace. When she came here, I silently vowed I would never make her go back but, I just can't stand for any more!

I'm ill, having to go under an operation in the very near future and I have been advised, by my doctor, that I am to have no excitement or aggravation of any kind. I don't think he figured on Phyllis.

She is very impatient, insolent, and disrespectful to me—not very kind to my older boy who is seven and, very obviously, not very anxious to please me one little bit.

I know this isn't a very kind thing to do under the circumstances but I hope you'll understand. Some day, when this horrible thing is all over, and you and your family are re-united, I hope I may have the pleasure of meeting you. Yours very truly,   Mrs. I. Jonah

My misery didn't last long. Soon I was sent back to the Home. I returned to Cottage 42 under Mrs. Goss and started Lincoln High School. It was good to see my old friends from Aptos who were going to Lincoln, and they greeted me warmly. I was glad to be back, even glad to be in Cottage 42.

Oct. 6, 1944

Dear Daddy,

I received your letter from Aug. 29, 1944 and I was awfully glad to hear from you and for once I didn't cry. By now you most probably have received a letter from Mrs. Jonah explaining why I left her. Well, I read that letter although she didn't know it. Believe it or don't but I don't want to say anything since I am always wrong anyway. I am back in the home again. I transferred to another high school which is called Lincoln. It is the best Senior High School in the city. I have loads of fun and a lot of hard work.

Today, I have finished all my homework and I am in my Study Period. I realize I didn't write last week but I was awfully busy with moving and all.

Tomorrow is a big football game. All my best friends are coming. I wish you could know my friends as they are real friends and we stick together all the time. One's name is Mil and the other Kay. They're awfully swell. Well, Dad, the bell's gonna ring any minute so this letter is gonna be kinda short.

Till next week all my love, love always Phyllis

Oct. 14, 1944

Dear Daddy,

I haven't gotten any letters from you this week but what a surprise. I got a letter from your brother. He is in Montreal. He said [he] *hasn't heard from you for nine months and I rushed him your address. The day he wrote me he said he had just arrived there. Well I sure was glad to hear from him. Right now I am in Study Hall or else I'd give his address, but I will next time.*

You know by now that I am in the home. So far I've been getting along O.K. ... Saturday night I went to a dance and I had the most wonderful time. I met the nicest fellow. He sure is swell. There is another dance next Saturday and boy am I looking forward to it. School is keeping me quite occupied.... Good-by for now all my love Phyllis

Nov. 13, 1944

Dearest Dad,

I received your letter with the money order (Sept. 24) in it and believe me that letter put all the courage in the world into me. To know that you really believe me and feel that I shouldn't depend on other people's kindness made me feel tops. I've been trying to get that point over to you for nearly three years. And at last it has impressed you.

Daddy dearest it's been wonderful. To know that you're with me is great and to know that you simpathize with me and believe that I'm not always in the wrong is better yet. You don't know [how] *I feel. Words cannot express it. Anyhow, I know that you will be able to get your visa this time, partly because I've learned to pray to God and I've prayed for you and because I feel it in my bones.*

When two people agree and love each other no power on earth can keep them apart, you'll see. Well, Dad, I don't know what else to say, I'm fine and I hope everything is all O.K. with you. I'm going to have some pictures taken and I'll send you some. Right now love and kisses Phyllis

Nov. 28, 1944   Mr. Bonapart seems to be on my side.

Dear Dad,

This week, Thanksgiving week a lot of things happened. For one thing I got a letter from you on Monday saying that you were very worried about me. Then on Thursday, Mr. Bonaparte wanted to see me. Whenever he wants to see me my heart jumps down thru my stomack. You couldn't guess what he wanted to see me about. Yes, he received your [letter] telling you were worried about me. He talked to me for 2 hours and when we were thru he told me to tell you to disregard in most ways the letter he send. For once we finally agreed at end. You know, Dad, I'm perfectly settled at Homewood. I've given them no trouble and everything fine but I guess you're used to that line. However maybe this time it will stick until you come. In fact I know it will, because there is not other alternative.

I am inquiring thru a refugee service to see if they can find momy.

I got another letter from Uncle Max and he's planning on returning to Europe after the war. Imagine that. He says he doesn't like Canada.

...Thanksgiving night we had a swell turkey dinner and all the time I was planning on the Thanksgiving we would have when you get here. It was swell. Please don't worry over me now I'm swell and I hope you are too. All my love till next time love and kisses, Phyllis

Dec. 4th, 1944

My Darling

I received your letter of Oct. 6, the news of your moving back to the Home did not surprise me as some two weeks ago I received the letter from Mrs. Jonah...Strange as it is, I was not shocked at it as I used to be on similar occasions before, your letters in the past few months seemed to indicate that something of this kind is going to happen...I'm not going to blame you, after all, maybe you are right this time, but now that your are back at the Home see to it that you can, at last remain there and try to get along with the people there. As you know Arno applied again, and I hope that this time I'll get the visa, so there is a chance of my getting over to you and ending this terrible nuisance of moving from one place to another. I'm glad to hear that you are so satisfied with your new school, let us hope that the success will be a greater one than before, and that year the "C" marks won't spoil your record card.

...All my love and best wishes, Your Dad

Dec. 18, 1944

Dearest Daddy,

I haven't heard from you for about three weeks. I supposed its the Christmas mail. I do hope you're fine though.

Right now we are having Xmas vacation, our second week and our last. I've had a swell week. The week before we received our report cards and this is what I got:

Geometry	*B*	*S*	*Biology*	*B*	*S*
Gym	*D*	*S*	*German*	*B*	*S*
English	*B+*	*S*			

I went up in Biology. You know Dad, that D I got in Gym is the first D I ever got. It really isn't my fault. It sure hurt but I'm awfully glad it was only in gym.

Anyway during our vacation I've gone to four movies and I'm going out again to-night. We had a Chanuka party and I got a lot of presents. One was a blouse and I like it but I am going to exchange it for a sweater. I've had a swell time. I wish you could have shared it with me. For New Years we are going to have a party and though you can't be here I wish you all the luck, health and a quick reunion. The usual wishes, you know, health and happiness, the same stuff I've wished you for years, perhaps this time it will come true, with a little of good behavior from me as an encouragement to God. I think of you more than ever now, realizing how much I need you.

I'm really fine and swell and I do hope you're the same. Till next time. All my love from your everloving daughter. Love and kisses Phyllis

December 22, 1944

My Darling,

Last week I received ...letters of Oct 14th, Nov. 6th and Nov.13th.....your last letter was very inspiring and I read it again and again as it revealed plenty of cheerfulness which I missed so badly in all the letters of the past months. That is exactly the state I want to see you always, keep your chin up and don't let others make you miserable. ...

Today I finished working and I'm going to have a vacation for 17 days. This is a fine break and I sure am going to enjoy it. I'd have gone somewhere to the country, the *places are so overcrowded nowadays and it is practically impossible to get accomodation unless you booked $^1/_2$-1 yr ahead, so I decided to stay here. After all we have got splendid beaches here and weather permitting I'm going to have a really fine holliday. So far I'm without further news from Arno, anyhow he made a new application...let us hope this time I'll get the visa...Love, Your Dad*

My father's reference to yet another application for a visa was once more encouraging news. Even as my troubles were relieved by returning to the Home, the war was beginning to turn in favor of the Allies and patriotism was running high as our victories were beginning to be more frequent. There was a widespread belief, or perhaps just hope, that the war would be over soon. I couldn't wait for that to happen!

18

HIGH SCHOOL

1945

Lincoln High School, located on a big hill in the Sunset District, was the newest high school in San Francisco—so new it hadn't been completed when the war broke out and all construction ceased. It was a very modern-looking building, two stories high, but it lacked a gym and a theater and had only a small playfield. School assemblies were held outside in a plaza where we sat on big, tiered steps like in an arena. Children at the Home could choose between Lincoln and Balboa High schools; Lincoln was more academic, but not as academic as Lowell. Theoretically, we would have been able to go there, but nobody did besides Mr. Bonapart's son.

It took me about forty minutes to get to school because I had to transfer street-cars. Going to school was fun because some friends were already on the streetcar, and at each stop new ones would get on, all meeting at the back of the car where we liked to sit. On the way home, I often stopped at the transfer point for a chocolate coke and a cigarette with friends. My smoking habit had started just a few months before. It was not easy to purchase cigarettes because of my age, as well as the wartime short-ages. Sometimes, I had to go into backrooms of shops to get them, although it scared me because I knew I could get into big trouble. Sometimes the store clerks who sold them to me were creepy, making me feel like I was "cheap," but I liked the sophistica-tion of smoking enough to continue with this bad habit for another ten years. Of course, the movies were filled with romantic scenes always accompanied by smoking, or intimate rituals of lighting cigarettes, thus encouraged our young habits.

Most of my friends from Aptos were at Lincoln, and some of the students from Lawton Elementary were there too—they had entered Lincoln in the 9th grade. I made some new friends and enjoyed the old ones too. I felt comfortable and at home in this school. High School was fun, especially the excitement at school about the athletic games between the high schools. The act of going to a football game in a crowded car, cheering for our team, the Mustangs, feeling happy or sad at the outcome filled me with a wonderful sense of belonging that I hardly knew, but craved intensely.

The Drama Club

January 7, 1945   Something was not going well, but I have no recollection of it.

Dearest Daddy,

Gee, I haven't heard from you for ages. I guess it must be a Christmas rush. How've you been meanwhile? I hope you're fine.

Honestly Dad, I'm not trying to complain but I miss you so much. I like the home so much now that I've come back and the staff is very good to me but I just need someone who is really interested in my feelings. I don't have a hard time getting along with girls its just that they are so utterly self-centered. And there are only a couple of those. But, otherwise I really don't trust the others. It's really terrible when you don't believe and trust anyone.

See Dad, if you don't come here soon, I'll come to you. I'm living in a dream, a dream when you come here and I'll live with you and maybe Mom will be with us. It's a dream, a beautiful dream. And Dad dear, you'll be proud of me. I am a good girl, you'll see.

With all this trouble about Russia, I mean, and Poland, I doubt if the war will ever finish. [Russia had recently invaded Poland]

Meanwhile we had New Years. We had a party here and it was swell, lots of fun. I was thinking of you and how it had been five and a half years since I had seen you and hoping that before the next year was at a close, you would be here. ... I went out with Aunt Laura —I call her auntie and we had some pictures taken. When they are finished, I will forward you a copy.

On Sundays from now on I am going to work at a hospital so I could help the war effort a bit. The nurse shortage is critical so, since I don't do anything on Sundays anyway, I thought I'd do something useful and important.

I hope you're feeling fine and I do wish I'd get some mail from you. It's been 2 months already and frankly I'm worried. I sure wish I knew. I'm feeling fine and swell and everything is O.K. So, until next time, take it easy and write soon.

Love forever from your everloving daughter,   Love + XXX (kisses) Phyllis

I can't recall who or why I distrusted some of the girls. It is not typical of my personality, and wasn't then, to mistrust people. Although I always wanted to be liked and popular, I was not sensitive to other kids not liking me or of them spreading tales. I didn't belabor "what will others think of me." On the other hand, I wanted to be doing what my classmates were doing. As it happened, in this time period the media was beginning to note teenagers' culture. With the advent of Frank Sinatra and the teenagers' idolization of him, the media began to follow the styles and habits of our generation. For example, the December 11, 1944 issue of Life declared: "Now no teenager dares wear anything but pure white sox-no hat, stockings or high heels." It noted our fascination with the telephone and high school sororities. I was a dedicated reader of Life for news of the war's progress, but also very interested in the articles on my age group as I identified with its culture.

However, my most important guidance did not come from Life. I was still reading classics such as Dickens and studied Shakespeare in one of my English classes. When we studied Hamlet, I took Polonius' advice to his sons to heart: (Act One)

> This above all: To thy own self be true,
> Then canst thou not to any man be false
> And this must follow as the day the night.

It was also advice my mother had given me in her farewell poem. I never lied to my father, although I didn't always tell him everything.

February 28, 1945   Received April 1

> *My Little Darling,*
>
> *At last a letter, and a good one at that....Anyhow it is good news to hear how satisfied you are now and that is most that matters.*
>
> *...A letter from Arno telling me he would try ...to get the visa for me. I often think that in case I should not be able to come over to you, to bring you here, but for the time being...immigration is completely stopped.*
>
> *Yes, you are right, Darling, it is already 5½ years since I left you and dear Mami, you were then 10 years old, and even now in spite of your pictures...showing a girl in her teens, before my eyes there is still the little girl ...and I cannot picture you otherwise.*

Finally, some words about his life in Melbourne

> *I'm all right, Darling, just doing the same kind of work as before.* [shipping clerk in a woolen mill] *It is sometimes monotonous and trying, but then there is a Saturday and Sunday every week, two days to do whatever one likes, to have a good time and rest. As a whole life here in Melbourne it is quite pleasant, from time to time I go to the pictures and we have here some beautiful picture theaters such as we did not have in Vienna, though on the other hand there is no opera house, or any theater where you could see classics, and the first is what I miss most.*
>
> *All my love and heaps of kisses, Your dad.*

March 2, 1945

> *Dear Dad,*
>
> *I finally got a letter from you after 5 long weeks. I received it last week along with one from your brother and one from Arnold. I'm sorry I haven't written sooner but really my studies keep me up till 11 or 12 o'clock at night. You see I don't take a study anymore, instead I take sewing and all my homework keeps me awfully busy. Well anyway how are you? Your letters are few and far away. I'm inclined to worry all the time when I am without news form you.*
>
> *Yesterday we had prize day. I got $5 for helpfullness around the house and good behavior. See, I'm improving.*

Your brother also seems to be making progress in Canada. He, too, works in a material factory. I was very touched. He wrote me, that he worked hard and that his pay is very little but when Easter rolls around he'll have saved enough money to buy me a dress. Arno always does that too. I think that is so sweet of them.

Aunt Laura's son entered the Navy last month. I see her about once a month.

My cottage mother her name is Mrs. Goss is a very sweet lady and we are getting along splendidly. If you remember, I lived in her house before and we didn't meet. Now that I have understood her, and found out how swell she is, living with her is grand.

Till next week then,   Love XXX kisses,   Phyllis

Once more I received a prize for helpfulness; this helped me to feel better about the accusations of bad behavior of my previous year. It is also comforting to me now to know that I really wasn't lazy or uncooperative, but just a rebellious teenager wanting to control her life. I remember liking Mrs. Goss.

April 1, 1945   Good news at last!

Dearest Dad,

Oh how I love you. Today is the happiest day of my life. We were sitting in our bible class and Mr. Bonapart was lecturing us about war effort which is lacking and then he told me that I got a letter from you....Then he said that your visa had been approved. (He had just got the cablegram from Arno.) He said it in such a way that I almost didn't believe him and I asked him to repeat it. He did and he said you would soon be here. I began crying and I couldn't stop. Here I was in front of everyone crying but I didn't even care. I was thrilled. All I could do was to thank God for his kindness.

We went to services and I prayed and thanked God again. You see in the last few months I have thought of God and Religion and I also found that my ideas and ideals in Atheism were wrong. I found that if you really believe in something, regardless whether it's good or bad it usually will give you something to live for, to work for, and to hope for. I found myself believing in God and wanting to be helping him and I gave myself some hope and courage and a true ideal. I figured if I followed his wishes and his laws I'd find a good, clean way of life, the kind you'd be proud of and mother, Mr. Bonaparte and everyone who was interested in me. I also thought how hard you had worked for me and I had to think of someone else for a change except me. I'm awfully grown up, Daddy, but I can still act fifteen. I'm so glad you're finally coming.

In your letter [2/28] you were thinking of having me come over there (etc.) but I know you'd never think of going back (Australia) if you were here. It's heaven. Today is a bright sunny day and I feel like a million dollars and today also marks my fifth year in America... There have been many happy days, many sad and weary days, but on all of them I have thought of you. I'll really be glad to see you.

I reported on my grades—all C, C+ and one B, in sewing. I promised to do better.

I don't know whether I've told you this before but I saw Carmen about two months ago. It was very good. It was surprising to hear that there are no Opera houses in Melbourne. We have a nice one here and Opera season is in the fall.

Today is Easter and vacation is over and we go back to school Monday. I am feeling fine and I know you must be too after such splendid news. Uncle Max sent me a dress and it's very pretty. I owe him a letter.

Till next time then, Love & kisses, Phyllis

For some time I had been thinking that there was no God, and I had become bored with the ritual of religion. Perhaps my dislike of Mr. Bonapart made the religious service over which he presided uninspiring and uninteresting. One day as I was sitting in Temple while Mr. Bonapart was giving a sermon, I thought, "there is no God! There is no bearded man in the sky directing our lives!" I fully expected and waited for something awful to happen to me at that moment, but since nothing did, I had the courage to continue exploring the idea. I thought of religion often, and was drawn to books about religion and spirituality, but they did not deepen any faith I had, rather they diminished it. I liked the ideas and some of the values—such as caring for others, being truthful and kind—but I never could believe that worshipping God had anything to do with how I behaved or what happened in the world. I don't remember talking to my friends about it, perhaps they wouldn't have approved of my wayward thoughts. In the letter above, however, I had tempered my thoughts, at least for the time being. I had recently read *The Robe*, by Lloyd Douglas, (a story about Jesus) that could account for my present inspiration. In a later letter I refer to this book.

April 2, 1945   JOY! The Visa is finally granted! My father explains his lack of letters and mail, revealing desperate feelings.

> *...Oh, Darling I'm so happy now, yesterday I received a telegram from Arno that my visa was granted, you can imagine how overwhelmed with joy I am. ...soon, very soon I'll be with you. It is such an awful long time since we parted that I wish I could get a ship now, right away. How do you like the idea of having daddy soon over there with you?*
>
> *Well, now I can tell you why you did not get many letters from me lately. It was simply because I could not pull myself together, being in such a desperate mood I was unable to concentrate myself on writing. Some three months ago, Arno wrote me that he had another interview in the State Department and though he did everything to help me, yet he thought that there was very little chance of getting the visa and told me not to be very hopeful. When reading this I was sure he was preparing me for the next letter which would tell me that my application for a visa was rejected. Now you can imagine how I felt about this, I had seen all my hopes, for joining you in the near future, shattered and as there was not chance of bringing you over to Australia during the war, there was nothing left for me but utter despair. All these years I have striven to come over to you, and there comes a letter which puts a sudden end to all my hopes.*
>
> *Yet, what I did not believe nor expect anymore came to pass; the visa was granted. ...And all of this thanks to Arno, only his untiring endeavors made all this possible, and had he not helped me I'd have never been able to come to U.S.A. I cannot yet tell you when I'm going to leave, it depends on when shipping accommodation is available, sometimes one has to wait 2 months and sometimes, even 6 months. ...In the next weeks I'll have a lot of work with getting everything ready for the departure.*
>
> *All my love and heaps of kisses, your Daddy.*

✦ ✦ ✦

On April 12 when I was in Social Studies class, an announcement came over the public address system informing us of President Roosevelt's death. Some people in class began to cry, and I felt very sad. He was the only president I had known and I loved him uncritically. Immediately, I began to worry about the next thing that would happen—would it delay the end of the war? The papers had been very optimistic about a quick ending, and in fact it did happen on May 8 as V-E was declared when the Germans surrendered. I celebrated along with everybody, feeling that the European war was especially important to me. Perhaps I would hear from my mother now.

The United Nations Conference was in San Francisco April 25 to June 26. I followed the proceedings in the paper with great interest. I wanted there to be peace since more than half my life so far had been in war. I believed in the possibility of a United Nations, and was very pleased when the Charter was ratified by Congress.

✦ ✦ ✦

May 6, 1945

Dearest Dad,

What's the matter with everyone? Does everybody have writers cramps? NO mail from you or Arno. [His letter of April 2 hadn't reached me yet] *I thought maybe after you had received such good news (about your visa) you would be eager to write to me. Every day I look forward to mail form either you or them, but it does me no good. Gee, maybe you are busy, but you can't be that busy that you can't even write a little note to your daughter. You used to tell me that you'd worry if you received no mail from me. Now how do you think I feel after five weeks of no news.*

I had done a lot of planning and imagining about what we were going to do after you got here and once when I was talking in my daydream, Mr. Bonapart came and shattered it. Now what? He said you couldn't get any transportation. Is that true? Gods, Dad, it's almost been six years and every time I think this is it...somebody wakes me up. How much longer can this go on? It isn't that I don't get along here, because I am too perfectly. I just get exhausted from disappointments. Mr. B. is swell to me and there isn't anything he wouldn't do for me.

Another obstacle in our unification! At this time, I seem to have a good relationship with Mr. Bonapart, despite his forecast that Dad wouldn't be able to get transportation. The letter continues:

Two weeks from today, I'm getting confirmed. As I've told Annie, Arno, your brother and as I'm now telling you, I wish you could be here to witness this important ceremony. I'll send you a invitation anyway, because I still haven't lost my power of imagination.

Tell me Daddy, do you have any American books in Australia? If you do, I suggest that you read "The Robe". It is a story of Jesus Christ and about the best book I have ever read. It is written by Lloyd C. Douglas.

Although getting confirmed meant embracing the Jewish faith, I was searching for other opinions.

Today is a terrible day. It is cold, foggy, windy and I'm just miserable. Last week it was real sunny. I fell asleep in the sun. I got a sunburn but by now it has turned into a nice tan. How are you enjoying your weather over there?

...I am going to talk to Mr. B. about working summer vacation someplace. I want to earn some money so that I will have it easier when I go to college.

Well, I'm feeling fine and I hope you are too. And if you have enough time for your daughter, please drop me a line. Love and Kisses, Phyllis

My father's response to my suggestion that he read *The Robe,* (July 9, 1945) was:

I would prefer to see you getting acquainted with your own religion before starting comparative studies of others.

About confirmation he was confused:

Would you tell me more about it, as I'm quite unaware of the meaning of it, usually boys of 13 have one, but we never had any for girls.

✦ ✦ ✦

In Spring my age group would be getting confirmed, a religious rite of transition for 15 year olds. This Jewish Reform ritual is meant to be more democratic by including girls whereas in the Orthodox tradition they would be excluded from a coming of age ceremony. We had additional classes to prepare us for this event that would take place in May. The service would take place in our Temple located on the second story of the administration building, and Mr. Bonapart was our Rabbi. Members of the confirmation class were assigned special parts.

It was a special honor to read a beautiful, dramatic prayer, "Grant Us Peace,

Oh Lord, Thou Eternal Source of Peace..." and usually was read by the best speaker of the class. Although I was not the best speaker, far from it, I was chosen to deliver the special passage. It was the only privilege I remember Mr. Bonapart bestowing on me. Unfortunately, I was extremely poor at public speaking, lacking both the drama of presentation as well as the bodily carriage to portray self-assurance and poise, caused, in my opinion, by his frequent criticisms of me. Of course, I wanted to say that prayer because it would satisfy my unquenchable thirst for attention, so I was pleased when I was asked. However, according to the 1945 Year-end letter to myself, I "balled up my speech—was scared as hell, but the service was swell." I can remember leaning all over the podium, my knees shaking, and voice trembling, and feeling ashamed of my poor performance. Perhaps he gave me that part to show me how inadequate I was. My letter to my father says nothing of my feelings about my part, but the rest of the day seemed to have been wonderful.

May 31, 1945

> *My Darling,*
>
> *I have received your letter of April 1st and can well imagine how you felt when receiving the news of my visa being granted... In the meantime, I wrote you twice about it. [no letters received]...Oh, dear, it is a grand feeling to know that in the nearest future I'll be over there with you. ...the prospects of getting a ship in 3-4 months are good. ...You were quite right that I would be disappointed with your report card... I'll have a little talk about it when I'm over there as I'm in such a good mood and don't want to spoil yours with ...my "preaching". ...All my love and best wishes, Your Dad*

June 3, 1945

> *Dear Dad,*
>
> *I don't think I've had any mail from you except two weeks ago. I got 10 dollars from you and thank you so much for it. Meanwhile I got confirmed. The ceremony was beautiful and I had a real perfect day. I won't ever forget it. Arno sent me a beautiful bracelet. It is real dainty and it is just wonderful. From your brother I got $5 and a real good pen from the god-parents. Then we went to dinner and a show. By the way, I, as well as everyone else, got a swell new outfit. Anyway I missed you. I hope that you will be here real soon.*

In a couple of weeks school will be over and then I am going to work during the summer.

With the peace conference [The United Nations] *here the whole town (or city) is a bit excited. I've seen a few Russian soldiers, two delegates, no four but that is all. I wanted to see Molotov and though I wrote away for tickets I didn't get them yet.*

The United Nations Conference drew delegates from 50 nations. It convened April 25 and ended June 26. It had been Franklin Roosevelt's brainchild, but he had died just a couple of weeks before. The letter continues:

Last nite I went to a party and I came home real late. I had a real swell time. If I've made too many mistakes please forgive me but I am awfully tired.....So till next time, all my love and kisses, Phyllis

Aug. 2, 1945

Dearest Dad,

I'm hoping that your on that ship bound for here and that is you're excuse for not writing. I haven't heard form you for months. I mean it. Every day I look forward to a letter from you but I never get it.

Today is Thursday. 2 days from today will be the 4th of August. Marking six years since I last saw you. I don't think I could ever forget. Daddy doll, and I sure hope that it will be the last time that we will be apart. I'm anxiously awaiting your arrival here. I hope it will be before Xmas.

My summer vacation will be over in five weeks. I hope the time never passes. I hope to go up to the Russian River for two or three weeks with Alyce. She is a very nice girl. ...She's Irish and we're real good friends. I'm anxious for you to meet her. Well your birthday is nearing and I wish you all the luck in the world but you know Dad I've told you that often enough what I really want to wish is that we will be together real soon.

Next week I'll be 16. I'm not looking forward to it because I've had such a nice 15th year. I hope you'll be here to witness my 16th one. I miss you very much. Please come soon. I love you, Phyllis

As I recall my life in high school I changed friends frequently. First, I met Alyce at one of the football games and we became friends. I think the expression we used was: "I go around with—." Alyce had not gone to Aptos; she may even have been a newcomer to San Francisco when we met at school. Her parents were deeply involved with a religious group that Alyce was not happy to be part of, so we encouraged each other with our anti-religious opinions. In the summer I spent a couple of weeks at her place on the Russian River, a beautiful resort area north of San Francisco. Two young men from the Philippines were visiting her family, perhaps as part of their missionary work. I cannot remember much of them, but they had been fighting in the war, and were the only men I had met who had seen action and talked about it; it was mystifying as well as horrible. They were politically active for some cause in the Philippines, but that went over my head, and I just enjoyed their maturity, different from the boys at school.

✦ ✦ ✦

Thursday, Aug 9, 1945 This was the first letter that I wrote to myself, "to be opened 10 years later." I followed this practice for several years.

> *Today I am sixteen. I've had a lot fun my fifteenth year. So many joys and so many tears. Leaving the Jonahs—Herb, Xmas, Alyce, the basketball season. I've learned a lot and taught a lot. Ella has improved a lot.*
>
> *The Atom bomb was discovered, we won in Europe, Roosevelt died and Russia's declared on Japan.*
>
> *I've begun a record collection and read many good books such as the Green Light, The Robe, Magnificent Obsession, Valley of Decision, A Tree Grows in Brooklyn and Black Boy. I've gotten lots of new clothes. I love Perry Como, Gregory Peck, Dave Clark. I know a lot for my age but I hate Mrs. Boughner she's too know it all.* [She once was my favorite house-mother.] *Mr. and Mrs. Liebhoff* [the assistant director of the Home] *are swell and I love Alyce and Fonda & Mrs. Riehl is good to talk too.*

The next few days were very momentous and exiting because Japan would be surrendering. The possibility of it had begun the day after my birthday, but Japan had conditions, so there were negotiations. I was glued to the radio, waiting for the moment when the war would actually be over.

August 14, 1945 Another letter to myself recording what happened that day.

August 10th we heard a peace offering. Today, 4 days later its been made official. Friday the 10th I cried. Today I could not. In the morning we knew; at 4:00 p.m.PWT [pacific war time] we heard the first real announcement.

Dear God, please let this be the very last war and teach us humble creatures to live together in friendlyness and brotherhood. Grant us peace..etc.

We were all dressed and ready to go the Bal Taberin [Theater Restaurant]. Betty, Eda, Emma, Marion, Irene, Miss Lewison, Mrs. Boughner and I were all excited. We took the station wagon and started towards town. On Van Ness we saw so many drunken service men. Still I didn't cry. It meant that the war was over. I kept on repeating it over and over & the heavy hammer of surprise, happiness, gratefullness and gladness would not penetrate my thick skull. Yet it was true. I was afraid I was dreaming only to wake up again and find myself in war. Most of my years have been in war. I wondered what it was like to be living in peace time. All day I'd been cleaning out drawers and in my cold room, I rekindled some old pleasant and otherwise memories through the aid of notes. Two cigs were smoked out while I reminisced.

Of all this I was thinking on Van Ness [St.]. We then came to a stop sign. There was a church there and while we waited for the signal to change, I noticed one lonely sailor slowly mounting the steps. Soon I could only see his feet. I ducked down in my seat so that I could see him once more. I saw his feet cross the threshhold and once again he was out of my life. I would have liked to have known him. ...As I saw him disappear, I could not conceal my joy anymore and among everyone I began to cry. On the streets all the sailors were kissing any girl they could get a hold of. We were in a car. Everyone was in the middle of the street, making noise, tooting horns, getting drunk.

And still it did not sink in: The war is over. I bought two papers with those head-lines. We drove around. I didn't say anything. I was thinking how glad I would be to [have] my Dad here and a little easiness came to me. ...How's it going to be to wake up this morning (its 1:00am as I write) and find myself in a world of peace (we hope) instead of strife.

Then we went to dinner at Grison's instead. Liquor was forbidden 2 hours after the announcement. Yet I was afraid to cross the street in fear that some drunk would jump or follow me.

Maybe 10 years from now I'll believe it but I don't now. And if it's a dream it certainly is in detail. ....Well, it's over. War's over. Peace; War ends; Japs surrender these words—I know their meaning but I can't hold them. And if it true, let me be a part of a great world, a world of peace and happines and share the results. He'll be here soon and the war's OVER. IT'S OVER, CAN'T YOU UNDERSTAND? IT IS OVER

It was a memorable day—the crowds, the joy, and for me a greater hope that my father would soon be here, and perhaps we would get news about my mother.

Saturday, August 18, 1945

Dear Daddy,

I haven't heard from you in weeks and frankly I'm slightly worried. Now that the war is over I guess you'll be able to come here even sooner. I sure miss you Daddy darling. Before I never let myself think of how much I missed you but after six years I forgot all my willpower and down I went.

I was supposed to go on a vacation today for 10 days, but I can't go since I have a bad sore throat. That's life. I wait all summer to go and then when the time comes, I'm sick. It's nothing serious, only that it's catching and Alyce (she's the girl who's taking me) has a 3 month old baby and I don't want her to get it.

Today is Monday, I'm all well now. I learned that Alyce won't go to the river till next week. That makes me awfully glad.

About ten minutes [ago] I got a letter from Rose Engel. [My parents' friends from Vienna.] Do you remember her? I haven't heard from her for 3 1/2 years. … She and her husband are U.S. citizens now. They have a nice home in Brooklyn, both are working and very happy at that.

You know Daddy I never did know if your birthday was the 20th or 21st of August. But whatever day let it always be a happy one, the one day at least that you can be in perfect peace and easiness.

Till next time, all my love and kisses, millions of them (10,0000,000 ect. From now on the censors won't have to butt in)   Love, Phyllis

I have no recollection of the baby, nor of Alyce's pregnancy—perhaps she was able to hide it, but it wouldn't have bothered me if she did have a child without the benefit of marriage. I personally was firm in my intent not to have sex before marriage, but my resolve was never challenged during my high school years. I remember another friend showing a big belly who told me that she would be out of school for a while for a stomach operation, and I innocently believed her. I can hardly believe how naïve I was.

Aug. 21, 1945

Dear Dad,

As time goes on there seems to be less and less news from you. Why's that? Vacation has begun, in fact it's two weeks old. I've had so much fun. My report card was awful and I know you'll be disappointed, but it's been awfully hard without a study period. I'm glad that I took sewing in the study's place because I learned to sew and I'm going to keep up with it. I've made 2 dresses, 1 blouse and 1 jacket, a bathing suit and now I'm working on a suit. Many people have suggested that I take that up as my life's work but I think I'd like to sew only for myself. This is what I got on my card:

	3rd report	*Final*	*Citiz.*
Gym	*D*	*D*	*S*
German	*B*	*B*	*S*
Geo[metry]	*B*	*C*	*S*
Eng.	*C*	*C*	*S*
Sewing	*A*	*B*	*S*
Biology	*A*	*B*	*S*

Last week I went to Russian River with my girlfriend. We went swimming and I say so myself I'm pretty good. It's my favorite sport. Then we went horseback riding and bowling. We went to a dance, too. We had a real good time and are going there again this weekend and for a couple of weeks in August.

Now Dad, please tell me a few things, first, when you come what sort of work do you think you'll do? 2nd, do you intend to go to Washington or try your luck in San Francisco. I'm anxious to know these things. When do you think you'll get here? I hope to hear from you real soon and I hope you're feeling O.K. I'm feeling swell.

Till next time, lots of love, Phyllis

Sep. 25, 1945   A new semester has begun, as well as new troubles with Mr. Bonapart

Dear Dad,

I guess it's been a long time since I've had a letter from you and also a long time since I've written to you. But you know how the first three weeks of school are. I've had a lot of homework. These are the subjects I'm taking: English, US History, Alg theory, Chemistry.

Today 12 ships came in from Australia with many Australian war brides. When I saw it I was filled with joy. Maybe in a few ships you'll be on there.

Gee how I wish you'd hurry and get here. I won't complain but I get so lonely. And furthermore I hate this lousy dammed home. And believe me, I don't care what I ever said about Mr. Bonapart, I hate him with my whole heart and soul and the day I leave here I'll let him know [what] *I think.*

I had my picture taken a week ago and I'll have one for you though I don't think I'll send it. I'll give it to you when you get here. ... Love Phyllis

I don't recall what started the trouble with Mr. Bonapart again, but I remember resenting his dour predictions of my father's inability to support me or even to find a job. Of course, it never occurred to me that he would have trouble getting a job. Then, Mr. B. predicted that I would not be able to leave the home until I was 18, while I was hoping it would be before the year was out.

My father gave me no answers to my questions. Ever the planner, I was really concerned about what my life would be like when he did come. Having hoped and wished for so many years for him to rescue me, I had imagined a life like I was living—in San Francisco, going to Lincoln High. I had often asked him about the kind of work he would be doing; earlier on I had even suggested that he learn to be a "mechanist." I wanted some guidelines.

✦ ✦ ✦

Now in my junior year, I was asked to join a sorority. It was my greatest wish to belong to a group, especially this very prestigious sorority. The rush tea, held on a Sunday afternoon, was very exciting but nerve-wracking. I wore a black dress with pearls, like most of the other girls, since that was the uniform of sophisticated young women. I wanted to see if I made it before I asked Mr. Bonapart for permission, because I knew what he would have said: "Who do you think you are even thinking of a sorority—you are a poor immigrant, what makes you think you should or could join? Where would you get the money?"

I was thrilled to have been asked, but also deeply disappointed not to get voted in. It was a brash action on my part to even attend the rush, as I would not have had the money to join, and probably would not have been permitted to do so. I wrote in my year-end letter:

> *Thinking back on it now, I can't see any good reason for not making it, because I certainly am not a drip, and I still go around with the Phi Deltas. I guess I just didn't have enough self-confidence. I hope I make it when I go to college.*

It never occurred to me that my living at the Home, being Jewish, parentless and not having money had anything to do with being rejected. Instead, I felt I just wasn't good enough. Perhaps I should have been flattered and satisfied that I was even asked.

November 11, 1945 Disappointing news about his coming

> *Dear Dad,*
>
> *At last after waiting 12 weeks I got a letter from you. News saying that you most probably won't be here by Xmas. I was hoping for it very much but as you say a few more months won't matter. If you don't get mail from me every week please don't worry as I have a lot of homework and also because I work and my time is very short. Beside I have nothing to say except when you write. We know so little about each other that corresponding becomes a little difficult.*
>
> *Last week we got report cards and I thought mine was good since few teachers give "A" the first period.*

Chem	*B*	*S*		*PE*	*C*	*S*
Alg[ebra] *Theory.*	*C+*	*S*		*U.S. History*	*B*	*S*
Eng.	*B+*	*S*				

A new job!

> *On Saturdays I work in a department store. I wrap Xmas presents and I get 73 cents and hour. This of course helps a lot in my allowance and all. I do quite a lot of sewing now and I like it a lot.*
>
> *I had my picture taken and Mr. Bonapart should have sent it off by now. I'm not quite as big as I look there. A couple of weeks ago I had my bands off for a day and really my teeth look swell.*
>
> *Love,   Phyllis with lots and lots of kisses.*

In October a representative of the Emporium, a big department store, had come into our classroom and solicited us for work. The store was in critical need of Christmas help, and since we were 16 years old, we were not only eligible to work, but were desperately needed. He handed out applications and a few of us were very eager to accept this offer. I don't know if I requested to be a wrapper or was assigned by the store, but I liked wrapping. We worked in the basement of the store where a huge conveyor belt fed many stations of wrappers. When we finished one package we put it on the belt and took another one to wrap. In those days, when shoppers bought something, they typically had it sent home. This is hard to imagine today when service in stores is so meager, but in wartime and for some time after, "charge and send" was the typical transaction. Since most customers came downtown by public transportation, it was also practical not to have to carry everything home. We also wrapped them pretty if they were gifts. Some of the girls in my class went to work afternoons, but most of us just worked Saturdays.

It was fun seeing the things people bought and to learn the prices of so much merchandise. After Christmas, I "floated" around the store working on the floor in different cashier stations. The job I liked the best was in the millinery department at Easter time. Perhaps it reminded me of my first days in San Francisco at Aunt Laura's shop. Ladies always wore hats when they went out of the house, but a new hat for Easter was always beautiful and special. I loved looking at them, sometimes trying them on before I wrapped them for sending. I bought myself a hat for my next birthday. My least favorite place to work was the toy department at Christmas time because so many toys were difficult to wrap. I also did some selling in the yardage department, but the regular saleswomen resented me because my sale would take away from their commission; as a part-timer I wouldn't get commission anyway. I stayed with the Emporium for two years, mostly working seasonally or when I was called.

Through working at the Emporium I became friends with Helen and the twins, Barby and Joan. I had known them in school, of course, but now we became much closer. I often visited Helen after school where we practiced the newest jitterbug step.

Helen's family was Mormon, and I was invited to go with her to teen nights at her church and I spent time with her at her home. Her family was poor, but very generous, and even invited me to live with them. That Christmas Helen and I exchanged cashmere sweaters, the ultimate in fine clothing in our school. I think they cost $25.00—it was our way of buying something extravagant for ourselves, but calling it a gift made it more legitimate. I soon discovered that being around so many wonderful clothes ate up most of my earnings, even with the small discount.

The twins were one of eight sets of twins in my graduating class. Another set became famous by modeling perms—"Which twin has the Tony?" the ads asked, showing their identical hairdo's. Barby and Joan were very active in school government and on many committees and thus enrolled me for some school activities such as the dance committee. They lived near downtown, and later were responsible for helping my father and me to get an apartment in the house next to them.

✦ ✦ ✦

Many high school kids liked to go to China Beach, a small cove almost under the Golden Gate Bridge, to soak up the precious little sunshine in western San Francisco. It was unsupervised, no lifeguards, making it even more special for teenagers. However, there is a terrific undertow on that beach, as in many beaches along the northern California coast. I had a terrifying experience one time when Joan and I went swimming and maybe she saved my life. From one of my year-end letters:

> *I had just learned how to swim into the ocean, and Joan and I went quite a way out. The water was so smooth, and it was so easy to go far, far out. Then we became cold and decided that we should go back. However, we could not. I swam and swam but it was of no use. Joan managed to get quite a ways in, but when she saw that I was having trouble she came to help. I was quite scared for I didn't know how to behave in rough waters. I thought that I should let the tide carry me into the rocks, but she said that the pressure would mash me to pieces. We had to swim to the other beach which was about 2 miles away, [really only ¹/₂ mile] fighting against the current, the drawing force of the rocks and the undercurrent. We made it though. Then we had to hike*

back to China Beach. When we came back everyone was glad to see us because Barby had noticed her twin missing and everyone was frantically looking for us.

I am very respectful of California undertows, and though I became very strong swimmer, I limit my swimming to still waters.

✦ ✦ ✦

I had resumed going to the Jewish Community Center pool when I came back to the Home from the last foster home. Now old enough to be in the co-ed activities, I enjoyed playing in the water in the company of boys. I did not date much, and when I did it was only once or twice with the same boy. "My boyfriends," of whom I had written happily to my father's dismay, did not continue to be a reality. I wanted to have a boyfriend—it would have given me some intimate connection that I longed for, but even today I cannot explain why I didn't connect; I can only guess that I was too eager, perhaps too needy, or perhaps too picky. I always had crushes on some boy or other—I suspect anyone who talked to me nicely. Boys dominated my thinking. It bothered me that I didn't attract the boys and although I was overweight and sometimes quite self-conscious about it, I am sure that was not the only reason. I did have a long distance romance with Lefty, a boy from the Home who had joined the Marines. It made me feel good to talk about my boyfriend, but when he came home our relationship was not real—it had survived in my head through the correspondence, and I expect that my facility for writing letters played a role in that.

December 1, 1945

Dear Dad,

I haven't heard from you for a real long time. You told me not to worry, but how can I help it. I guess you're doing this just to punish me, but I don't think that's very fair because I suffer enough as it is. It would be silly for me to try to explain since we know so little about each other and you most probably would not understand anyway. You know Dad as much as I love you and want you here I know so little about you and visa versa. If it wasn't for the hope of your coming soon, to which I cling desperately, I don't think I'd last very long.

This point about knowing so little about him has appeared in a couple of letters. I began to worry about my future relationship with him.

I've got a very bad cold but I guess that when you get this letter I'll be O.K.

We got report cards:

Chem	*B+*
Alg Theory	*C+*
Gym	*C*
English	*C+*
U.S History	*B*

I am still working and I like it very much. The money I'll make during Xmas vacation I'll put into government bonds. That'll help, if only a little when I go to college.

I haven't heard from any one for a real long time. I guess everyone is busy. Well Dad, here's all my love till next time and please write soon. Love and kisses, Phyllis

December 31, 1945

My Darling,

At last another letter from you came in, and at the same time I have received your photo. Should I tell you how glad and pleased I'm to have it, oh, Darling it is really beautiful, I never thought my daughter were so good looking, placed on the mantlepiece it is always in front of me, and believe me it is an inspiring sight to look at. I wonder whether you see the difference between this picture and the last one I got last year. Well, now I can tell that I disliked it very much, that sad face and sorrowful look of your eyes made me feel miserable, whereas the new picture with your eyes shining is such as I want you to be and always dreamt of.

You know it is so strange to see you so well grown up, I cannot help it, but when thinking of you I cannot picture you out otherwise than as you looked six years ago when I left you, the small little girl that stood waving on the platform when the train carried me away. Of course, you must have grown in the meantime, yet when think-ing of you my mind does not want to take in any other picture. Isn't it funny? Well, I think I'll have to abide by this until I'm over there, which I hope will be very soon.

Yet other delays in his coming to America.

Today my visa expired. I'll have to renew it, let us hope that I soon shall be able to come over to you. There are still some 3000 brides of American soldiers waiting for shipping accommodation and it was reported officially last week, that they would be able to leave for the States within the next 3 months. When they have left the whole position will have eased up and our turn will come quicker. So Darling, this is the position today, of course, the unexpected often happens, and it may be just as possible to get the call to start sooner than expected. In the meantime you must have some patience and to look on life as cheerful as you do so well in the photo. You certainly must have wondered why I stopped sending you money. Unfortunately I could not get the permission...as there were no dollars available, but now as they got the loan (you certainly read about it in the papers) I hope I'll be able to receive the permission and send you something.

Apart from the terrible heat (104°) I'm feeling fine and hope you are likewise. ...All my love and lots of kisses,   Your Dad

✦ ✦ ✦

And so the year ended. I had made some good new friends, had developed skills and confidence by working, but had not been able to satisfy my quest for a boyfriend. However, it had been a very good year for the world. Hitler killed himself before Germany surrendered in June. Soon thereafter, in August, the war in the Pacific ended dramatically with the dropping of atom bombs on Japan, and surrender came quickly after that. In San Francisco, the delegates from all over the world, writing the United Nations Charter at the Opera House, created much excitement by their arguments and their agreements. Yet, despite the fact that the war was over, my father still wasn't here, and I was waiting impatiently for him to secure a space on a ship.

19

MORE TROUBLES

1946

I was looking forward to a quick reunion with my father, but it was not to be. Meanwhile, my war with Mr. Bonapart was accelerating again.

Jan 16, 1946   I ask many questions again about our future.

Dearest Dad,

After many weeks of waiting I finally heard from you. A day before that I received a letter from Arno and he too said you'd be here by Easter. You can't imagine how happy I was. I also got a picture from and of them and they still look the same. About finding you a room. It's very difficult to find rooms here, but you'll be put up when you get here—no need to worry. Incidently, I hope you don't think you're going alone, because I'm coming with you. I think[I] lived here in the home long enough when the time comes and you're here I'm going to stay with you. Do you think you'll go to Washington? I think that we ought to think of the picture right now. What kind of work are you going to try to get?

You're weather is exactly opposite ours. It is real cold here and were it snowing it would frosty and icy. I certainly do miss snow.

Report cards are coming up soon and I think mine will be pretty good. As I told you before I worked all during Xmas vacation and I got a little money saved. Mr. Bonapart said that I could not work anymore since I was indispensable in the house, haha. I finally found out why the kids were in such great awe before him. It's because he inflicts fear into their minds. Once you know that you can wind him around your little finger. (which I intend to do!)

My girlfriend and her family may take me up to mountains in the snow and I [will] attempt to learn how to ski.

Well, Dad, take care of yourself and I wouldn't work to hard. I do hope this time your trip won't be delayed to much.

I am fine and I hope you're too. Love and kisses Phyllis

January 23rd, 1946

My Darling,

I have received your letter of Dec. 1st …You are certainly wrong in assuming that the reason of not writing to you is to be sought in my desire to punish you. What a nonsense! This is sheer imagination, I have never had any such intentions and why should I want to punish you? Oh, darling how wrong you are, thinking I were so narrow-minded and revengeful. As it is, fate was severe enough with you and there is no need for anyone to add anything to it. Dismiss those strange ideas of your mind and if there is anything I'd like to see on your way, it could only be: profound happiness. That is what I want for you and nothing else.

So far nothing changed here. The prospects of soon getting away are obscure…they don't give any information, the usual answer is you must wait. … As you must know there are a few thousand brides of Americans waiting for shipping. According to the papers, the Amer. Government is sending a special ship to take them to the states, and when they leave, it won't be long until I can get transportation. So be a sensible girl and don't get desperate about the whole affair, in the next few months the separation will be ended.

Hope you are healthy and fine, write soon, and whenever thinking of me, know there is no one who wishes you better or loves you more than your Dad.

And so we waited for the brides to come to America. Meanwhile, my father was thinking about what work he would find in America, for the following letter from Arnold Bick, our friends from Vienna who had gotten him the visa, gives advice, but I knew nothing of this correspondence.

December 10, 1945

Dear Sigi! [My father's nickname]

I haven't heard from you since a long time until your letter arrived of 9/27. I think also that you should get shipping accomodations now earlier. I hope I will hear from you soon that you are starting your journey. I received last week a big picture of Phyllis, she is a very pretty girl, but I wouldn't have recognized her anymore. She is not looking like Lore [my mother] either.

With reference to your question don't be worry about your chance of getting a job; it might happen that you will have difficulties in getting a job as an accountant, because some firms prefer accountants, educated in United States, but you will certainly find work. Don't let fool you from newspapers—there is work for everybody for the present, not always the work, the people like, but everybody who wants to work has a chance to do so. There are always people without jobs, especially now in the time of reconversion. In a country of 130,000,000 people there are all the time some out of work or changing jobs and that is all.

When you come over I expect you to start working, even hard labor for a time to get accustomed with the feeling and thinking of the Americans. That is, as I see it, absolutely necessary and I had to do it too, and then I'll help you to go in business. If you prefer a clerical work and like accounting, than you have to take a low paid job and study at evenings, to enable you to grow; that is all up to you and I would not suggest to decide now. See at first America, see it with open eyes, look around and watch yourself and others and you'll get the push you need and decide what to do for the future. However it is don't worry about yourself before you are here. Everything will turn out O.K.

Here is everything in best order. ...I intend to open up a giftshop sometimes late next year, if the landlord is able to build; otherwise I have to leave my present business because my landlord here intends to raise the rent that much that I'm not able to pay for. So I have a lot of worries myself. ...Anny and Arno

When I discovered this letter a few years ago, I was overcome with gratitude to Arno and Anny for their steadfast labors on behalf of my parents. From the letter I inferred that Arno was impatient with my father's concerns, perhaps recalling that in Vienna my father had not been working. I had the feeling from this letter that my father might have been wondering, perhaps complaining or even whining about his future in America. Arno's advice was excellent.

I pondered gratitude again, considering that Mr. Bonapart and others had called me ungrateful. It seems that I've been grateful to people but did not express this feeling for lack of knowing how. That might also have been my father's problem; in his correspondence with the Bicks after he came to the United States, he surely would have thanked him over and over again, but what else can be done to show gratitude? I visited the Bicks in 1952 when I was traveling near Baltimore where they lived. However, it was not a joyful occasion of meeting after so many years and so many troubles; perhaps they were down on their luck at the time, perhaps they were angry with us for some omission of gratitude; perhaps there were other reasons that I could not know about. After that I lost contact with them, and I don't think my father continued to correspond with them very long. When I tried again many years later, they were not to be found in local phone books, and the old numbers did not work.

On the other hand, I know that I have done some big favors for some people, but did not like it when they continuously thanked me. I was satisfied with only one thank you, and never felt "I did so much for XXX, but never got any thanks." I am helpful because I want be, and don't need gratitude. I ponder this emotion. Still, I am sorry that my father did not keep up with them.

March 28, 1946

Dearest Dad,

I know that I didn't write to you for a long time but I've been so very busy and so much homework to do every night that I've had hardly a moment to myself. But anyway I haven't heard from you in ages. When do you think you'll be coming over. I certainly hope it will be soon. In one more week I'll be here 6 years. Quite a long time of you really think about it.

I got my report card and it was fairly good. This is what I got:

Chem	*B*	*P.E.(Gym)*	*B*
Trig	*C*	*Eng*	*A*
U.S.	*C+*		

Gee was I surprised to get an A in English. I worked hard but I didn't expect an A.

Easter vacation is pretty near and as I remember it, you should have been here by then. Oh well-

New troubles brewing with Mr. Bonapart. The letter continues:

Things aren't so good at Homewood any more but it doesn't matter because I decided long ago that I'd get whatever I wanted and that neither Mr. Bonapart or anyone else is going to stop me. I know that you like him, but if you know him as I do, you like me, would not have any respect for him. He just likes to tell stories about how much he knows. If he knew half as much as he thinks he knows, he would indeed, be brilliant. Enough for him.

You know lately I've been sewing clothes for the girls around home and thus I get a little bit of extra spending money. I guess I'm taking after mother a lot. Have you tried to inquire about her. I have but I haven't had any answer from the Red Cross yet. So I don't know.

Well Dad how've you been? You never tell me about yourself and I often think how little we know each other. Funny isn't it?

Write soon. Love, Phyllis

The last paragraph is very poignant. I knew very little about my father—what he liked or disliked, his current work or ambitions, plans for the future. Yet, I had written him so much about me. I was beginning to wonder what our life would be like together.

Even if Mr. Bonapart wouldn't let me work at the Emporium anymore, I found I could make some money sewing for some of the girls. I didn't do that much, but I was admired for my skill. Sometimes other girls or even the housemother would compliment me on my talents: "you're going to make a wonderful wife—you can cook and sew so well, you're a good hostess and you're smart." I loved these compliments, but worried deep inside if anyone would ever want to marry me, as I wasn't popular with the boys.

I was still thinking that there was some hope for my mother, and my father occasionally mentioned her in his letters when he wrote about our reunification. I had no answer from the Red Cross.

March 24, 1946 Complaints about my report card again, and a few thoughts about work.

My Darling,

I received both your letters of Jan 17 and Feb 18ᵗʰ ....There is no news concerning my leaving, but I was told...that all brides will be sent away by June, so there is every hope that I'll get the passage shortly after that....When writing about the room, I only wanted to have some place prepared to go to, and that was meant for the short time after my arrival ...The reason of my going to the States has always been to be with you. We have been separated long enough and the first thing I'm going to do is to make an end to this state...

Now about your report card! You say it was a pretty good one. Well, maybe I'm old-fashioned but in my school days a report card with "C"s in was not regarded "pretty good." I assume that it is a kind of a highschool you are attending, but I'd like to know how many more term you have to do in this school before you have qualified for College...And what are your plans and what do you intend to go in for? As to my future plans, I can't judge it from here what would be best ...as regards the job or the place of residence. ...I'll have to take any job offered and then I'll have time to look around.

All my love and heaps of kisses from your Dad

May 7, 1946

Dear Daddy,

I got your letter last week [of March 24] *but I couldn't answer sooner as this week we are having mid terms and I'm real busy studying so that I'll get better than C. C means average and last time I only got two and this time I doubt if I'll even get one. The older you get the harder the work gets. I most probably won't even be able to go to college as college is very expensive here and as of yet I've no money saved.*

I guess I might as well break the news now. Your daughter is such a detestable, selfish sneaky, rotten low thing (not to be called a person) and she has such a rotten charac-ter that she poisons everybody's mind by her bitterness and ruins everything she touches and every place she goes has to be cleansed afterwards—so the honorable Mr. Bonapart, the ass, says. So he decided to kick me out of the home, and again I have to leave and go into a fosterhome. I really don't believe what he said because I know what my friends think of me and certainly if I was that bad I would not have so many real true friends like I do. We are having a lot of fights lately because having gotten tired of Mr. Bonapart's bullying I tell him what I think of him and it isn't very nice. I guess his fat conceited makeup can't take it straight. Enough for that—and don't worry—I've been on my own long enough to know how to take care of myself. We are having a food drive in the U.S. for people in Europe and I am very active trying to do a little bit of my share.

Well Daddy, I hope you are well and that I will get a telegram from you soon telling me that you're coming. I'm very well and please darling have faith in me 'cause if you don't there is no use to our reunion. I have all the faith in world for you — you are my future and hope for the future so please believe in me and I'm sure everything will be O.K. in the end.

Love and kisses Phyllis

May 31, 1946, Thursday

Dear Daddy,

I'm leaving the home Saturday. My Foster mother and father are very nice people and I know I shall be happy. I know I've said that twice before but in the States we say: Third times a charm. I really hit the jackpot. They have a beautiful home, nice kids, I have my own room and every thing fits into my dream. I don't see how I can help but be happy but we'll see. I'm going to be away all summer. Maybe you'll be back here by the time School starts. Gee, I could see that.

While assembling all my stuff I ran into my letters and ran into those from you and Mother and you can't imagine how much I cried. It all seemed so close and yet so far away. Six and a half years passed by. It seems like yesterday because I remember everything and yet it seems like centuries past because I changed so much and have done so much to improve myself. I doubt if you'll recognize me. I'm very lonesome for you and Mother and though all probability says no I can't help hoping.

It seems that every time I moved I found his and my mother's letters and re-read them causing sorrow and tears. I may have remembered "everything" then, but now I have no recollection of my feelings. The last sentence about my mother may be the first time that I actually suggest that she may not be alive.

Well Dad, I'm fine and I hope you are too and I hope to hear from you soon. Love Phyllis... P.S. I love you, I miss you, Wish you were here.

So, I was kicked out once more. I have no recollection of a particular event or situation that caused this—probably more of my rebelliousness and bad attitude. My new home was very nice, on the edge of Saint Francis Woods, and opposite to my old school, Aptos. Mr. And Mrs. Caro—I would call them "Muz" and "Pops"—had two small children. I had my own room this time, which I really appreciated. The home was spacious with many rooms, and I didn't have too many chores, and was permitted to go out with my friends and to speak with them on the phone for a long time.

July 2, 1946

Dear Daddy,

I'm sorry I haven't written sooner but apologizing wouldn't do any good because you know all the excuses anyway.

I've been in my fosterhome for about three or four weeks and I love it. I know that is only a short time but long enough for me to know whether I like it or not.

Mr. and Mrs. Caro are really tops. Most probably you are saying that that is what I said last time. In the other foster home the people never bothered to try to understand me or talk to me. I was just there to do the work. But here we really know each and for once in my stay in the U.S. I feel like I belong to somebody. Its a wonderful feeling.

School is out and I got the following:

Chem	B	Eng	B
Trig	C	U.S. History	B
P.E.	B		

We went up to Yosemite and intended to stay for only a little while because my fostermother['s] appendicitis.

My fosterfather sold out his share of business and at the moment doesn't know whether to start in L. Angeles or up here. At any rate, I decided to go with them no matter where they went because I like them and I couldn't stand to go back to the home.

Daddy I swear it when you come here and I shall be out of the home legally I'm going to tell the honored son of a b——just exactly what I think of him and it's not going to very good. Believe me, although your opinion of him is pretty high, I have no [such] opinion. Truthfully I hate him like I've never hated anybody and he's not half as good as you think he is. Enough for him.

Well, Dad seems like I'm running out of words. I'm fine and very happy and at peace and I hope you are too. I'm anxiously awaiting your arrival and it seems its due pretty soon. Take care of yourself and write soon. I will, I promise. Lots of love Phyllis

I wonder what my father thought of these developments? Actually, he may not have received this letter as he might already have left Australia by then.

Aug 11, 1946, Letter to myself "not to be opened for 10 years."

Had a very happy birthday for a change. I am now seventeen. My presents were: a coat and hat from myself, a lipstick from Eda, material from Helen and also some from the twins, perfume from Nancy, stationery from Muz & Pops, sox from Michael and bubblebath from their grandmother—the bag. Anyway it seems silly to name so many incidentals but I when I read this letter I hope to have a couple of kids & believe me, they won't be able to count their presents. My hat is very cute—it is black and looks like a witches hat with a big satin bow in front. My coat is royal blue and I love it very much. I got my hat in the morning. (I also got a letter from Dad as I do on every birthday). When I came home I showered, did my nails, and got dressed. I wore my black dress, shoes, coat hat, purse, white gloves and Helen's jewelry. I think I looked very good —so did everyone else. Eda and I had dinner at Helen's house & then we went to the show with the twins and Barb. Robertson. We saw "Our Hearts Were Growing Up", then we went to the twins' house for tea and stuff and took a cab home which got here at a quarter to two. I was very happy.

I guess this has been a most successful year for me. It seems I finally got things straightened out with myself finally. I am very happy to say that I gave Mr. Bonapart a very unpleasant time and made Mrs. Goss quit her job. Alyce and I stopped going around together when I met Helen in October. We have come to be very good friends. My love as always was for Jerry with a slight crush on Dean. I got quite popular with everybody. This year I began to work at the Emporium and they have called me back a few times—I think they think I'm a good worker. I went to a sorority tea and didn't make it—gee I felt awful after that—finally I regained my confidence. Oh I forgot I went to a fosterhome in the beginning of June. For a while I was very happy, but as in all things the novelty wore off . I finally concluded that I would never be happy unless I was on my own. Maybe I'm too independent, who knows. Lefty & I had quite a lot of fun writing letters while he was in "boot" for the Marines.

We went up to Yosemite again—only stayed for two days Muz got appendicitis. I'm going to work tomorrow, Muz is having her nose fixed. Maybe I'll have mine done when I read this, although Toni thinks I'm beautiful. Well I guess I better sign off, next year I'll be free!

Lots of Luck till your 18 , Phyllis

I don't remember Toni or even if I spelled his name right, but any compliment was very important to me.

✦ ✦ ✦

My fosterhome hadn't turned out so well, after all. When Mr. Caro went south to find a new business, and the children were in a boarding school or perhaps summer camp, another man was a constant visitor. I didn't like him at all. He seemed sleazy to me, and sure enough, one night when I was doing dishes, he sneaked up on me and gave me a big French kiss—my first. The smell of alcohol on his breath and the disgusting open mouth nearly made me throw up, and I began to fear him, but I didn't know what to do about it. I surely couldn't tell Muz. I didn't know if he actually spent nights with her; if so, they were discreet.

Although I had written my father that I would be moving with them wherever they went, I knew that I didn't want to go anywhere with them. I also didn't want to go back to the Home.

August 8, 1946   Airmail for the first time, received August 12.   Good news at last!

My little darling,

At last, after all those years of waiting I've some good news for you.   Today I booked passage and I'm going to leave Australia on the 24th of this month, i.e. in about two weeks.   I have been told that the trip takes about fifteen days which means that I should arrive about the 8th of September.   They could not tell me the exact arrival there, but you would get the necessary information from any shipping office.   The name of the ship is "Marine Falcon".

A few days ago it was exactly 7 years that I left you, who would have thought that we would be separated for so long a time, yet now this is coming to an end.   Oh my girl, am I happy, wonder if I would recognize you, though I hardly think so.   This is going to be my last letter.

It is very important that you should find a room for me so that when I arrive, there is some kind of a place where to go.

...And now again I want to send you my heartfelt wishes. May this birthday of yours bring to you happiness and a bright future and help you forget those last ugly years of sorrow and disappointments. ...Now Darling, Keep well, heaps of kisses (for the last time on paper) and cheerio, Your Dad.

That night Muz and I had an altercation about some French dressing her boyfriend had made for dinner that I didn't want to eat. One thing led to another, and before I knew it, I was told to pack my bag and that I would be returning to the Home the next morning. We had a big scene in Mr. Bonapart's office the next day: (From a letter to myself in August, 1947, reviewing the past year.)

I hated him [Bonapart] *so much that I was crying, as I often did when I talked to him. He talked of deporting me, and I very calmly answered that I did not give a damn, that someday I would be able to do things the way I wanted to and he wouldn't be able to interfere. Muz burst out crying, ran over to me and asked to be forgiven, but I pushed her away. She certainly didn't spare the details when she told him of all the petty things I did while living with her. She told him I was rude to her guest because I wouldn't eat his salad!*

A few days later, I was called to Mr. Bonapart's office again. This time Mr. Caro was there and wanted to have some details of what had been going on while he was gone. I suspected that he had some inkling about her lover. I was truthful, but I failed to tell about the man kissing me. After this discussion Mr. Bonapart seemed to be much friendlier, so I guessed that finally I was not to blame. This two month foster home episode was really weird. I wondered why people wanted to have foster children—today I know that few of them do it for charity, but rather for the money they receive, or for the services the children are made to perform. Perhaps it was Mr. Caro's idea to have a watchdog for his lovely, but perhaps unfaithful wife.

✦ ✦ ✦

I was put in Cottage 22 where Mrs. Bloomgarden was the cottage mother. I had known her before I went to the fosterhome, so I requested that I become part of her house. She had only recently come to the Home. Mrs. Bloomgarden was a very tall woman, had wavy gray hair, wore glasses and spoke with a very slight southern accent. She was not Jewish but had married a Jewish man. Recently widowed, she was supporting her daughter, Rosemary, who was just a year older than I. She liked me, which felt good.

So, although I would still be living at the Home until my father and I could live together, my life would be very different as my days as an orphan came to an end.

THE POST-WAR
PERIOD

20

LIFE WITH FATHER

September 1946 to February 1950

634 Fell Street, as it looks today

*I*t is 8:00 on this cool morning as I stand on the pier in San Francisco. Although it is Friday, the 13th, usually considered an unlucky day, it will be a lucky day for me as I await the arrival of my father on the SS Marine Falcon from Australia.

*M*ore than seven years have passed since I last saw him and I am very nervous about our meeting. Will I recognize him? I've often asked him for his picture, but none came, and I didn't even have a snapshot. Will he recognize me? I have sent him two portraits, but I've changed even since those were taken. I am already seventeen, starting my last year in high school and in charge of my life—will my father want me to be his little "puppele," the girl of nine that he last saw? How will we be with each other?

*O*f course I am happy that he is at last coming to rescue me from my plight as an unwanted, difficult child, but I am very scared—more frightened than I've ever been. I've been worrying about our life together. Mr. Bonapart had warned me that I would not be able to live with my father because he would have no money, so I worried about finances. What scares me most, however, is our future relationship. In our letters we had argued about my vocational choices and also about religion, and I know these subjects will create problems.

✦ ✦ ✦

It would be another three hours before the ship arrived at 11:00. Mr. Liebhoff, the assistant director of Homewood Terrace, accompanied me that day. We stood on the pier scrutinizing the people cramming the ship's deck, searching for a familiar face, and to me everybody looked like my father. Surprisingly, it was Mr. Liebhoff who somehow picked my father out of the crowd. Even when he pointed to the man he thought was my father, I did not recognize him.

Six hours later, at 5:00 p.m, he finally disembarked. We met with an awkward hug. I hadn't been hugged by anyone in the intervening years! I started crying. We didn't know what to say to each other. This moment—for which we had been waiting for so many years— dissipated into an unmemorable event by the long wait and Mr. Liebhoff's presence. It was like having a TV reporter zeroing in on a very emotional moment—I hate looking at such private scenes. After our meeting, we still had to wait three more hours while the customs procedure dragged on and on before my father could gather suitcases and leave the pier. Later he complained about my cool reception.

I had made arrangements for Dad to spend the first few nights at my friend Helen's home. Her parents were extremely generous in their concerns for me and for my father; despite their small place, they had offered to have him. After a week, he found a room to rent in the Richmond district for $20.00 a month and began searching for a job. Apartments in San Francisco at that time were at a premium, and anyway, he didn't have enough money to pay for one, for he had come to San Francisco with only $100, less than a month's wages, and nothing more than a small trunk and suitcase.

He was now 45 years old, in good health, but balking at having to get glasses. His English was excellent, still with a slight accent, but very understandable. He quickly found a job as a shipping clerk for the Royal Typewriter Company at $165 month where he was to work for several years.

✦ ✦ ✦

Meanwhile, I continued to live at the orphanage, but now—like most of the other children—I had a Sunday visitor. We spent our Sundays together going to the Zoo or Golden Gate Park, or a movie and then, dinner. We enjoyed smoking and drinking coffee. We were becoming acquainted almost as two strangers, and almost immediately my worst fears about potential conflict began to emerge. The first disagreement had to do with clothing. Custom at that time demanded that high school girls wear bobby sox and dirty saddle shoes, but he insisted that I wear stockings and clean shoes.

"I insist that you dress properly," he said. "A young woman must always pay attention to her appearance."

"I can't afford stockings," I replied curtly, "but most of all I don't want to wear them. Besides it's not fashionable to wear stockings or to have clean shoes. High school kids wear bobby sox and dirty saddle shoes and that's what I want to wear."

"I don't want to be seen with you looking like that. You either dress properly or I won't take you out."

"OK, we won't go, then."

And we didn't go out that Sunday, both of us stubborn. I don't remember how that conflict was finally resolved, but I think I must have won, since we eventually resumed our visiting, and I didn't wear stockings.

Fortunately, we had many very nice times getting into involved discussions about politics—we both liked the Democrats—my experiences at school, and even religion, but we never talked about the past, either in Vienna, Australia or about my mother, except in the most superficial way. I was so self-centered that I never brought these subject up, but he most likely would have said, "Let bygones be bygones." Now I resent my father's failure to bring up old times, thus depriving me of family history. The future was the main topic of conversation: when we could get an apartment, where I would go to college, the things I had been dreaming of and planning for during the years of our separation.

We also argued about trivia. At a certain point of the discussion, he would wrap it all up by saying: "It's a known fact that..." For instance, discussing movie stars, "It's a known fact that Maureen O'Hara is the most beautiful actress" or "It's a known fact that the male body is more attractive than the female, you can see it in the animals." After that, the discussion was finished, period.

Our Apartment

In spring of 1947, my friends, the Twins, helped us get an apartment in the house next door to them at 634 Fell Street in the Hayes Valley district. Our flat was on ground level of a two-story building, the Russian landlady living above us. Another apartment just like ours was on the other side of the entry where a young couple, Wilma and Wesley, lived and with whom we became friends. Like so many other old flats in San Francisco it was a railroad flat with no hallway—that is, you entered through the living room, through the next room, then to the back of the flat where the kitchen and bathroom were. There was no shower, only an old-fashioned tub standing on feet. The kitchen, big enough, but poorly designed wasn't modern either. The ancient stove was not very reliable, and the only counter, about 30" wide, was near the laundry-like tub. Next to this sink stood a cabinet for dishes, and on the opposite wall was space for a table. An ironing board folded down from a small wall near the table. There was no refrigerator, but a cooler—a three-shelved cabinet whose screened back opened to the air and worked well enough in naturally air-conditioned San Francisco.

It wasn't great, but I was thrilled: this would be <u>my home</u>. I was ecstatic about buying furnishings and deciding on paint colors. No longer would I need to be grateful to strangers for their charity in accepting a "war orphan."

The flat, with its very high ceilings, had probably not been painted in decades; the walls were dingy, and black above the gas heater. I chose gray and sunny, bright yellow as my colors, and my father with enthusiasm, but no prior experience, began an immensely difficult job of painting the walls yellow, the wood trim gray.

We selected two sofa sleepers in cheap furniture stores in the Mission district, a tailored navy blue one for me for the second room and a brown velvety one with matching easy chair for the living room which doubled as my father's bedroom. The simple wooden kitchen table and chairs were so poorly made that in a short time the backs of the chairs fell apart and we sat on stools instead of chairs. We bought a blond console radio with record player, an extravagant purchase at the time, and stained a chest of drawer to match. Blond was then in vogue as the modern finish for furniture. We should have bought a full-length mirror, but somehow that hadn't seemed important at the time, so I had to stand on a chair to see the lower part of me in the small medicine-cabinet mirror in the bathroom. All of this was bought on credit, as we had only $250, barely enough for a down payment.

I was sure that I was the luckiest girl alive, living in the nicest of circumstances! In reality, the stuff was all very cheap and broke down quickly; the neighborhood was on the edge of the Fillmore district, the worst neighborhood in San Francisco. In fact, all my foster homes and the orphanage were more nicely furnished and in better neighborhoods, but I never made comparisons. I wrote in my annual birthday letter, August 9, 1947:

> This little apartment is my home. It is a wonderful feeling. I can have anybody over, at anytime, and I can do with it just what I want to. I hope that this feeling of loving my home will always be with me. It is one of the keys to the big room called happiness.

We settled into a pattern of daily living. I finished my last semester in high school commuting to the Sunset district, worked at the Emporium on Saturdays, shopped for and usually prepared meals. On the way home from school I stopped at a little corner grocery store and purchased items for dinner. I made friends with the butcher and enjoyed lingering over choices and discussing the news. I usually cooked dinner, sometimes with help from my father.

After dinner, sinking into his brown easy chair, Dad would listen to classical music—"Pledger at the Opera" was a frequent favorite—read the paper, and often fell asleep. I would be in the kitchen studying. Around 10:00 he would make a pot of coffee, and we spent some time chatting about world news or my homework and smoking a couple more cigarettes.

Dad was meticulous. After work, he would take off his good clothes, press his pants, brush his jacket, and clean his shoes. He kept all of his things very tidy, and became impatient with my lack of order. Sundays he often spent the day cleaning our apartment, polishing the wooden floors till they shone; I helped with housecleaning too. Dishes had to be done immediately, usually he washed and I dried.

He took our laundry to the launderette two blocks away, bringing it home wet to save money on the drying, then hung it on the wire clothesline off the kitchen that attached to another apartment house. He wore a smock over his clothes at work, a gray cotton smock which often tore and which I impatiently patched. For years after his death, I kept such a smock hanging in the garage ready for the few really messy jobs I might engage in, reminding me of his fastidiousness and my lack of it.

✦ ✦ ✦

The first six months were like a "honeymoon" as my father and I became acquainted, set up housekeeping with all of its attendant chores of living a joint life. For the first time in seven years somebody actually cared about what I thought and what I did and wanted to please me. He loved bringing me little surprises and I enjoyed getting them. He cared how I looked, complimenting me on new creations I sewed and within his means allowed me to buy new clothes. I sometimes bought him ties. He helped by pinning hems up for me, sometimes ironing my blouses and by washing my hair. He loved my shoulder length, black, wavy hair, I suppose because it was like my mother's. Once a week, over the kitchen sink, he would wash and scrub my hair with Breck Shampoo that guaranteed a shiny outcome. I enjoyed being part of a family, so long absent from my life.

✦ ✦ ✦

Before graduation in June, I acquired a middle name. Invitations and personal cards were to be printed for this significant event, and I wanted to have a middle name like everybody else. I asked my father for suggestions. He explained how Jewish children are named after deceased relatives, and so he mentioned some names, including Helena. I modified it to Helene, but I have no clue now who Helena was. I wasn't excited about the graduation nor about staying out all night, but it is a rite of passage I endured. A friend had arranged a blind date for me, so the four of us spent the night riding on the Ferry, kissing because it was what people did, but it wasn't fun. The ceremony took place on the next morning.

After I graduated from high school in June, I got a job at Standard Brands as a clerk-typist. It seemed like a good job, and at first I flirted with the idea of working for a year to save some money, but typing invoices quickly got boring and as September drew nearer, I wanted to start school.

Of my 18th birthday, nearly a year after my father came to the U. S., I wrote my usual letter to myself on the typewriter he gave for a present:

August 9, 1947

> I had a very happy birthday with lots of presents. I also got a Birthday cake. Dad got it for me, and it was a complete surprise. To some people that isn't very much. But to me it was the beginning of a wonderful life. It was my first birthday cake. As I blew out the candles, I knew that from then on Dad and I would be getting along a lot better. I had such a feeling of completeness, of being loved, and of somebody trying to help me and wanting me.

I had already forgotten the nice cake Aunt Laura had made for me on my first birthday in the United States. I loved the typewriter, the best portable that Royal Typewriter produced; it would serve me for many, many years.

It was a given that I would go to college, but also that I would have to work part-time. I had planned for it, and my father wholly approved. I found another job in September—part-time—at Wells Fargo Bank headquarters downtown on the corner of Montgomery and Market Streets. One of the famous Wells Fargo coaches, housed in a small museum off the lobby imparted history and prestige to the bank and made me feel important to work there.

I worked thirty hours a week, six days a week, from 8:00 to 1:00. The first hour of the job required me and several other girls to open and sort the mail; a bank officer who stood behind us, supervising us as we sat in a row opening letters. We chatted while working, and he sometimes told us jokes. Otherwise, the hierarchy at the bank was very rigid. The tellers, all males, literally worked in cages, had to wear dark suits, could not do anything without approval, and though they looked very professional, were only high-school graduates who had worked themselves up to this prestigious position, but didn't make much money. They complained about the high cost of the required clothing and their low salaries. The officer, who supervised us in the mailroom, also walked the lobby, greeting patrons and approving transactions for the tellers. My job was as a messenger: if a teller needed some signature, or some information, I ran to the appropriate office or person to do his bidding. I liked the job because it was mobile, and interesting. I made some nice friends there, but working there never inspired me to get into the banking business. My salary was helpful in meeting expenses for school and helping with the household as well.

✦ ✦ ✦

I started San Francisco State College in 1947; then it was on Haight and Buchanan Streets, and only a few blocks from where we lived. After work, I went to school from 2:00 to 5:00p.m. and I carried 12 units of solids—Chemistry, Algebra, English, and French. The college was crowded with young men returning from service and getting their education through the G.I. Bill. They were more mature than us eighteen-year olds, and were often excellent students. That was especially true for Algebra—many of them thought it was an easy course, but I struggled with it. There weren't many girls in my math class, but I met many in English and French. I joined the College Theater to make some friends, as few of my high school friends went to State, and it turned out to be perfect group for me. Many weekend nights were taken up by the performances, and I also had to participate in dress rehearsals as I did the make-up. The College had a very active theater with many productions during the year. The best part of this activity was the cast party on the last night of the production. I met many stimulating, intellectual and exciting people I really liked, I fell in love with several of the men, but nothing serious came of it—except fun for the moment.

My father encouraged me to get good grades, but did not nag me to study. He also believed in enjoying life. When I studied too late and too long, he would urge me to do something for pleasure. "A time for everything in life," was one of his sayings, so at first he didn't mind my participation in the Theater. My first major was Chemistry, which he suggested and endorsed; but when I nearly flunked algebra, I switched to Psychology for which he had little use. When I received mediocre grades, he was quick to blame it on all the time I spent on the Theater production. Of course, I was also working 30 hours a week, which had some effect on my grades.

✦ ✦ ✦

My father was satisfied with his life—of course, he would have liked to make more money, have reserves in the bank, but he was not a workaholic. He found some friends from Vienna—I don't know how they found each other, but one man, Max Schnittlich, came over almost every Saturday night and the men would sit at the kitchen table with a pot of coffee and discuss and argue; sometimes I joined in the arguments—I would call them philosophical discussions except that Max and my father would interrupt each other, sometimes shouting, banging fists on the table, and pointing fingers at each other. These discussions would last way past midnight as neither was willing to the let the other have the last word, but there seemed to be no hard feelings, as the same thing happened next week. Max liked to argue with me too, especially about religious ideas. Max introduced Dad to some other friends who had cars, and this group often spent Sundays together in Marin County, walking the trails. He liked getting out of town to scenic places, but if I had nothing else to do he would go someplace with me. I fondly remember many enjoyable outings to the Zoo, the museums, Stern Grove, and Golden Gate Park sharing pleasures of nature and culture. Now I lead a hike in Golden Gate Park once a year, and we spend some time at the Band Shell listening to the concert. The musicians, some now very old men, are still—as they were fifty years ago—wearing red uniforms with military style caps; some of them, were players at that time, too. Now there are few people who listen, but when I went with my father, there were many more rows of seats, all filled. When I sit there, listening, I am reminded of my father and the pleasant times we had on such Sundays.

Except for Max, none of his friends ever came to our house. This was a vestige of his Viennese culture, where only family exchanged visits in homes and all other social engagements took place in the coffee house. He also found some friends to play bridge with. Writing to myself in my annual birthday letter, I wrote: (August 9, 1947)

> I wanted him to have a host of friends, so that he would not have to depend on me for friendship and companionship. But that didn't turn out at all. I soon realized, with a heavy heart, that my father's only ambition was me; to do everything for me. And though it made me feel good in a way, for I had never had anyone feel that way towards me, I felt awful in another way, for I knew that I could never return that feeling, and when I told him so, he felt miserable. For too long a time, I had had a barbed wire fence around me, and it was very hard, if not impossible, for anyone to penetrate...it wasn't a matter of secrets, but a matter of affection, but affection with no strings attached, and his life revolved around me. He had come here for me...willing to give me everything, wanting only a little closeness in return. And hard as I might have tried, and am still trying, I could not give him that.

✦ ✦ ✦

My friends, on the other hand, were frequent visitors. In fact, when we had barely moved in, I invited almost everybody I knew for dinner, including Mrs. Bloomgarden, my recent housemother from the orphanage. At first he didn't want to have company because he felt our place wasn't nice enough, but I was so enthusiastic about showing off my own place, that he soon accepted the steady stream of friends who came. When I wanted to invite Aunt Laura, he demurred, insisting that he would be ashamed to invite her to our poor apartment. I think it must have hurt her terribly that he never went to see her and thank her for accepting me into her home, and I thought his reason was vain and foolish. I feel it was ungrateful and unsociable of him, and I am very sorry that I couldn't convince him otherwise.

My friends found him pleasant, easy to talk to and interested in our chatter. He preferred my Jewish friends, but was hospitable to all. He joined our conversations at the kitchen table, even though he was sometimes opinionated and narrow-minded. One time a Hindu schoolmate came to visit, and as we sat at the kitchen table talking, the subject of the boy's vegetarianism came up. My father was interested in his dietary restrictions, but then ended the conversation with his typical "It's a well-known superstition, not eating meat," but said in a friendly way. I don't know how my friend received this dictum, but I couldn't believe my father's narrow-mindedness in view of his own dietary restrictions of not eating pork, nor eating meat and dairy products at the same meal!

He didn't share my enthusiasm and trust in friends. He didn't believe that friendships lasted forever, best exemplified by this statement: "Friends are friends as long as things are going well, but just watch, when you need them, they are nowhere to be found." He had said this to me often in our warring years in response to my veneration of friendship. I reminded him how the Twins and Helen had helped us to find shelter and how the Bicks, our friends from Vienna, had worked so hard for many years to get him a visa. It was my father who forgot his old friends.

◆ ◆ ◆

For my second year of college, starting in September of 1948, I changed jobs, working twenty hours a week as a cashier at Joseph Magnin, fondly known as JM, an upscale department store downtown. Working there, I was able to observe some of the societal changes of the postwar era. For example, television had just been introduced, and instead of TV programming just on the weekends, Thursday night was added. People arranged their social lives around the programs, hosting TV parties—dinners on TV trays so all could watch. I actually didn't see my first TV program for several years, too poor to buy this fancy toy, and not knowing anyone else who had one. The papers were full of things to do as a result of the TV. The downtown stores responded, too. They had been open on Thursday nights, itself a new idea, but had to change to Mondays to allow people to watch TV on Thursday. Then, towards Christmas, JM opened its novel Lion's Den where men were treated to appetizing hors d'oeuvres and drinks while beautiful girls modeled lovely clothes from underwear to fur coats. My cashier station serviced that department, and I was amazed at how much money was spent. I enjoyed the festivity of the lounge and thought it was a novel idea for improving sales, although today I would label it as sexist. Sometimes, the men tipped me generously for wrapping their purchase nicely, even though the service was free.

✦ ✦ ✦

Christmas accentuated our problems about religion. Thoroughly American-ized, I was involved in the great commercial Christmas tradition. Exchanging pre-sents with my friends was bad enough, but when I admired Christmas trees, I was admonished, especially since I showed little interest in the Chanuka tradition. Nev-ertheless, he and I exchanged presents as part of Chanuka, but he made no effort to enlighten me or educate me about these ritual events. He gave me my first watch, which I loved, and I gave him a red-striped Pendleton bathrobe that he kept to his dying days.

Only a few months later, however, a burglar stole my watch, along with the very few valuable things we had—cigarette lighters and fountain pens. It happened early in the morning just about the time I would be getting up. It was our pattern that my father usually got up first in the morning, walking through my room to the kitchen and bath. When he was dressed, (the only walk-in closet was in my room) he would wake me, sometimes, by tickling my toes. On this morning I also woke gently to toes being tickled, but this time when I opened my eyes, I saw a black man sitting at the edge of my bed tickling my toes instead. I screamed, he ran out the front door, and my father, who had still been asleep, awoke startled, but too late to stop the guy. We always felt it was a good thing that he didn't try to stop him, thus at least avoiding physical harm. The watch, which had taken much scrimping on my father's part, was precious to me, although its monetary value may not have been high. The worst effect from this incursion would be the nightmares I had for twenty years of a man coming to rob me which would wake me with a scream stuck in my throat and my heart racing.

◆ ◆ ◆

The most important facet of my father's life was his religion, and the source of our contention. He had acquired his orthodoxy in Australia, as I don't remember his religious devotion when we were in Vienna. To his pleasure, he found an orthodox synagogue just a few blocks away in the Fillmore district. Poor and older Jewish people remained in this district after the war while the more affluent moved to other districts. Although it was becoming a Black neighborhood, some Jewish shops and the synagogue remained for a few more years serving an ever-diminishing aging population. Saturday mornings he dressed in his best suit and went to Temple (I was working), and in the afternoon he would listen to his beloved Metropolitan Opera; after it finished, he would take a long nap. This constituted his Sabbath, and nothing altered this routine. He did not cook on Saturday, nor do any physical labor, nor would he take a bus to the park. He would have liked to keep kosher, but saw that it would be difficult for lack of shops selling kosher food nearby, and that I would not have gone along with it. Still, he would delight in preparing Jewish "soul" food, such as chicken soup with matzoth balls or borscht, goulash, or Wiener schnitzel. With great glee, as though it was a special treat or surprise for me, he often brought home some Jewish bakery goods or kosher hot dogs. "At least you like Jewish cooking," he would say. We observed the Passover and the High Holidays in dietary ways, but I never went to the Temple. The issue of religion was deeper than Christmas or dietary restrictions. I had denounced my faith a couple of years before, and I was not interested in anything Jewish. When, in a conversation, I said: "I don't believe in God," he would shake his head in disbelief and say: "How can you say that? Oh, what they taught you at that Home!"

It's not what they taught at the Home, I retorted. I came to this conclusion myself. I've been studying about religion in my Anthropology class, and I think all religions are bunk. Religion just causes a lot of trouble, look at what happened in the war—it all started over religion. I think people should believe what they want, but keep it to themselves.

Shocked, he replied:

But the Jewish religion is different. It was handed to us by God, and although we've been persecuted for thousands of years for our beliefs, we are still holding strong to it. It makes us who we are.

The argument continued. I didn't want to be *just* Jewish, couldn't be, if I tried. I had already chosen my friends from many religions and races. Just in that one year I was asked to be a Maid of Honor in three weddings—one Protestant, one Catholic and one Jewish. Although I gladly accepted the honor, I was disenchanted by the fuss and the rituals of the weddings. I vowed that I would get married quietly without it. I believed in assimilating. I wanted to be American, belonging to that Whole, not be confined to one group of people. Furthermore, I didn't believe God had anything to do with our lives—we lived them according to old habits, and I wanted to change them, to be more modern and more practical. Besides that, I didn't like God—why was He jealous as it says in the second commandment? True love isn't jealous. If religion were based on love instead of fear, I might have been more interested.

My father rebutted:

You don't know what you're talking about. You've learned some silly things in that class of yours that all religions are equal—but they are not. How can you compare the Jewish religion with that of the primitive tribes who worship stones or mountains?

I responded, passionately:

Why not—the stones or mountains are real and have no less control over our lives than God. If I pray to God to help me get something—like I did when I prayed for you and Mom to come here—the result wasn't any better than if I'd prayed to the mountain. Besides, I think all that ritual is meaningless. I don't like sitting in Temple listening to somebody (and here of course, I was thinking of Bonapart) mouthing of about our behavior. I don't like that dreary singing. If I were to want to pray, I would do it by myself.

Today when I think of those arguments, I have to give my father credit for being gentle with my blasphemous ideas, for not forcing the issue of my not going to Temple. He patiently hoped that I would change my opinions, but I never did. What disturbed him most, however, was that I was not dating Jewish boys, his fear being that I would marry a *"Goy,"* a non-Jew. Although he didn't mind my having non-Jewish girlfriends, he liked the Jewish ones best; and he would point out to me, sarcastically, that they went to Temple and observed Jewish traditions, and dated Jewish boys. "Just why do you, <u>my daughter</u>, have to be so different?" he'd say pointedly, but I liked being different.

Religious differences became the problem that I had feared when I wrote in my year-end review (Jan. 1, 1947):

> *If, by the time I read this, I find myself without a father, it will be because I married a non-Jewish boy. Isn't that silly? He is quite stubborn, like myself.*

After some arguments, he would become despondent and bitter as he realized that I would not listen to his counsel about dating Jewish boys. The truth was that Jewish boys didn't ask me out, but I made no effort to find them or be liked by them. Finally, I had a Jewish date to go dancing. The fellow turned out to be obnoxious and tried to force me; I jumped out of his car in Golden Gate Park, lucky to be near a bus stop and a bus was coming, and that I had a dime, "mad money," in my pocket for the fare. I came home late at night, frightened by my narrow escape and having left my purse with key in his car, I had to wake my father. I didn't explain—I wouldn't have known how to tell him, but the next night, the fellow came over and wanted to go out! When I opened the door and saw him, I told him to leave, but my father came to the door and asked him in. "Go home", I shouted and he left, but my father didn't understand why I was so rude. When I told him—with great difficulty since sex was not on our discussion list—he shook his head, sighed several times and said: "Yeah, Yeah, this is what happens to Jews in America!"

In conjunction with my rebelliousness about the Jewish faith, he had another problem with my independence as I decided to major in Anthropology. Not only was this a worthless subject with strange ideas of evolution and culture, it didn't have a market. "What would you do with such a degree?" he asked. "What kind of a job will that get you? "I could become a college professor, teach at the Junior College," I replied, to which he shook his head incredulously, not being able to imagine his daughter, a woman as a professor.

However, my grades had improved as I became truly interested in this field, and all of a sudden I began to get A's instead of C's. I started making plans to go to Berkeley to finish my degree, and to his great disappointment I was going to live there instead of with him and commuting. I don't think I was much different from other 20 year-olds wanting to establish their independence, but because of our history, and with no other family to buffer my assaults on his dreams, my father became depressed often, treating me with silence. Once, after a terrible argument, I ran away. With few dollars in my pocket, I went to the YWCA and took a room and with the paltry remaining money had a bowl of chili for dinner. It was a most sobering experience, as close to homeless as I could imagine. But my father hadn't worried because he thought I'd gone to my friends. When I returned the next day, he was glad enough to see me. When I told him what I had done, his frustration with my rebelliousness was aggravated. "How could you even think of leaving like that? Is that what I came to America for? We are family, small enough, but we must stay with each other."

◆ ◆ ◆

I had plans to go to University of California, Berkeley in September of 1949 after working all summer and saving for the additional expenses of living away from home. I had even gotten a small scholarship, but alas, there were no jobs that summer. My first experience with unemployment brought some unexpected consequences. When I told my father that I had applied for unemployment, he was furious—"We don't take charity," he said. "It's not charity," I argued, "I paid for that out of my paycheck." However, the argument was solved by the unemployment office when it denied my claim because my job had only been part-time work. I ended up having some occasional work that summer, but not enough to allow me to live in Berkeley.

I signed up for a course in keypunching at IBM, a very new office skill, and after passing an IQ test, they agreed to train me and then place me in a job. Big, somber "THINK" signs in gray and black stood on every desk and larger ones decorated the IBM office walls. They accepted only single women. Everybody dressed in dark colors. After completing the month-long course, I was referred to the Del Monte Corporation, the giant food company. I didn't like keypunching—if typing was boring, keypunching was even more so, and our keypunch operation was very regimented. There were six of us women, and our supervisor literally watched over us from a podium. The pay was good, however, and I saved a lot of money so that I could go to Berkeley in February.

My rebelliousness again created a problem. We were given ten minute smoke breaks, but were not allowed to leave the building. I did anyway, for I had discovered a little coffee shop next door. Our supervisor's boss was having coffee there, and when he spotted me, I was called to his office afterwards and he scolded me for my offense. After being reprimanded, I went to the personnel office complaining that it wasn't fair that we couldn't leave the building if he could. There I was again, that stubborn, defiant child, refusing to abide by the rules. Politely, I was given two weeks termination pay and had to leave the company immediately. I didn't mind, however, since I was going to leave in two weeks anyway to start school in Berkeley.

✦ ✦ ✦

And so it was that I was on the move, again, this time not kicked out, but choosing to leave so that I could be independent. My father and I continued to be in touch by phone, I came home for some week-ends and summers, but I loved my independent living.

21

SEARCHING FOR MY FAMILY

L-R: Netty, Golda, Arthur, Eva, Heini, Susi & Peter (1970s)

My father and I didn't talk about our life in Europe, so I forgot all about the family left in Europe as I went about my Americanization, my studies, and my social life. We never talked about my mother or other relatives, their whereabouts or their fate, which may seem strange, but it is common among survivors of the Holocaust not to have talked about the horrors at that time. However, my father knew, through inquiry to the Vienna Jewish Community Center, that my mother had died in May 1942, but he did not tell me. I found the inquiry among his papers only after he died, although at some level, I knew that she was not alive.

✦ ✦ ✦

We received the letter below from Dzuniu, my mother's younger brother. I infer that my father had been able to contact Dzuniu first. His letter is full of pain from the horrible massacre of his family.

Vienna, June 26, 1947   Translated from German.
My Dearest!

I am looking for you already since 1945 and I have found you with trouble and sweat. You can't imagine my surprise when I have received a sign of life from you; unfortunately I am the only one left of your family. The [my] *good* [wife] *and child and my good mother have been destroyed on one day. Heshiu* [his older brother] *was the first in our family who has been killed; Stella* [Heshiu's daughter, my age] *was shot when she started to run; Hella and Bella* [wife and other child] *were killed a few days later. You can't imagine this if you haven't seen it; my mother was chased to death barefoot; over here all people were shot at the cemetery. I can't explain it if I had a full month. I can't write now how I saved myself because I'm very nervous; I will explain next time. ... The family from Lawoczne is all in Vienna...*

I am living in Vienna and I am thank God all right. Now I am looking for a possibility to emigrate, I don't know where to yet. I will inform you about everything. Now I ask you to tell me everything about Sigfried [my father's nickname] *and Lizzi. I hope that I'll meet you all in life. Dzuniu*

My father translated the letter for me, leaving out the gory details, saying only that there had been a "massacre" in Stryj. He didn't even mention that the Lawoczne family was in Vienna. (I only recently found the above letter.) In 1947 I had appreciated that Dzuniu made the effort to find us in the United States through a Red Cross search, thus linking us to our family. In addition, he later sent us $100, a goodly sum then, which we appreciated even as we wondered how he had so much money when people in America were sending CARE packages to their relatives in impoverished Europe.

My father continued to correspond with him, although infrequently. My father did not relish writing letters, perhaps the years of writing to me had made him weary, or perhaps he had some reticence to communicate more intimately with his deceased wife's family. Surely, he had to feel some discomfort in having survived, perhaps guilty that my mother hadn't, but I never heard him say such words, nor did I think them in 1947. Shortly before his death in 1971, my father returned to Europe for the first time and was wonderfully received by Dzuniu and the rest of the family, making him wish that he had gone before.

◆ ◆ ◆

In September 1955, I was twenty-five, still single, living in Wisconsin, but not liking it. I had attended the University, leading to a Master's degree in Anthropology, which led to a job as a social worker in Kenosha. I decided to quit my job after a year and a half and go to Europe. It was to be a survey of European cities including two weeks in Vienna to see Uncle Dzuniu. Very few people were traveling to Europe at the time, especially young women traveling alone. Europe was still very poor, and trying to rebuild its cities. I was very proud of what I had accomplished by my own efforts in the United States, and that I had been able to save $600, enough money to go for two months. My father was pleased that I wanted to go to Europe to see Dzuniu, so I don't know why he hadn't told me of the relatives living in Vienna.

On my way, I went to Montreal to see Uncle Max, my father's brother, and Aunt Tillie again. I loved these people, and they were very warm to me. We had been corresponding, and I had visited them once before. They were very poor, and struggling to make ends meet which must have been very difficult because they had lived such a comfortable life in Germany before.

The ship left Montreal via the Lawrence Seaway to go to Liverpool. I spent two weeks in London, one in Paris, a few days in Zurich before going to Vienna. Austria had been divided into zones administered by the Allies and Russians until that August when it had became a sovereign county. Bombing by the Allies had destroyed many buildings and those that hadn't been affected, were dark and dingy. Rebuilding was going on everywhere, even as it had been in London and Paris.

Not until then, having seen many world-famous cities, did I appreciate Vienna's beautiful architecture. The precious Opera House was the first building to be rebuilt when Austria became its own master again after the Russians left early in 1955. Heralding the rebirth of Austria, the opening of the Opera in November was to be a symbol to the citizens that Vienna would become noteworthy again among world cities, and created great excitement.

I walked through the 1st district, amidst the scaffolding and busy workmen, trying to recall the buildings of my youth, and to my surprise, many things I had thought I had remembered, were not that way at all. For example, I wanted to see the statue of the "Spinnerin am Kreuz," which I had "remembered" as a woman sitting in front of spinning wheel weaving, based on an old Austrian legend. The monument was in fact a fancy metal-sculpted cross marking the spot where the woman had sat spinning for thirty years while waiting for her husband to return from the Thirty Years War in 1648. The cross was nothing like the statue I had remembered! It impressed on me how fragile and inventive memories are without the renewal by pictures or stories. However, I did remember many buildings, such as our apartment, my school, the place where my friend lived and the Volksoper where I had attended plays of fairy tales.

I was very excited about seeing Uncle Dzuniu, his new wife and child, Heini then 5, and to my great surprise, I found almost the whole family from Lawoczne—the Schleifers, Golda and Bernard, Yetty Rothman and her daughter Susie, now married. I was greatly astonished, but pleased, to meet these close family members whose very existence I had entirely forgotten, even though I had spent summers with them before the war. The biggest problem I had in connecting with my relatives was language: I spoke broken German, but German wasn't their first language either. Some knew a little English, but it was much effort for them, so, like my early visits to the farm, I wasn't able to communicate with them. Even Uncle Dzuniu had little to say to me, language being but one problem, his depression another. At that time his business was not going well, he and his wife barely talked to each other, and when I asked him about my mother, he began to cry, but would tell me nothing although he must have known what happened to her. Thus I was very disappointed by my first experience in Vienna—strangers on the train had been more communicative than my family.

Even as I was visiting in Vienna in 1955, the Rothmans and the Schleifers would be immigrating to the United States within a week; their children, Eva and Arthur were already in New Jersey. By 1971, my next visit, most of them had returned to Vienna. I couldn't understand why they had returned—it was inconceivable to me that they would prefer Vienna to the United States. This time I had brought my children and husband who were welcomed by my relatives. Although they were polite, they told me privately they were sorry that I had not married a Jew, but they did not shun him as they later shunned Heini's Italian, but converted, wife. They were nice enough to my husband; in fact, Cousin Heini, Dzuniu's son, then 22, even wanted to do some business with my husband, a real sign of acceptance. Two years later in 1973, I, divorced by then, returned with my children, 11 and 14. Without knowing any of the details or reasons for divorce, they disapproved of my action. "See, you should have married a Jew," they said, although some of them were also divorced, but from Jews.

Planning for a trip to Europe in the summer of 1979, I had taken a German class that academic year, hoping that I'd be able to speak with Uncle Dzuniu more, to hear more about my mother and the rest of the family. Unfortunately, he had died that March before I came, a great disappointment for me.

That year I stayed with Eva and her mother, Golda. Well into her 80's then, she was a tiny woman always busy doing housework, never sitting down, not even for meals. She was a wonderful cook and was very interested in me, but we had trouble speaking to each other—her language was Polish, Yiddish and some broken German like mine, but we tried. When her husband, Bernard, had died in New Jersey, Eva, by then married and divorced, decided to return to Vienna, although Golda did not want to go. She had liked America. She was the only one who treated me with love.

Eva Schleifer and her mother Golda, 1985

Eva was a seamstress, a dealer in antique jewelry and a great gambler. She was beautiful, with dark auburn hair, twinkling brown eyes made-up to highlight them, beautifully dressed, even at home, and very clever. She disdained my plainness and lack of class, criticizing everything I did, wore and said, as though she was the only one who knew anything; she treated me like a poor relative from America, refusing my contributions to meals and outings. Once, after I had failed to know something that was well known history to her, she rebuked me with condescension, "So, what did you learn in school?" Then she said with sarcasm and envy, "You were always so smart, doing those crossword puzzles when you came to Lawoczne in the summer. My mother always chided me for not being as smart as you, but I see you aren't so smart after all!" Eva had harbored this envy of my "smartness" for a very long time—although I had only copied those crossword puzzles in Poland for lack of companionship or other activities. Perhaps it was her misplaced envy that prohibited our being as warm and intimate as I longed for. I found her to be sophisticated, clever, and I admired her despite her criticism of me. I wanted to have a close cousin, but it was not to be. When I visited her she took me to café houses where she played cards, for hours, while I sat nearby reading books, not what I had come to Europe for.

I often asked her to tell me about the old pre-war times in Lawoczne, and of her family's experiences during the war, and occasionally some stories came out. The Schleifers, Eva and Arthur and their parents, as well as Yetty and Susie Rothman had escaped from Lawoczne by walking through the Carpathean forests for many nights as the Germans were coming to Poland in 1941. They had gone separately, so that if discovered, they would not all be found together. They fled to Hungary where Eva's brother, Arthur, also fought with the resistance. How they survived there after fleeing, how and when and even why they came to Vienna after the war, nor why they returned to Vienna after being in the United States for several years I never found out. I persisted with my questions because I wanted to hear more, but Eva quickly wearied of talking, and wouldn't allow me to record her.

Once she told me how Shoniu, the oldest Rothman son, had been conscripted by the Russians into military service when they had invaded Galicia in 1939, but was later put in prison in Siberia for ten years. When he was released he returned to Poland, already married and with two children. He placed ads in many cities' newspapers looking for his sister and mother and luckily found them in Vienna. They quickly got him out of Poland and he ultimately went to New York, where he still lives, but returning frequently to Vienna to see his family. Shoniu is now in his mid-80s, ten years older than I, healthy, vigorous and enjoying his life in New York. His memory of those times seems to be excellent, but it is not something he cares to speak of, although recently, he told me that the Rothman family had comprised 150 members and they, on the whole, were well-to-do. So many potential relatives! However, when I was small child visiting them, I cannot recall what we would today call wealth or a life of luxury, nor did I experience being a part of a large family. One of his sons, Joseph lives in San Jose, so we see each other periodically.

Suzy still lives in Vienna; her mother, Yetka, died just a few years ago, living to a ripe old age. Suzy and I can hardly communicate because of language. Her younger brother Teddy, the youngest Rothman son, whom I had not met in Europe, lives in Israel and I visited him there. He and wife, Mimi, speak English, so our visit was very cordial, and they were very hospitable to me.

In my previous visits Uncle Dzuniu had been unhappy and never seemed to have any joy in life and I wanted to know why. Finally, Eva told me short bits: he had lost his wife and child by the Nazis, or more likely by Poles, when the Germans invaded Poland in 1941. Apparently he had been out of town, and when he returned he discovered everyone had been killed. His baby son had been thrown into the house wall, killing him brutally. Dzuniu immediately joined the undergound resistance in Hungary, just over the border from Stryj, and although captured several times, had escaped. He married again and moved to Israel after the war, but then moved to Vienna, and later to Frankfurt. Later, he became quite wealthy as a hotel owner and real estate dealer, but never happy. His second wife died in the 1960's.

His son, Heini, who lives in Frankfurt, Germany, with his Italian wife, and two wonderful girls, speaks excellent English and for a while was often in touch with me. He is the only relative that came to visit me in California, once in 1978 and again in 1996, and I visited him in Frankfurt several times, but this relationship has ceased as well, not by my doing. Since his last visit, we have not had any communication; he doesn't answer phones and doesn't respond to my letters.

I begged Eva to take me to see the farm and Stryj, then part of Russia, but she had no desire to revisit her past. However, after the disintegration of the Soviet Empire in 1991 when Galicia became a part of the Ukraine, I pressed harder and she finally agreed to arrange a trip the next year.

✦ ✦ ✦

Vienna in 1992 was more beautiful than ever, still exuding *"gemuttlichkeit,"* a word especially associated with Austria, meaning charm. The gray and dingy stone buildings had been sandblasted to be white or pastel, sparkling with pride and elegance. The little streets with old buildings in the central district were now lined with new and fashionable shops with enticing merchandise, the café houses with their outside tables were full. It is a great walking city, for some of the old streets have been converted to walking malls. The people walking or strolling in this area were very fashionably dressed, women with ostentatious jewels and silk dresses, men in suits. Yet amidst the high fashion there are still people wearing a national costume, a suit of gray trimmed wool with loden green lapels—men and women alike, except the women wear skirts—topped off with a very characteristic gray felt hat which often has a feather in the band. Only in Austria have I seen this national costume amidst the urbanites. I, wearing comfortable travel clothes, was clearly recognizable as a tourist, but I was happy to see that Vienna had restored itself to its former beauty.

Our trip to Galicia was a short four-day trip, much of the time spent on the way. Eva's brother Arthur, who had lived most of his life in New York after emigrating in 1955, was living with Eva in Vienna at this time and would be our driver. The countryside was abloom with sunflowers, a big crop in Slovakia. We had adventures with getting lost, locking ourselves out of the car, and having trouble finding restaurants that were open. Crossing the border into the Ukraine was a long, drawn-out procedure taking several hours, reminding us of the closed-door policies of the Russian era.

Nevertheless, we were able to visit Stryj, former home of my grandmother Hannah and her sons, Dzuniu and Heshiu. Arthur, who had lived with her while he was in high school, was able to find her house and the candy store she and Heshiu, her other son, had owned. It was located by a small walking mall—one that Arthur had remembered as a grand boulevard where families had promenaded with their children. Again, an "enhanced" memory! I recognized the back stairs of the house, and was thrilled with the idea of putting a picture to my dim memories. The area of my well-remembered stinky outhouse had been replaced by a big apartment house.

We tried to go to Lawozcne, but there was only a gravel road, and the little Citroen couldn't negotiate the rough road. I was very disappointed not to be able to visit the homestead, but it probably would have been replaced anyway as most of the houses in the area looked relatively new. However, I did see the little stream, which I had remembered as a big river behind Great-grandfather's house, flowing in the vicinity.

In L'viv, where my other grandparents had lived, we went to a museum of Ukranian house types, and there my cousins remembered their past. A big, hive-shaped clay oven in one house with built-in ledges surrounding it reminded Arthur of sleeping on such a ledge, getting warmth from its sides when he was a young boy. Eva recalled that the local farmers' houses had dirt floor, whereas her house had had a wooden floor. Implements hanging on the wall reminded them of how they were used for everyday chores.

At last, I got some details! In the end, they said they were glad that they had gone on this journey of remembrance, and were pleased to recall at least some parts of their past with some fondness, but alas, no new memories came to me. I was impressed with their remembrance of languages they had not used for decades—Slavic, Polish, Ukranian and even some Russian.

Although I had hoped that they would recall some things from the times I had spent on the homestead in my youth, they told me little about me as a young summer visitor. Not surprising, since my visits were only a small part of their early lives; I had not remembered them as the children of my summer times at all!

I was disappointed that we didn't get to Lawoczne, their home village, but satisfied just to see the houses sporting TV antennas in the countryside; the old wooden churches, complex to the eye with their many cupolas; the women still wearing babushkas and boots and herding their one cow as it grazed on the road while young girls wore high heels and modern clothes. Large horse-drawn carts still carried the hay, and water came from central wells. There wasn't much car traffic, but our Austrian license plates attracted the police who charges us with speeding, several times, even though we weren't. Yet, it was always scary to be stopped by the police. A five-dollar bill held with the driver's license covered the "fine," the simplest way to get by. Our biggest anxiety was finding gas stations that had gas to sell.

◆ ◆ ◆

I loved seeing the lovely landscapes—the forested mountains still providing timber, and the gentle fields now filled with their distinctive haystacks and the fragrance of fresh cut hay. The scene did not look like 1992, but more like the dim memories I had clung to. My cousins blamed the Russians for keeping the area so primitive, but for me its simplicity made the journey to my past complete, even if the people who came from this landscape of my childhood are not part of my present world.

I had made several trips to Vienna over the years, hoping to reconnect with this family, but it never happened. Although they were all cordial, hospitable and very generous to me in Vienna, they never wrote or communicated with me after I left. My letters went unanswered. I was a stranger in their midst, one that they didn't particularly approve of. Having shared life in Lawoczne and in refuge in Hungary, Vienna and New Jersey, they had remained close to each other, although I didn't see much love between them.

I had been an outsider even as a child by living in Vienna, seeing them only in summers and without a common language; I was not part of this circle. They were not interested in my life or my experiences in the United States, nor in my father's story. My relatives never asked and weren't interested in how I had survived without a family in America nor did I impress them with my academic accomplishments. Perhaps they expected to me display wealth or to bring more elaborate gifts (I did, but very modest ones). Perhaps in their minds, a person who could travel must be rich. Aunt Netty once asked, "Don't you wish you could live in Vienna again?" I was startled by the question, it was a ridiculous notion—I was so glad that I didn't live in Vienna! I couldn't even imagine living there, even if the buildings were beautiful—I loved America so, and found Vienna distasteful for its superficiality. The war, creating very different experiences and lifesytles is much to blame for our extrangement, and I am sad not to have found my family.

22

I NEVER CRIED
FOR MY MOTHER

Fifty years after the Holocaust the media have taken to display the horrors of it. Recently, three big movies, *Schindler's List, Life is Beautiful,* and *Jacob, the Liar,* have shown in a dramatic form what documentaries failed to do earlier. New films highlighting different aspects of the Holocaust keep reminding the world of its brutality. This recent public interest has made it easier for me to begin to come to terms with my mother's death. If I had wanted to forget the Holocaust previously, now I seem inundated by the accounts and ready to think of the horrors, and how my mother, in particular, may have experienced them.

Furthermore, recently I have received many reminders of Jews' personal losses besides life itself—money, property, businesses and art works. These reminders come from Swiss and Austrian banks that are required to distribute millions of dollars to Holocaust survivors who have a claim. Germany had been paying reparations for many years, but only in 1990 did the Austrian government begin to accept responsibility for its part in the genocide when it began making some reparation payments for victims. Victims are able to receive some social security payments, and retribution payments have recently begun. I have been the recipient of such retribution payment for the death of my mother. Ironically, in the early post-war period my father engaged a lawyer to get compensation from Germany for her forced labor and death, but it was denied because she was "stateless," a condition imposed on her by the Nazis. At the time he was making these claims, I did not approve; I wanted nothing to do with Germany, the reparations, or even the history. I feel differently now, perhaps because I am older and hopefully wiser, and can deal with these subjects and see that they are important and just. In addition to personal losses, Austria or Germany, even Switzerland which banked those factories, must pay some retribution for the slave labor imposed on the victims, but not to their descendants.

My mother was such a slave in a factory in Germany. She wrote she was working in a tobacco company, but to me then a twelve year old, I had no idea what that entailed even though she described her misery in her translated letter of Oct. 7, 1941

I am still working in the cigar factory, which is very strenuous. At 6 o'clock in the morning the work begins until 5:30 in the evening with one hour recess. I would be already satisfied if I could be at home. I work with 120 women who also came from Vienna, we have dormitories and one dining room together. It is not nice and nothing pleases me.

Later, I had thought that "cigar factory" might have been a cover word for the real kind of factory—perhaps munitions, perhaps something else, but now I know it was cigars. Then in late 1941[1] she wrote me that she was going to Poland, and that too I had not understood to mean death. And then I stopped hearing from her.

I've had trouble dealing with my mother's memory, even identifying the pain. I tried not to think of her. I expect that it is sorrow mixed with guilt that I tried to repress for so long. My mother was not my favorite parent; I was definitely Papa's girl for my father had spoiled me; yet from her letters there can be no question of her deep love for me and her desire to join me in San Francisco.

To compound those feelings, I wonder why my father and I had not spoken of her when he finally joined me in San Francisco—or anytime after that. He actually made an inquiry in 1947 to trace her and was informed that on May 6, 1942 she was forced to go on Transport #142 to Minsk, but he did not share it with me; I found it among his papers later. The report did not mention if she was killed, or when or how. Neither she nor her fate was subject of discussion, and, even if not forgotten, kept carefully hidden in those intervening years. Of course, I realized sometime during the war that she probably was not alive anymore, but I did not acknowledge it enough to grieve for her; moreover, I did I know how to grieve.

In 1978 I had some of her letters translated onto audiotapes but not transcribed. It was heart-wrenching to listen to the voice of an Austrian lady as she translated the letters, her whining accent helping to create the idea of my mother talking to me, pleading with me to be good, grateful and to help her find an affidavit. I could hardly bear it then, but now I am more able to listen to or read these letters, but never without tears. How could I have been so callous as a child? Perhaps I really didn't understand her misery, didn't know how to read beyond the

---

[1] Her last letter to me from November 23, 1941 is in Chapter 10, pg 122

words or just didn't want to know because it was too painful.

I had all of her letters translated in late 2000. In addition to the letters to me, I found a few of her letters sent directly to my father and others sent to my Uncle Max who had forwarded them to my father. I found them among my father's pile of papers and had them translated too.

October 18,1941   From my mother to my father who is interned in Australia:

Dear Sigi!

I have just received your letter from August 8th, lately the mail comes faster. I thank you very much for that. I am now in Vienna on vacation. With great difficulties I was able to get 14 days. I have already written to you several times from there and I am wondering that you haven't received my letters yet. Unfortunately I have been through a very, very hard time and I do not know what else lies ahead.

Thank God you are so far in good care and I — I am here. For your information I can just tell you that when I came here a few days ago I had the strong intention to follow the example of my father. I do not know if I should say thank God or unfortunately to that: I have temporarily postponed it. I tried everything to get to our child, the good Anny and Arnold have been very good and helpful but it was of no use, the affidavit is now invalid. Yesterday I have sent a telegraph to the foster-parents of our beloved Lizzy, to send the entry [papers] to Cuba. It is hopeless cause like everything else has been for me until now — but I will try everything so that I have nothing to blame myself for.

I am happy that you have a picture of me, in those days I looked good, but now I do not look that good anymore. It is no wonder with all these worries and sorrows and in addition to that to live in a community. [slave camp?]

Now I have complained enough, do not let yourself get in a bad mood, you cannot help me and pity does not help me either.

I wish so much that you will be united with our beloved child soon; unfortunately for me there is no hope, I do not think that I will be able to outlast all this; I do not have the emotional strength for that.

Your lovely parents wrote me a few weeks ago, all were healthy. My parents had to suffer a lot but besides that they are healthy. From time to time I hear from Max and Tilly, thank God they are healthy, too. I will write all about you.

And now farewell, have a good time and think sometimes about your desperate

Laura

I don't know when my father received this letter—perhaps 6 months later. Her reference to the example of her father refers to his suicide—so she must have been thinking of it, and I cannot blame her for that. Her hopelessness in this letter is distressing and foreboding; surely it must have affected my father that way, but he never mentioned it—again probably too painful. Of course, I didn't read this letter until this year, I couldn't help but cry with belated deep sorrow for her suffering and her courage.

◆ ◆ ◆

My mother's last letters were written to Max, who was in Portugal at the time, telling of the bad news of his sister and parents, and finally of her own misfortune.

March 3, 1942   From Nordhausen [translated from German]

My Dears! [To Max, Tillie, and her sister Julia and husband Irmhold]

I have thankfully received your nice letter from March 11 [1941?]. A letter from me was already on its way — came back, however, and now I will tell you that I have received a very desperate letter from Hanny [my father and Max's sister]. To you she writes the following:

> *"What concerns our dear parents I cannot tell you anything right now, I am already five months without a message, the good lord knows how they are and also I will not live long, I don't look good. You would not recognize me. Day and night my thoughts are with our good parents. Where should I look for them? I was thinking about walking to them, unfortunately it is not allowed. Now you my dearest brother are my father and mother, advise me what to do, I do not have the nerves anymore—I am very sick and besides I am feeling bad overall. Maybe it is possible for you to send me a kilogram of cocoa, almonds or coffee. My poor kids have to suffer a lot and they do not look good. Louis is 8 years old and Dzinmia will get 4 years on June 26th. Don't be angry with me when I ask you for that, if possible do it, it would help me a lot, otherwise one cannot do anything. .... Hanny"*

My mother's letter to Max continues:

I am very miserable about her letter and I am not sure what for God's sake has happened to our poor, dear parents. Even if it would be like she suspected, God forbid, there should be a message from the neighbors. In a word, it is a terrible disaster. I have sent your letter to aunt Cilly and I ask her to write me a few lines, until now I haven't heard from her. A few weeks ago there was the transport from Leipzig to P.[Poland], therefore I think that they have been on it, too, otherwise I would have heard from her. I have written her again yesterday, as soon as I get a message from her I will write you.

Also from Siegfried I have not heard anything for a few months, hopefully he is healthy and well. On March 20th it has been already 2 years since our loved child has left. You write me that my letters are so hopeless, unfortunately I cannot write you something pleasant from us who have been torn from their families. You do not have to worry about me as long as I am here because I am working, earn for life and feel well and I hope that it will come the time where we all will be together again with our dearest. I have heard from my mother and brothers thank God. I just don't want to visit them, you can imagine. [The Germans had occupied Poland in Sept. 1941.] *I am glad that you are thank God healthy and earn the necessary. What's about your trip to Jamaica? How are Jula and Irmhold? Do they earn money as well? Give my best regards to them.*

The good Hanny has gotten a birth certificate for you, dear Max, but she did not get the home [country?] *certificate, I will enclose it.*

With this letter I cause you a great grief that I am feeling deeply, too, and I am feeling with you. If God only wants that something different happens to our poor parents.

I wish you all the best! Regards and kisses,   Your Laura

April 21, 1942

My Dears! [To Max and Tillie]

Unfortunately I have to inform you today that I will leave Nordhausen tomorrow. I will be transferred to the collecting point in Vienna and from there I will go to Poland. On my way through I will visit Aunt Cilli and Herta. I am very prepared and calm; you just cannot escape your fate. I am just happy that Lizzchen and also Siegfried will be spared from this. Should God protect them and you and help me to get together with my dearest while I am still alive, Amen!!! Write my child that I am fine and that she should remain a good child and honor and respect the good people who replace her parents temporarily. I do not know if I will be able to write from there but I ask you to not to leave the child without mail; write the dear Siegfried the truth.

From Hanny I have received mail, unfortunately—unfortunately, with very terrible news. Since November your poor parents do not live anymore. It does not make sense to conceal it from you, it has hit us very hard and we have to bear it. Dear Max, it hits you as a child very hard and I feel with you, because I have worshiped your good mother so much and I will never forget her. Be brave and bear with dignity what cannot be changed anymore!! They have it behind them and they do not have to suffer anymore.

Stay healthy and happy for me and I kiss you as well as Jula and Irmhold and I remain

Your faithful Laura...I write you as soon as possible

Actually, I had not learned of her exact fate until the summer of 2001, although I had suspected something like it when, in 1991, I read that Russia released lists of fatalities at the hands of the Germans. The news reports indicated that huge mass graves had been found in Minsk, in what had been Poland, but is Belarus now. I started another Red Cross search. In 1992, while visiting in Vienna, I inquired at the Kultusgemeinde, the Jewish Community Center, no new information there. Why Minsk, I wondered, as I looked on the map—that was nowhere near her family in Poland. Why did she go to Minsk? I had not heard of a concentration camp there. I continued my search.

In 1994, I searched for her at the Yad Vashim, Israel's Holocaust Memorial, but found no trace of her, so I filled out a *Page of Testimony*—regarded as symbolic tombstones—giving information about her, her brothers and mother to add to the Books of the Dead, stored in hundreds of binders on many 6-tiered shelves in a room full of such stacks. That gave me a visual picture of how many Jews had perished in the war, and I did not want her or her family to be unremembered. The Holocaust Museum library in Washington, D.C. also had no further details about her, but had information in books documenting how thousands of Jews had been killed in Minsk. In January, 1995, the Red Cross only acknowledged her departure from Vienna, but had no further information:

✦ ✦ ✦

Since that time, much new information has surfaced, and I became more determined to get some answers to my questions—how they knew she died, and how she died. The answers finally came in an e-mail in response to an inquiry to Austria, along with an attachment from the Encyclopedia of the Holocaust, Vol. 3, p. 940-41. It was shocking, to say the least.

Subject: Re: Laura Finkel
Date: Mon, 23 Jul2001 10:10:37 +0200
From:gisella wibihail@doew.at

Dear Mrs. Mattson

In April, 1942, the head of the security police and the SD, Reinhard Heydrich, visited Minsk in person and informed Strauch, the local KdS (commander of security police and SD), that the Jewish transports from the West to Minsk, interrupted at the end of 1941[when America had declared war on Germany] had to be resumed, and that from then on these Jews were to be killed immediately after arrival.

On May 6th, 1942 a deportation train with 998 Jewish men, women and children on board left Vienna Aspang Station for Minsk. Between May and October 1942, altogether 16 trains with over 15,000 people from Vienna, Koenigsberg, Theresienstadt and Koeln arrived in Minsk. The Office of the KdS Minsk had made extensive organizational preparations in order to be able to exterminate these people as quickly and efficiently as possible. As the place of execution a small pine wood at a few kilometres distance from Maly Trostinec estate was chosen, a former colchose [a collective farm]—which the KdS office took over in April 1942. The estate was situated about 15 km southeast from Minsk. By keeping in close contact with the main railway administration "Mitte" in Minsk through a special liaison officer, the KdS made sure to be informed well in advance of the exact arrival time of the transports. As a first preparatory step big trenches were then dug, measuring up to 3 m [10ft] depth and 50 metres [165ft] length (about 1/2 football field).

The executions themselves followed a pattern and relied on the participation of 80 to 100 men, including members of the Schutzpolizei and the Waffen-SS. After arrival of the trains at the freight station in Minsk generally between 4 and 7 a.m., a detachment from the KdS office disembarked the newly arrived persons and their luggage. The people were then herded to a nearby place of assembly where another detachment from the KdS office relieved the Jews of their money and valuables. At this place of assembly KdS members selected those very few—between 20 and 50 people per transport—whom they deemed suitable for forced labour on Trostinec estate. Finally the deportees were driven on lorries from a loading point at the edge of the place to the trenches which were situated about 18 km away. This process remained unchanged for the first 8 transports. ...

Deportees from the first transport were shot directly at the trenches. For this purpose up to 20 marksmen were placed at the individual trenches who in the course of the shootings had to be exchanged several times with members of the prison task force. From about the beginning of June 1942 onwards "gasvans" were also used, of which the KDS had three at its disposal. In that case the victims were crammed into the cars at the loading point, i.e. first on the train of the freight in Minsk and later next to the branch line in Maly Trostinec, and taken to the trenches. Only there were the exhaust tubes connected and the gas fed into the cars. Due to technical problems and frequent defects, but also because of the necessary and labour-intensive cleansing of the "gasvans" after each murder assignment, those "gasvans" were not in constant use, and with later transports there were mass shootings too. The transport from Vienna on May 6th, 1942 mentioned at the beginning, was until October 1942 followed by 8 further transports carrying about 7,500 Viennese Jews, in addition to several hundred Austrians taken there from Theresienstadt. Only 17 people are known to have survived among the almost 9,000 Austrian Jews deported to Maly Trostinec.

sincerely

Gisela Wibihail

✦ ✦ ✦

In 1986, before I had received this gruesome information, I had worked with a hypnotist to uncover some memories of my mother. We worked for about an hour, she leading me on with questions and taking notes, I lying on a table, in the darkened room, in a deep, but conscious state of relaxation, responding. No great surprising breakthrough occurred, but the door to memories opened just a crack. With her prodding, I engaged my mother in conversations hoping to hear some words from her—for it is impossible for me to "hear" her words in my memory because I no longer speak German. Afterwards, she suggested that I write about my experience, but I felt the urge to write a letter to my mother.

German words came to me.

"*Meines Liebsten Madchen*"—I am imagining a letter from my mother, and I try to think in German. "*Warum schreibst du nicht? Ich warte und warte!*" (Why don't you write? I wait and wait!) I think these would be some of the words that she would write to me, as she had written me many times before, and I begin composing in German, but I switch to English as I reply since I cannot recall enough words in German:

Dearest Mutti,

Although some German words come to me, I will write you a letter in English now, almost sixty years after my last letter. Though I have often thought of you, I have blocked out much to remember you by. Of course, it is painful to think of you; instead of thinking of warm fuzzies and hugs and kisses, what I remember is your scolding me a few times over things that are normal children's unpleasant behavior. You were right to scold me, but it is unfortunate that that is what I remember about our relationship. It is painful to know how you suffered, how desperate your situation was, and that despite several people sincerely trying to help you, constant obstacles were put in your way. How brave you were to continue trying, and writing to the family to keep us all together.

You used to sign your letters, "your strict Mutti;" did that mean that you really were strict, or is what I thought about you? Yet, in the middle of my core, I know there was more to us than your scolding. I am a warm, loving, thoughtful woman and mother—characteristics that would be impossible had we only had conflict and discord. I know that the earliest relationships imprint on the child; I, therefore, know that you loved me dearly. I know it from my heart, and from your letters although I do not remember it in my memories. Scenes of my childhood with you are almost all of my bratty behavior.

I even went to a hypnotist to uncover our relationship. The first thing she asked me was to find was a scene in which we were close. I pictured myself in front of a mirror with you standing behind and to the side admiring me in the pretty new dress you had made for me. It is velvety and resembles a spotted fur. I recall that when I was younger still, I carried a piece of such cloth around with me and rubbed my face with it when I went to sleep. Today I wonder if you made a dress of this material for one of your customers, and made mine out of scraps. That scene reminded me of doing the same thing with my daughter—a hundred times over. I named her after you—almost like Laura—Laurel. She is forty-two now, and when I sew things for her, I feel close to her; perhaps in my unconscious I am thinking of myself as a little girl with you. She has often been impatient with fittings and I can't help feeling that it must have been like that for me, too. I still have two dresses you made for me; one is the maroon velvet with lace collar and ball buttons down to the waist that must have been the last thing you made. I had wanted to have Laurie wear it when she was around ten, but it never fit—I was fatter than she at around 10 or 11 years. The other dress I still have is the black, silky dirndl with the hand-painted flowers on the hem. When we still lived on Nussdorferstrasse you exchanged sewing something for our artist-neighbor's wife to have him paint the dress, and I can recall your excitement over the dirndl. I know that you must have loved me to do such things for me. I also remember that you bartered sewing for piano and dancing lessons. These are surely acts of love—perhaps we just didn't hug and kiss—because I can't remember any of those.

In the course of the hypnosis, during which I was totally conscious of myself, I was led to another scene: we were living with Gusti—I have always wondered who she was. Was she a friend who kindly took us in after we were forced to abandon our apartment by the Nazis? I didn't like living there. Gusti didn't like me; perhaps I was willful, fresh or ungrateful—I don't remember, but I was disliked for such behavior later when I lived in foster homes. You and I shared a room and a bed and we didn't go out of the house much. I can't even remember going to school at that time. I remember that I told you of my friend's mother who was bleeding from the stomach—obviously menstruating—but you didn't tell me what that was about, although you should have.

One morning you woke me to present me with a poem you had written for me—a poem that would guide me as I departed alone to a world of strangers. I was annoyed with you for waking me, and quite uninterested in your poem. When I read it now,

I feel that I as a mother would have given the same advice, and besides the poem is really very beautiful. Unfortunately, I didn't treasure your words, and I wasn't grateful for your effort at the time, although I am now.

I can't remember at all if I was afraid of leaving you. People always ask me if I wasn't afraid to leave you, to go to America, if I wasn't sad, but I don't recall those feelings. Perhaps you had made my journey to America, with all of its modern miracles and opportunities, so promising that I couldn't wait to go. Or perhaps, having left you often before to go to your mother's in Poland, I was inured to separations.

Of course, it was not your will to send me to a far away place to make my own way-indeed, not; it was your intention to give me a life when life itself wasn't assured if I stayed with you. You did not expect it to be a permanent separation, just for a short time until you could come to San Francisco to join me, but fate would have it otherwise.

In my hypnosis, the therapist asked me to recall the last time I was with you. I couldn't remember. I felt terribly about that—how could I not remember the last time I saw you? I came up with a scene at the train station the day of my departure, but later I learned that you were not allowed to come to the station with me because of the nighttime curfew for Jews, so perhaps we didn't have a chance to say a tearful good-bye, although in one of my letters to Papa, I mentioned that we both cried. I have often wondered why I didn't remember; perhaps it was just too awful, too emotional. In my life I have avoided farewells. Did I learn that from you? Did you hide your tears from me when I left you? When did I learn not to cry? I cannot stand to drag out saying good-bye to anyone.

This is what I would say to you now if I could say good-bye, after hugs and kisses and tears: "I hope that your life after I left had a few bright moments and that your death was easy, if there is such a thing. I hope you found some friends to share your misery, to comfort each other, to hold hands. In your horrible death was there somebody with you to share that pain? I wish I had somebody to share the pain I felt when that e-mail came to inform me how you died. How can there be such pain, so long after it happened? Now I feel guiltier than ever for not trying harder to find someone to help you out of your hell. I am so sorry that you had to suffer so much.

I wish that we had shared emotional moments like this—and that I could remember them—so that I could escape the emotional desert of my family life. I wish I'd had a mother all my life, even now, I'd like to know what it's like. I hope your spirit comes back to me in memories or dreams to tell me things about you and let me see you and us as we were.

I write this letter with great difficulty, tears running down my face, blurring the screen. As I write, I am listening to a CD playing opera arias of Madame Butterfly repeatedly, intensifying my desolation and deepening the emotion I feel from your loss. You must have felt like she did, sending your child away to a strange mother, perhaps wondering if you really would see me again, if you were doing the right thing.

As I think of us, victims of war, at last I am crying for you, but it is small comfort, for I cry alone, not with family and friends over an untimely death, but alone at my computer trying to tell our story.

With love, your Lizzi

23

VISIT FROM MY DAD

Thanksgiving 2003

Dearest Dad,
Last night I heard somebody fumbling at my door. I was scared and tried to keep the
door from opening, but I couldn't, but when the door opened it was you, and I was
delighted to see you. You were considerably stouter than how I had remembered you,
but your smile and your joy at seeing me were wonderful. As I reached to hug you, I
awoke. The dream was so vivid, that I could not return to sleep, so I got up to write
my thoughts and to review what happened since I last saw you.

✦ ✦ ✦

More than thirty years have passed after your death and I still have dreams of you! It is not the first time; you enter my dreams occasionally, sometimes to argue about our differences, but this dream felt like reconciliation. It is Thanksgiving. It was another Thanksgiving, in 1971, when you were very ill and I had to put you in a nursing home. You could not speak at that time, but your eyes told me that you didn't want to go. Your cancer had progressed to the lungs and to the brain, and you couldn't get out of bed on your own. You died a month later, in December, but I didn't mourn for you then. I was mourning for my life because that night was also the death of my marriage, and once more I was to be an orphan, without family.

My loneliness at that time was excruciating. How I wished I had a mother or relative to go to, but there was none, and it was difficult to speak to friends about divorce. So, as I had done in my youth, I escaped. I went to Mexico, deep in the interior, spending a week at a hotel where Anthropology professors stayed when they were doing fieldwork, at Casa Bloom in San Cristobal de las Casas. It was my week of mourning, not exactly sitting Shiva, the Jewish mourning custom, but in spiritual quality it was the same. I had to think about how I would live my new life without a husband and a father. Hearing the professors at meals, and walking among the colorful natives in the town, reminded me that I loved anthropology and that I would try to resume that career. It also reminded me that you did not approve my choice of anthropology as a career, and that we had had many arguments about the uselessness of such a subject.

You would not have approved of my getting a divorce. Although you didn't approve my marriage fourteen years before, because my husband wasn't Jewish, you finally accepted it, and enjoyed my family life—you liked my husband and his family, and they liked you; you loved your grandchildren. When you had leave from your job in Korea every year, you came to stay with us for several weeks, and we had happy times. Those years were my happiest; at last I was part of a family—husband, parents, in-laws, children—I didn't feel like an orphan.

During your seven-year stay in Korea, again we were corresponding, but this time, keeping up with the technology, we spoke our letters on tapes. I made a production of sending you a tape weekly, more or less, telling you of our life, and having the children sing and talk to you. They loved you very much, and they have not forgotten you. Like before, your tapes didn't tell me much about your life in Korea, rather there were complaints that I didn't send tapes often enough, and that I didn't keep you properly apprised of your affairs, such as your checkbook and stocks. I kept the tapes for a while, but when the recorder broke and new technology replaced those tapes, I threw them away, and unlike the letters you wrote from Australia that I now treasure, I have no record of your time in Korea.

On one of your last visits, you wondered why I didn't get a job. "With your education would it not be more meaningful than doing dishes and cleaning house?" you asked. I was shocked at your suggestion—I enjoyed being a housewife, and furthermore, it was the role women played in the 1960's. I defended my life style. But after you died and I was separated, I would have to work, not so much because I needed the money, but because I needed a purpose, I needed to go to work to start a new life. Many friends deserted me; they just didn't know what to do and how to be with a divorced person. You would have predicted that, and I would have stubbornly argued that my friends would be friends forever. I didn't plan to leave my house, a house you loved because it was big, beautifully decorated and in a lovely neighborhood, but I finally had to because being single in a married neighborhood was painful.

✦ ✦ ✦

In your last years, at 60, you went to work for the Army in Korea so that you would have a retirement income. Among the papers you left behind were commendations from Army generals for the great job you were doing. At last, after a lifetime of underemployment, you finally reached your potential. Your progress was fantastic, advancing to a GS-12 from a grade 2 in just a few years. You loved your job, in charge of the accounting department with very new computer technology. You liked living in Korea, making friends with people you worked with, perhaps even a lady. Also you loved the opportunity to travel with tours from the Army recreation department to places such as Vietnam, Hong Kong and your favorite, Japan. You always brought treasures for me from these places—jade, pearls, china, paintings, carvings, vases—these are still in my house, a constant reminder of your love. You had scrupulously saved money, but you hardly got to use it, and I was the lucky recipient of all your work. I was so grateful then that I didn't have to worry how I would survive as a single parent. It was wonderful for the first time in my life to have some money in the bank.

There were very bad economic times for several years, and 1972 right after you died, seemed to be the worst. I had several jobs in the next few years. In 1976 I sold my house, and the kids went to live with their father. Their turbulent adolescent years were no better than mine had been, not having a stable family, a war in Vietnam, political unrest, drugs and rock and roll, a music style you would have disdained, but which your grandson loved and now plays for a living. I went back to school to pursue a Ph.D. in medical anthropology, but I didn't finish. In the end, I found my niche. I taught anthropology and health science in community colleges, like I had dreamed of when I was a student. I did research on the holistic health movement, and wrote a book about it, published in 1982. I traveled a lot. I bought a new house with a magnificent view of the Cupertino hills, where I still live. Seeing the evolution of the seasons each morning as I prepare breakfast, inspires me and makes me feel close to nature. You would have liked this house too.

✦ ✦ ✦

I've been writing my memoirs using our letters as the focus, so I've read and re-read your letters several times. Reading them from today's perspective, I realize how sweet and tender a father you were, and even when you were angry with me, you usually found something positive and up beat to end the letter. I took your love for granted, as children often do.

It took me twenty years to look through your papers, only then discovering what a nightmare you lived through on the Dunera, being a prisoner instead of a refugee—why did you not talk about it? And why did we never talk about my mother? At least I learned a lesson from this silence, and I have made it a point to discuss my history with my children, and to discuss their disrupted family during their adolescence.

✦ ✦ ✦

The night the nurse called to tell me that you had died, after I had hung up, I said out loud, "he really loved me." I said it with a heavy heart because I knew that night was also the end of my marriage. Now, what I am really sorry about is that I never told you how much I loved you, how sorry I am that I hurt your feelings by rejecting your love when I was 20, then wanting to be on my own, to make my own decisions about careers and religion.

Had you lived, you would have disapproved of my divorce, disapproved of my children's adolescence. You had once forecast that my children would give me trouble as I had given you trouble, and they did. Nevertheless, we survived, as you and I had survived before.

Thank you for visiting me in my dreams last night, and allowing me to reminisce about you and those hard times long ago. All has turned out well.

24

EPILOGUE

On the 4th of July 2000 I commemorated my 60 years in America with a party as a tribute to America and its opportunities. More than 100 friends, my American family, came to celebrate with me my luck in having landed in California, and to have experienced a life not possible for a forsaken child in most other places in the world. Friends from different, important parts of my life attended— school friends, neighbors, my writing group, my bridge group, the China Friendship group, and the greatest number, my hiking buddies from the Sierra Singleaires. The latter has been the most significant group of my life for thirty years. As we hiked the trails each Sunday admiring the bountiful and beautiful nature of our Bay Area while revealing and sharing the joys and pitfalls of our lives, we formed lasting bonds, and at last I belonged to a group. As I mingled with my guests at the party, I recalled each friend's contribution to my life, and I was thankful for their years of friendship, for listening to me and liking me.

The warm notes thanking me for making this celebration meaningful for them, the guests, pushed me purposefully and seriously into the task at hand, the writing of my memoirs. It has been a difficult endeavor—for years—difficult both physically in the hours at the computer, and emotionally by examining my youth through my letters and those of my loving parents. I had traveled to the places I and my parents had lived, searched libraries for material related to that period, and interviewed many people who had some connection to my story. My friends always encouraged me, even when I thought I must have bored them by my self-absorption.

As I read the letters that I wrote so long ago I often had the feeling that the writer was a stranger—not me. Sometimes, I was aghast at her rudeness to her father, her rebelliousness, yet other times I was delighted and admired this girl who tried to be so self-sufficient, who tried to analyze her behavior so as to be likable, who took chances to make her voice be heard, and who loved to have fun. After re-reading my parents' letters many times, for the first time I recognized how much they had loved me and how heart-breaking it had been for them to have me alone in another country. I regret that my father and I had not been able to discuss the years of separation.

In my first decade, loving, doting parents encouraged me to be independent, curious, honest, dependable and worthy of their pride. In the next decade—between ten and twenty—I expanded and developed those characteristics and then some. I became even more independent, more than those in charge of me could stand. On the other hand, being without parents during those critical adolescent years, notwithstanding the long letters from them, I was deprived of being a child and feeling loved in spite of my inadequacies. My father told me how much he loved me via letters, but it wasn't enough. His criticisms, added to Mr. Bonapart's are the words that lingered in my memory. I unconsciously assume responsibility when things go wrong or don't turn out, even when the failure isn't my doing.

✦ ✦ ✦

Those teen years made me an adult, perhaps prematurely. I became decisive, determined, rational, and self-assured that I had the ability to cope with life's surprises. These qualities have been useful in years of trouble, but still, I was forever hungry for family connections, even though I observed that many families' relationships are not to be envied. I had felt somehow tainted, perhaps unlovable, for being without a mother, and even without many memories of my mother. The spiritual, *Sometimes I Feel Like A Motherless Child*, speaks to me—I feel vulnerable when I hear it, sad that I lost my mother, ready to shed tears. Because of those feelings, I made the acquisition of friends the dominant purpose in my life. Friends became my family, and my community, and I was nourished by that support.

Unfortunately, those years without hugs and kisses also made me somewhat remote and I found it difficult later to accept affection even from my father who was so anxious to give it to me. I learned to hide my most delicate feelings, instead becoming pragmatic, business-like and objective, making others think that I was very strong. One friend accused me of wearing an armor to keep others from knowing my most tender feelings. Coincidentally, I chose to identify with the turtle as my totem—hard on the outside and soft on the inside; willing to stick my neck out to move on, and although slow, finally reaching my objectives. These are also my characteristics. Inanimate turtles, given to me and purchased on my travels, inhabit my house to remind me of those qualities.

◆ ◆ ◆

My early success in traveling alone—meeting people on the way, discovering other customs and practices and learning bits of the languages—led me in pursuit of new cultural experiences all over the world. Although in my adolescence I had yearned to belong, when I travel, since I don't belong, I enjoy the experience of being an outsider, of not being bound by some repressive customs. I love the feeling of being in a strange country, discovering its secrets, making friends and entering into the lifestyle; of being in "the present," with heightened awareness, and surprised every hour and around every corner. I enjoyed the lack of responsibility, as well as the challenge of planning and surviving the trip. I relish that kind of consciousness, hard to achieve in the everyday world of work, so I yearn to wander.

Moving continued to be a constant in my life, even though I have lived in my present house for more than two decades. After I left my father to attend the University of California, Berkeley, I continued to be on the move thereafter, to pursue education, adventure and to comprehend the world. My curiosity about cultures, races, religions, mountains, rivers and famous places around the globe, always present in my adolescence, directed me to major in Anthropology, and sent me on the move frequently. The experience of being kicked out of so many homes taught me the lesson that leaving, or moving on, is a possible solution. Thus, my travels were as often escape as well as wanderlust. Whether it was getting out of a job, a marriage or boredom, I learned to retreat from difficult times by leaving home.

My favorite place away from home was China where I spent my sixtieth year, in 1989-90 as a teacher of English at Shandong University. I love the Chinese people and admire their ability to endure hardships and to laugh despite their burdens. I returned to China three times by leading tour groups to share my love and enthusiasm of that incredible country.

Despite my travels, I found no place I liked better than where I live now, in the San Francisco Bay area. I have no soft spot for Vienna, even though I returned there several times. Each time I was thankful that I had landed in San Francisco when I was ten.

✦ ✦ ✦

I didn't start my career as a teacher, but in fact, I always was one, even as I was always a student. I enjoyed sharing information and knowledge and thus ultimately found myself in teaching situations, whether as a college teacher, a tour guide, volunteer ranger or as a resource for my friends. I am still teaching, and still learning.

I am proud of my accomplishments and not ashamed of my failures. I am so lucky that I can live my life creatively, satisfying most of my desires, savoring the beauty of nature, the warmth of friends and the love of my children. My life is rich.

Many traits and delights from my adolescence persisted and are still with me, but I am not rebellious anymore. I still value friends; I am still attracted to new experiences and new people and searching for fun. I still swim, sew, read a lot, like to give parties, love to be with my friends, especially in nature, and I am still looking for new journeys.

Time Line

August 9, 1929	I enter the world
March 12, 1938	Hitler takes Austria
November, 1938	We have to move to a stranger's apartment
March, 1939	Father is taken to prison for being "stateless"
May, 1939	He is released from prison, goes to Kitchener Camp in England
? 1939	Mother and I move to a friend's apartment
March 20, 1940	I leave for America
April 6, 1940	I arrive in San Francisco, begin to live with Aunt Laura
June, 1940	Father is sent to Isle of Man as Prisoner of War
July, 1940	Father embarks on the Dunera
September, 1940	He arrives in Australia, goes to P.O.W. camp at Hay
September , 1940	Mother has to move as the friend she lived with has died
November, 1940	I go to my first foster home
May, 1941	Father moves from Hay Camp to Tatura Camp
June 6, 1941	Mother sent to Nordhausen, Germany, to work in asparagus fields and later at a cigar factory
July, 1941	My first visit to Yosemite
December 7, 1941	Pearl Harbor, U.S. declares war on Japan, Germany & Italy
February, 1942	I move to Homewood Terrace, an orphanage, Cottage 42
April 21, 1942	Mother returns to Vienna from Nordhausen camp
May 6, 1942	Mother is killed at Maly Trostinec, near Minsk, Belarus
December 12, 1942	Father is released from internment, moves to Melbourne
June, 1943	I move to Cottage 24, at Homewood Terrace
February, 1944	I move to another foster home
October, 1944	I return to Homewood Terrace, Cottage 42 again
May, 1945	Father's visa is finally approved
June, 1945	Germany surrenders
August, 1945	Japan surrenders, World War II is over
May, 1946	I move to another foster home
August, 1946	I return to Homewood Terrace, Cottage 22 this time
September 13, 1946	Father arrives in San Francisco
February, 1947	We begin to live together in downtown San Francisco
February, 1950	I move to Berkeley to study at the University of California

References Cited

Allen, Robert L.: *The Port Chicago Mutiny.* Warner, 2000

Bartrop, Paul R. and Gabrielle Eisen: *The Dunera Affair: A Documentary Resource Book.* Jewish Museum of Australia, 1990

Baumel, Judith T.: *Unfulfilled Promise: Rescue and Resettlement of Jewish Refugee Children in the United States, 1934-1945.* Juneau: Denali Press, 1990

Bukey, Evan Burr: *Hitler's Austria: Popular Sentiment in the Nazi Era, 1938-1945.* Chapel Hill & London: Univ. of No. Carolina Press, 1999, 2002

Chappell, Connery: *Island of Barbed Wire,* Corgy Books, 1986

Clare, George: *The Last Waltz in Vienna.* New York: Holt, Rinehart & Winston, 1980

Harris, Mark J, and Deborah Oppenheimer, (Ed): *Into the Arms of Strangers: Stories of the Kindertransport.* New York; London: Bloomsbury Pub.: St. Martin's Press, 2000 (page 9)

Jason, Philip K, and Iris Posner, (Ed.): *Don't Wave Goodbye: The Children's Flight from Nazi Persecution to American Freedom.* Greenwood Publishing Group, 2004

Orgel, Doris: *The Devil in Vienna.* Dial, 1978

Shirer, William L.: *The Rise and Fall of the Third Reich.* Fawcett, 1959

If you enjoyed this book and would like to pass one on to someone else, please check with your local bookstore, online bookseller, our website or use this form:

Name _____

Address _____

City_____ State _____ Zip _____

Please send me:

_____ copies of *War Orphan in San Francisco* at $14.97 $ _____

Shipping: $4.00 first copy and $2.00 for each additional copy $ _____

California residents please add Sales Tax — $1.23 each $ _____

Total Enclosed $ _____

Payment must accompany orders. Allow 3 weeks for delivery.

Send orders to:
Stevens Creek Press
PO Box 305
Cupertino, CA 95015

Visit our website at: www.stevenscreekpress.com
or email us at: stevenscreekpress@pacbell.net

_____ I am interested in having Phyllis Mattson speak at my association, school or organization. Please send me more information.